American University Studies

Series IX
History
Vol. 48

PETER LANG
New York • Bern • Frankfurt am Main • Paris

For the General Welfare

Frank Annunziata, Patrick D. Reagan,
and Roy T. Wortman

For the General Welfare
Essays in Honor of Robert H. Bremner

PETER LANG
New York • Bern • Frankfurt am Main • Paris

Tenn. Tech. Univ. Library
Cookeville, TN 38505

Library of Congress Cataloging-in-Publication Data

For the general welfare.

(American university studies. Series IX, history ; vol. 48)
  Bibliography: p.
  1. United States — History — 20th century. 2. Public welfare — United States — History — 20th century. 3. Charities — United States — History — 20th century. 4. Bremner, Robert Hamlett. I. Bremner, Robert Hamlett. II. Annunziata, Frank. III. Reagan, Patrick D. IV. Wortman, Roy T. V. Series.
  E742.F67   1989   973.9   88-9115
  ISBN 0-8204-0796-8
  ISSN 0740-0462

CIP-Titelaufnahme der Deutschen Bibliothek

For the general welfare : essays in honor of Robert H. Bremner / Frank Annunziata, Patrick D. Reagan, and Roy T. Wortman. — New York; Bern; Frankfurt am Main; Paris: Lang, 1988.
  (American University Studies: Ser. 9, History; Vol. 48)
  ISBN 0-8204-0796-8

NE: Annunziata, Frank [Mitverf.] ; Reagan, Patrick D. [Mitverf.] ; Wortman, Roy T. [Mitverf.] ; Bremner, Robert H.: Festschrift; American University Studies / 09

© Peter Lang Publishing, Inc., New York 1989

All rights reserved.
Reprint or reproduction, even partially, in all forms such as microfilm, xerography, microfiche, microcard, offset strictly prohibited.

Printed by Weihert-Druck GmbH, Darmstadt, West Germany

Table of Contents

	Page
Preface: Robert H. Bremner, An Appreciation by Frank Annunziata, Patrick D. Reagan, Roy T. Wortman .	ix
A Classic Revisited--II: Mr. Bremner's Modest Masterpiece by Richard Magat	1
Federal Welfare for Revolutionary War Veterans by John P. Resch	15
Sarah Josepha Hale, Matron of Victorian Womanhood by Angela Howard Zophy	61
Origins of Welfare in the States: Albert G. Byers and the Ohio Board of State Charities by Robert M. Mennel and Steven Spackman	91
J. Sterling Morton and the Conservative: Jeffersonianism on Trial by Ronald Lora	131
Populism's Stepchildren: The National Farmers' Union and Agriculture's Welfare in Twentieth-Century America by Roy T. Wortman	161
James Thurber's Columbus by J. Mark Stewart	203
Peace-Church Conscientious Objectors and the War Department in World War I by Albert N. Keim	223
The Black Legion: A Paramilitary Fascist Organization of the 1930s by David J. Maurer	255
Governmental Planning in the Late New Deal by Patrick D. Reagan	271

Ambassador Claude G. Bowers and the Chilean Decision to Break
    Relations with the Axis Powers, September 1939–January 1943
    by Jack Ray Thomas 303

Aid to Families with Dependent Children in Texas, 1941–1981
    by James H. Conrad 337

C. Wright Mills' "Letter to the New Left":
    A Radical's Critique of American Liberalism
    by Frank Annunziata 361

Robert H. Bremner's Publications 375

Robert H. Bremner's Ph.D. Students 381

Contributors 385

Preface: Robert H. Bremner, An Appreciation

Americans have always been known as a generous and optimistic people. Yet American generosity has assumed varied historical forms ranging from the famous spirit of voluntary association noted by the nineteenth-century French traveler, Alexis de Tocqueville, in <u>Democracy in America</u> through the charity organization movement of industrializing America to the mixed forms of private and public philanthropy which emerged over the course of the twentieth century. Few scholars of the American philanthropic impulse have been so knowledgeable, so wide ranging in historical scope, and so insightful as Robert H. Bremner.

Robert H. Bremner was born on May 26, 1917, in Brunswick, Ohio. He received his undergraduate degree from Baldwin Wallace College, Berea, Ohio, in 1938 and earned the M. A. (1939) and Ph.D. (1943) degrees from The Ohio State University. During World War II, he served as a civilian job analyst in the Quartermaster Corps of the U.S. Army. From 1946 until his retirement in 1980, Professor Bremner taught at The Ohio State University where he is now Professor Emeritus. His doctoral dissertation, "The Civic Revival in Ohio: The Fight Against Privilege in Cleveland and Toledo, 1899-1912," reflected his interest in reform activities. This continued as a scholarly lifetime interest in the history of social welfare and philanthropy in the United States. Starting with his 1950 study with M. Adams and L. Greenberg, <u>American Red Cross Services in the War Against the European Axis</u>, his publications reflected a continuing interest in how Americans care for their fellow citizens in time of need or crisis.

American Philanthropy (University of Chicago Press, 1960) and From the Depths: The Discovery of Poverty in the United States (New York University Press, 1956) set the scholarly foundation for his reputation in the academic community. From the Depths was a perceptive study which had a major impact on the historiography of Progressive reform in the United States. He held a North Atlantic Treaty Organization Fellowship in 1961, won a Social Science Research Council Fellowship in 1963, served as a Huntington Library Fellow that same year, received a Charles Warren Center of Harvard University Fellowship in 1967-1968, and was a National Endowment for the Humanities Senior Fellow in 1973-1974. Among his numerous works are the massive Children and Youth in America: A Documentary History (Harvard University Press, 1970-1974, 3 vols.) and The Public Good: Philanthropy and Welfare in the Civil War Era (Alfred A. Knopf, 1980).

Professor Bremner's scholarship reveals his breadth of knowledge and enthusiastic research in wide areas of American society and thought including social welfare, the history of the New Deal, the connections between literature and history, and other aspects of American history. Robert H. Bremner's career is marked by prolific research, which he carefully integrated with classroom teaching, and an extraordinary concern for the educational advancement and well being of his students. His abilities as a teacher are complemented by a wide knowledge and use of research materials and tempered by his innate curiosity and a keen interest in students as individuals. As a teacher of both undergraduate and graduate students, he has the skill of perceiving the special talents and intellectual concerns of the individual and encouraging them. His enjoyment of students--as keen as his research interests--continues through lectures and seminars which come alive with probing intellectual depth, catholicity of conceptual breadth, and a rare gift of a wry, sparkling sense of humor.

Robert H. Bremner is one of those most rare of academic mentors with talents of equal strength in both teaching and research. Never losing sight of his primary mission as a teacher, Bremner always encourages his students to reach their maximum potential. His guidance of graduate students extends beyond the academic role to encompass his gentle, strong presence based in human decency and personal friendship. Throughout these years, many of us have been graced with the caring presence and quiet competence of Kay Bremner, his wife of thirty-seven years. The generosity and hospitality of the Bremners has made a noticeable impact on all of us. The Bremner home served as the scene for numerous celebrations of the completion of general examinations, the successful defense of the dissertation, and for the good fellowship of many informal reunions. A Bremner-made vodka martini on-the-rocks is reputed to be the best in all of Ohio.

Robert and Kay Bremner share a passion for neighborhood and local history. A ride with them through the local environs takes the form of an encyclopedic treat in local lore, whether in James Thurber's old Columbus neighborhood, examples of modern residential architecture, or on the way to a convention far from the hometown of Columbus. Bob Bremner always provides commentary about a given neighborhood, an architectural style, or the industrial history of an area. His special affection for small towns and their history always illuminates a point while relating to a broader interpretation of history. The informal sessions we have had with Dr. Bremner have proven as enlightening as our formal classroom experience with him. His amazing ability to explicate texts and interpret primary sources sheds light on the chosen topic while at the same time educates and, at times, inspires his students to constantly remain curious about people, places, and ideas. His professional guidance has been recognized and appreciated by all who come in contact with him. Professor Bremner has made a point of inviting his graduate students to various professional conventions and meetings where he would introduce them to other historians. His support and loyalty for students seeking employment has been thorough and helpful, well above and beyond the call of vocation. More than one graduate student has been told how fortunate he or she was to be working with Bob Bremner. His special brand of teaching evokes the ideal of a genuine calling manifested in his unusual sense of responsibility to his students outside the confines of the classroom. His loyalty to students and to teaching serves as a model and an inspiration for all of us who have experienced the pleasure and privilege of working under his direction. Significantly, he dedicated his 1980 work, The Public Good, "for students past and present." His humane capacity for arousing historical curiosity, for energetically assisting his graduate students in seeking source materials or their first teaching position, and his ongoing interest in the lives of his students reveal a rare and precious quality in this modest, brilliant teacher and scholar--

Robert H. Bremner--who enriches the lives of all those he touches.

This collection of essays arranged chronologically is intended as a tribute to Bob Bremner for his lifelong dedication to teaching and historical research. While the primary focus of the essays is on the social history of the United States in relation to the general welfare clause of the U.S. Constitution, the reader will notice a diversity of subject matter and approach reflecting Professor Bremner's wide interests noted in the list of publications below. Not surprisingly for a scholar with such a catholic curiosity, Bob Bremner inspires students to examine a variety of topics over the whole sweep of American history. These essays mirror Professor Bremner's encouragement of intellectual interests which range across diverse topics and over the chronological course of American history--from national welfare efforts at dealing with the problems of Revolutionary War military veterans through the post-World War II challenge of C. Wright Mills to the reigning faith of American liberalism.

The editors would like to thank the people who made this work possible. The idea for this work stemmed from efforts of Professor Ronald G. Lora of the University of Toledo and Professor Robert M. Mennel of the University of New Hampshire. Each of the contributors, except for Richard Magat, worked under the direction of Professor Bremner while completing doctoral work in history at The Ohio State University. A list of doctoral students under Professor Bremner is included below to give the reader an idea of the longterm commitment and dedication to the craft inherent in Professor Bremner's career.

The editors would like to thank Jody Curtis and Richard Magat of <u>Foundation News: The Magazine of Philanthropy</u>, 1828 L Street, N.W., Washington, D.C. for permission to reprint Magat's essay on <u>American Philanthropy</u> from the July/August 1985 issue; The University of Chicago Press and John P. Resch for permission to reprint the article from <u>The Social Service Review</u> 56 (June 1982), pp. 53-58; and Robert L. Daugherty, editor of <u>Ohio History</u> for permission to reprint Robert M. Mennel and Steven Spackman's article from <u>Ohio History</u> 92 (1983), pp. 72-95. We also would like to thank the Committee for Faculty Research, Tennessee Technological University, Cookeville, Tennessee for funds allowing time to complete the project. Our thanks to Cathy S. Hunter and Mary Cay McKelvey of Cookeville, Tennessee for typing and proofreading drafts of the work. Dean Joseph Lerner and Associate Dean Robert Briggs of the College of Arts and Sciences, Tennessee Technological University; the Department of History, The Ohio State University; and a number of individuals provided financial assistance in publication. Reed Browning, Provost of Kenyon College, graciously provided funds for telephone calls. Mostly importantly, we--editors, contributors, Bob Bremner's graduate students, and those historians who have worked with him over the years--express our lasting gratitude and appreciation to Robert H. Bremner--teacher, scholar, and friend to us all.

                                            Frank Annunziata
                                            Rochester, New York

                                            Patrick D. Reagan
                                            Cookeville, Tennessee

                                            Roy T. Wortman
                                            Gambier, Ohio

A Classic Revisited--II:

Mr. Bremner's Modest Masterpiece

By Richard Magat*

When it was published 25 years ago, Robert H. Bremner's American Philanthropy showed few signs of becoming a classic. It ran only 186 pages, and we expect heft in landmarks of scholarship. Nor did it read like a work of scholarship. Not a single footnote marred its pages. The prose was easily digestible as well as informative. "A pleasant narrative, seasoned with humorous comments," a critic wrote in The American Historical Review in faint condescension.

Moreover, it was not a book the author had planned. Rather, it was made to order. To be sure, the commission emanated from respected auspices--the University of Chicago Press History of American Civilization series, edited by Daniel J. Boorstin, even then a noted historian and later to become Librarian of Congress.

The series consisted of 7 works covering American history chronologically and 16 topically. (The other subjects ranged from religion to the Supreme Court, labor, railroads and American newspapermen.) And Bremner was in eminent company, with such authors as Marcus Cunliffe, John Hope Franklin and William E. Leuchtenburg.

Still, a slim commissioned work is not calculated to win academic acclaim or to last very long. American Philanthropy has proved to be an exception on both counts. It lives in every bibliography of voluntarism and philanthropy. It is the starting point for both casual readers and academic scholars. And, unlike many classics, it is still available, thanks to a reprint in 1982 (University of Chicago Press, 230 pages, $11.00 paper).

Its author retired in 1980, but that year he published an important scholarly work, and is now embarked on an audacious new project that would daunt many scholars half his age.

How to account for the durability of American Philanthropy? For one thing, although it was not a scholarly work, it was a scholar's work. The 13-page "Suggested Reading" appendix is a fascinating map to American and British writing on philanthropy, from John Winthrop's "A Model of Christian Charity" (1630) to Andrew Carnegie's "The Gospel of Wealth" (1901) to the then recent scholarly article, "American Philanthropy and the National Character," by Merle Curti, one of Bremner's mentors.

Bremner wrote American Philanthropy during one of his forays from Ohio State University--a backwater in the minds of highfalutin' historians--to more prestigious scholarly precincts. In this instance, he was associated with the History of American Philanthropy project, which Curti headed, at the University of Wisconsin.

"Curti would have preferred me to do a monograph on philanthropy in the Progressive Era," says Bremner, "but he respected my intent to do something wider and less detailed, and he read and commented on my work in progress."

Henry Allen Moe, then president of the John Simon Guggenheim memorial Foundation, said he wished American Philanthropy hadn't been published, probably because he felt Bremner's modest volume might take the wind out of the sails of Curti's large, well-funded History of American Philanthropy project.

Boorstin on a Limb

But Boorstin went out on a limb and called American Philanthropy "A pioneering volume." He wrote in his introduction that Bremner "is neither a sentimentalist, a cynic, nor a muckraker. He is a ruthless and sympathetic historian."

The book was published only a few years after worried foundation officials, who had just emerged from two congressional investigations, convened a conference of scholars in Princeton to discuss the gaps in research on philanthropy and to set an agenda for nudging the subject into the mainstream of scholarship.

As Bremner himself noted, "American historians have only recently begun to regard philanthropy as an interesting and profitable subject of research."

One of the most vigorous goads to the production of more knowledge about philanthropy and voluntary effort is Robert L. Payton, president of the Exxon Education Foundation.

Payton pairs American Philanthropy with James Douglas' recent (1983) and very different Why Charity? as "the two essential works for anyone who takes an interest in the subject."

Its brevity and absence of academic baggage accounted for some of the qualified praise of American Philanthropy in learned journals when it appeared. In the Annals of the American Academy of Political and Social Science, F. Emerson Andrews said the omission of footnotes and scarcity of financial data "will distress students in the field but probably delight general readers."

John R. Seeley of York University in Toronto, wrote "Perhaps something more like 'A Short History of American Philanthropy' would have raised hopes less high and dashed them less."

Still, he noted, "Only a very ambitious or competent man would have attempted to cope with so large a topic in so small a book: only a master can cover a domain in a few words, more especially so where the field covered is a virtual terra incognita."

The debt to Bremner is acknowledged by present leading historians of philanthropy, such as Barry Karl of the University of Chicago: "What American Philanthropy does that is genuinely significant is to extend the meaning of philanthropy in its American context back into the origins of American history."

Survey of Voluntary Activity

The book surveys voluntary activity in charity, religion, education, humanitarian reform, social service, war relief and foreign aid. The account is peopled with representative donors, whether of money or service, with promoters of moral and social reform and with the institutions and associations Americans have founded to conduct their philanthropic business.

In addition to hardy perennials such as Benjamin Franklin, Clara Barton, Dorothea Dix and Abraham Flexner, American Philanthropy tells of such figures as Squanto, the escaped Indian slave who aided the enfeebled, bewildered Pilgrims in the dreadful Plymouth winter of 1620-21; A.T. Stewart, a New York merchant prince who organized American relief for victims of the Irish famine of 1846-47, and Mabel Boardman, an heiress who made the

Red Cross a national organization.

While Bremner applauded the American philanthropic tradition, he noted "something about philanthropy that seems to go against the democratic grain. We may be willing to help others but we are not humble enough to appreciate the efforts of those who would bend down to help us."

Looking back a quarter century, Bremner recently traced the sources of skepticism about philanthropy--"from a lower middle-class cynical attitude of H.L. Mencken ('You just can't believe there's anything like altruism. Everybody must be out for themselves'), to the populist view represented by the late Congressman Wright Patman to the leftists or radicals who are suspicious even of the public uses of wealth."

Then, adds Bremner, "There are some contemporary historians who think that if the reform doesn't work out as the reformers hoped, there's something the matter with them. They were nuts or crooks or both. This view blames the past for the failures of the present: nothing works; everything has gone awry, and so they wonder whether the whole concept of doing good is wrong."

At the opposite pole of the tendency to sneer at philanthropy, Bremner says, is the tendency to overpraise it.

Thus, "I don't give two hoots about bequests. Some people would say that research on philanthropy requires that you go down to the courthouse, read every tenth will and see what people did with their money. That's perfectly respectable, but I'm not interested. Likewise, fund-raising is important, but it's not my major interest."

Student of Progressivism

Except for World War II service and sabbaticals at scholarly centers, Bremner has clung fast to his native Ohio. Born in Brunswick, Ohio, the son of a lawyer for a Cleveland title insurance firm, he was educated at Baldwin-Wallace College and received his master's and doctoral degrees at Ohio State University.

He lives with his wife, Catherine, in Worthington, 15 miles from the campus. They have two daughters, both graduate students; one taught at the University of Peking, the other is a freelance writer.

Bremner's work on philanthropy arose from his well-regarded research on the Progressive Era in the early 1900s. He had written his dissertation on the "civic revival" in Ohio, the urban version of Progressivism, which he maintained was different from Theodore Roosevelt's brand: "It was much more influenced by Henry George's Single Tax movement, involved more direct services for people, and much more direct democracy."

"The writing of an article about Progressive attitudes toward wealth got me to thinking about attitudes toward poverty," Bremner says. He reached back further in American history and the result was From the Depths: The Discovery of Poverty in the United States (New York University Press, reprinted in 1965. 364 pages. $12.50 paper), the work of which he is most proud, and which many historians say is his greatest achievement.

From the Depths shows how philanthropic movements added to public awareness of poverty:

By the 1920s, insufficiency and insecurity had come to

be regarded as even more disturbing issues than dependency; the industrial causes of misery were recognized as more important than the moral; and social rather than individual reform was being urged as the appropriate remedy for want.

Twice as long as American Philanthropy, the book is fully footnoted and contains a 37-page bibliography and a portfolio of photographs, etchings and cartoons on poverty. Although it preceded Michael Harrington's highly publicized The Other America and although Bremner and Harrington had met, Harrington inexplicably fails to cite From the Depths in his book.

A former student of Bremner's, Professor Robert Mennel of the University of New Hampshire, says From the Depths provided many research leads for other scholars.

It also accounted for Boorstin's choice of Bremner to write American Philanthropy. Boorstin recalled in a recent interview, "I was looking for good scholars who were good writers and knew relatively neglected areas." While he had not known Bremner, they developed and have continued a friendship.

Boorstin, author of the notable Genius of American Politics, was a midwife and editor of the series, "but Bremner didn't need much editing and revision. He seemed to be able to do it with his left hand."

Interest in Children

Bremner's work on American Philanthropy kindled his interest in public programs for children. In the last decade of his active teaching career, Bremner presided over the birth of another important new scholarly sub-discipline--the history of families and children.

He was general editor of Children and Youth in America, a

three-volume, 2,600-page work sponsored by the American Public Health Association, financed by the Federal Children's Bureau and published by the Harvard University Press.

The series consists of documents on the subject from the 17th century (e.g., a request from the Virginia Company to officials of the city of London in 1619 to send 100 needy children from England to the new colony as servants or apprentices) to the present.

The first volume was completed in 1969. The series enlarged and revised a two-volume, 1938 documentary history that had ignored the treatment of children from minority racial and ethnic groups.

The new work paid attention. Thus one section deals with "Negro and Indian Children," including such documents as an 1818 advertisement for a school for black children in Washington and Eleazar Wheelock's plan in 1754 for a school for Indians, which later became Dartmouth College.

In the Harvard Educational Review, Joseph Featherstone called Children and Youth "a comprehensive and often somber presentation of the place of childhood in our national life--far and away the best chronicle of public policy toward children we now have."

The call to edit the series interrupted Bremner's research at the Huntington Library, under a grant from the Social Science Research Council, on philanthropy and welfare in the Civil War era.

Assisted by The Rockefeller Foundation, Bremner completed

the work at that consummate study center, Villa Serbolloni in Italy. It was published as The Public Good in 1980. This too was commissioned, from a series planned by Allan Nevins for the Civil War Centennial Commission.

In this work, Bremner seems to have responded to one of the few criticisms of American Philanthropy--that it did not clarify the relationships between voluntary and governmental activities. Bremner characterized their relations as "cooperative and complimentary rather than antagonistic."

Yet, in The Historian the reviewer J.P. Maddex, Jr. says, "He urges that wartime philanthropy, by marshaling private aid to uphold the state in its crisis, conditioned postbellum Americans to rely on private chairty rather than government." Another reviewer said "Bremner's lucid account...documents what has been perceived but not pinned down before."

But Kathleen McCarthy, a scholar who happens to admire Bremner's work generally, was disappointed. "Although an excellent overview," she wrote, "[it] provides few fresh insights into the mechanics of specific organizations, regional variations, gender differences or changes in the philanthropic role."

War and a Burgeoning Career

Bremner did not embark on his scholarly career until after World War II. Having been classified 4F because of poor eyesight, Bremner took a civilian job in the Army. He was thoroughly mismatched to a job in the Quartermaster Corps as a job classification analyst, he recalls.

"Here I was, a bookish young man, more at home in the library than any place else. I had never seen a carpenter at work, hardly, or a lift truck operator, but it was my job to go around and decide whether this was a Grade 4 job or a Grade 5.

"The most controversial were officers' secretaries; the higher the officer's rank, the more the secretary's was supposed to be, and I, this little inoffensive thing, was stuck on such a decision. They would be impatient and say, 'You're holding up the war effort!'"

Bremner was a sort of "scholar for hire" from the beginning. He had just started teaching at Ohio State in 1947 when the American Red Cross asked him and some other young scholars to write a history of the organization. His slice was a detailed administrative history of Red Cross services to the armed forces in World War II.

The resulting monograph was not published; it was for the Red Cross's own use--"to learn from the past," as Bremner puts it, "to enlighten future Red Cross administrators." However his and other monographs, which are available in the Red Cross archives, were the ingredients of a published work on the American Red Cross by Foster Rhea Dulles.

Three decades later, after retirement from the university, Bremner took the assignment of ghosting a history of the Battelle Memorial Institute Foundation, a research center in Columbus that had been created through court order because the nonprofit institute had not been distributing enough of its income.

In the intervening years, Bremner's major projects were interspersed with teaching and such scholarly chores as serving as as the editor of various series. One, called the Modern

American and published by the Ohio State University Press (1968), was a vehicle for publishing original scholarly articles in all areas of recent American history. He also edited "Essays on History and Literature," which explore "the usefulness of literature to history and the way in which history recreates and literature renews the universal elements of human experience."

Free of Pomposity

Having devoted his working life to explorations of human wretchedness and efforts to compensate for exploitation and poverty, Robert Bremner himself stands free of the pomposity and self-importance that too often mar the character of scholars of high achievement. Frank Annunziata, professor of history at the Rochester Institute of Technology, who took his doctorate under Bremner, contrasts him with other academic mentors. "In seminars, he demonstrated tremendous intellectual tolerance," Annunziata recalls.

"Unlike some other professors of high reputation, he was not acerbic, not a wisecracker at the expense of running down people or scoring points. Rather, he appealed to the better angels in our nature. We learned an important lesson in civility from him. And with all of this, his seminars were stimulating and intellectually rigorous."

"Bremner is the soul of kindness in dealing with colleagues and students," says Marvin R. Zahniser, chairman of the history department at OSU. "He takes a deep personal interest in all of his students, following their progress for many years, taking pride in their accomplishments and attending sessions at historical conventions when they present papers."

One of those students recalls that in addition to being "humorous but endlessly informative, [he was] persistent in seminars until you got the drift."

Robert Mennel of the University of New Hampshire recalls his mentor's compassion and occasional sly humor. Bremner can turn that humor against himself, even in talking of the deprecating behavior of academics who hail from fancier environs than Ohio State.

Thus he recalls the remark of an assistant to the noted Harvard historian Bernard Bailyn, who had asked Bremner to write an introduction to a book on the 19th century bluestocking Anthony Comstock. Pleased with Bremner's essay, the assistant said, "Why, we haven't had nearly as good things from really good people."

"Although he was de facto a member of the intellectual meritocracy, he had absolutely no interest in status," one colleague observes. "He was just the opposite of the academic scrambler and pusher."

Stanley N. Katz of Princeton, a leading student of philanthropy, says, "He is such a quiet and self-effacing fellow that I sometimes think the academic profession has not recognized the tremendous contributions he has made. He strikes me as one of the most admirable human beings I have met in the profession."

Bremner is "one of the most thoughtful and sensitive people I have ever met," says Independent Sector President Brian O'Connell. "He keeps sending me material beyond the call of duty. The message I keep getting from him is, 'History has neglected this major aspect of American life, and we as a society will be worse off if we don't repair that.'"

Unreconstructed Liberal

Although Bremner has sometimes been criticized for qualifying his judgments, he is an unreconstructed liberal. He recalls lecturing at another university in which two clean-cut young men in dark suits stood at the back of the hall.

"They listened intently and took notes, and I began to think they were F.B.I. men who somehow had learned that I had voted for Henry Wallace in 1948. Not so. They were just from the university development office. Having heard that I was lecturing on philanthropy, they thought they might pick up some tips on fund-raising."

His liberalism did not spill over into activist politics. "He was essentially contemplative," recalls a former student, "and in a letter to me he reported that during the campus unrest of the 1960s, while there was a tremendous amount of noise outside his office window, he thought it best just to continue his work."

But advocacy plays a central role in philanthropy and social policy, Bremner believes. In a recent summary of his current work, he wrote:

> To some extent all philanthropic acts involve advocacy because each reflects the donor's attitudes and values, and constitutes a vote for or against some issue....Acting either as individuals or in association with others, American philanthropists have promoted temperance, peace, and woman suffrage, opposed slavery, assisted fugitive slaves, and protected children and animals against abuse.

Bremner applauds such recent efforts as the work of the

Children's Defense Fund and the Roman Catholic Bishops' pastoral letter on the U.S. economy. His own concern with the welfare of children was reflected in a 9,500-word post-retirement article, "Other People's Children," in the Journal of Social History.

Drawing on sources ranging from the diaries of Cotton Mather (1681-1708) to writings of Daniel Patrick Moynihan (1982), Bremner summarized and analyzed centuries of American debate over policy toward child welfare:

> Some people think the way to help children is to help their families. Others believe both families and children will remain in a bad way until all the gross injustices and inequities in society are eliminated. Still others assign the interests of children lower priority than such matters as increased outlays for weapons, tax relief, balancing the budget, reducing deficits, and shifting the balance of power from the federal government to states and local communities....Until greater recognition is accorded children's rights...they will continue to be neglected, not only by some parents, but by many public officers and servants. [This neglect] will have grave consequences for American life and civilization.

*Reprinted with permission from Foundation News, (1828 L Street, N.W., Washington, D.C. 20036, $29.50 per year) July/August 1985, pp. 53-58. Richard Magat is president of the Edward W. Hazen Foundation and book review editor of Foundation News.

Federal Welfare for Revolutionary War Veterans

by John P. Resch*

The 1818 Revolutionary War Pension Act combined features of a pension plan and poor law provisions to reward and assist impoverished Continental army veterans. The act included a means test which was administered with the aid of a national poverty line. Approximately 20,000 veterans applied for benefits. Their claims produced a national survey of poverty conditions experienced by a large number of elderly men and their households. This article examines the pension act and offers the first systematic study of the claimants and their households who sought relief under the act.

Introduction

In 1818 both houses of Congress passed, by overwhelming majorities, the Revolutionary War Pension Act. The bill provided $96 a year for privates and $240 annually for officers who served at least nine months in a Continental line and who swore that they were "in reduced circumstances" and "in need of assistance from [their] country for support."[1] Congressional pension advocates were responding to a public outpouring of sentimentality toward Revolution veterans which was an integral part of a growing national spirit in the aftermath of the War of 1812. By embracing a common patriotism founded upon the legacy of the Revolution, Congress rejected the traditional argument that republican principles were incompatible with the creation of a military pension establishment or with federal charity to a "rank of society."[2] The new attitude stressed that the Republic's heritage would be dishonored and its principles tarnished unless the nation aided its "heroes of the Revolution"[3] who were suffering in poverty. Furthermore, some congressmen believed that the country owed a debt to these soldiers who were scantly rewarded for risking their lives and property to secure liberty. Finally, a large surplus in federal revenues, combined with assurances that the pension program would be brief and inexpensive, contributed to the bill's popularity. Fewer than 2,000 veterans were believed to be eligible for the program at a cost of $115,000 for the first year.[4]

Historians have correctly identified this act as a milestone. It shattered nearly forty years of resistance against awarding lifetime pensions for completing military service. It created the first military pension plan, and it set a precedent for later veterans' programs.[5] However, scholars have overlooked the act as the first federal effort to aid some of the nation's poor; the 1818 pension act combined features of a pension plan and poor-law provisions to reward and assist impoverished Continental army veterans.[6]

The charitable intent of the 1818 act was explicit. Pensions were awarded to veterans "in reduced circumstances" who swore that "they were in need of assistance from their country." In 1820, because of a flood of applicants, Congress tightened the poor-law provisions of the act by adding a means test. Veterans wishing to continue on the pension rolls as well as new applicants had to report their residence, occupation, health, income, debts, and an inventory of real and personal property to the War Department. Also, they were to provide the age, gender, physical condition, and relationship of all others in their household and any sources of aid rendered the applicant. Furthermore, the War Department required a codicil containing a court's assessment of the value of the veteran's property. Finally, the War Department established an unofficial poverty line to help separate deserving from undeserving applicants. The attorney general ruled that only applicants "in the lowest grade of poverty" deserved the benefit.[7] Over 18,000 of the 20,000 applicants passed the means test. One result was the first federal program of direct assistance to some of the nation's poor. A second result was the largest federal relief effort until the twentieth century. Recipients and an estimated 60,000 members of their households received aid for an average of nine years at a total cost of $22,000,000.[8]

The amended pension act implemented a social policy resembling recent proposals for a guaranteed annual income for persons below a national poverty line. The act established that economic need was to be measured by wealth, that is, income plus assets; it affirmed that eligible persons had a vested right to benefits; and the War Department included a national poverty line as part of its means test.[9] Finally, the $96 annual payment provided enough aid to allow an individual a "comfortable and frugal" existence.[10]

This article seeks to develop historical perspectives on early federal poverty policy by answering three questions: Who were the poor veterans? What was the nature of their poverty? How were they affected by federal aid? These questions will be addressed first through statistical analyses of the applicants, noting their wealth and conditions of poverty, the compositions of their households, and the differences between applicants above and below the federal poverty line. Second, statistical data will be combined with case studies, relying on testimonies in the applications, to further understand the conditions of poverty and to see how claimants viewed the aid. Finally, a single applicant's "life course" will be studied to illustrate in detail some causes of impoverishment and results of extended aid.

Statistical Analysis

The statistical data come from the 20,000 pension applications filed under the act as amended in 1820. A structured random sample of the claims produced a representative group of 877 applicants. All personal, household, and information about assets found in their claims were recorded on a standard form for each case and then codified for analysis, using the Statistical Package for the Social Sciences (SPSS). In addition, about a third of the sampled claims included testimony, usually by the veteran, which was recorded on the standard forms.[11]

Statistical analysis revealed the general characteristics of the claimants. Most of them had joined the Continental army by 1778 while in their teens or early twenties and had served one to three years as privates. At the time of their application, 81 percent of the veterans lived either in New England or in the middle states. Despite this concentration, the applicants were highly mobile geographically. A third of the total no longer lived in the regions where their units originated, and another 20 percent appeared to have moved to a different state within the same region. This last figure, however, has to be taken cautiously because units routinely recruited men from nearby states. Half of the applicants were sixty-five years old or older, but only a small portion, about 3 percent, were in their eighties or nineties. About a third used a mark to sign their form and slightly more let a scribe affix their names to the claims. The use of a mark or proxy is sometimes interpreted as a measure of illiteracy. However, it may also have resulted from the effect of age or ill health, the latter being reported by eight out of ten applicants. Eighty percent of the applicants had wives who were on the average eight years younger than themselves. But, in most cases, they were reported to be suffering from infirmities. Over two-thirds of the veterans reported that they had no occupation, worked as laborers, or were tenant farmers. The remainder were almost equally divided among tradesmen, yeomen, and business proprietors. Nearly 25 percent of all applicants swore that they had once received, were receiving, or would soon be forced to seek charity from their family, friends, or town.

A series of tables gives a more precise picture of the veterans' wealth and poverty. Table 1 provides the distribution of wealth for all claimants, using the official court figures as well as those assessed by the applicant. The latter were derived by subtracting all reported debts not deducted by the courts from the official estate value. Courts determined the official figures by adding the values of the personal and real property cited on the applicant's estate inventory and subtracting the amount owed on a first mortgage. The War Department's regulation allowing the deduction of first mortgages was probably intended to reward frugal veterans, to protect investors, to deter fraudulent claims of debt, and to ease the court's work. Only 3 percent of the applicants benefited from this regulation. Most inventoried estates consisted of household goods, a few farm implements, a couple of animals, some tools, and an occasional decorative piece. Real property was reported in one case out of five, and only one veteran in twenty-five claimed income. Applicants averaged $129 in court-assessed wealth, but half had less than $37 in property. And, as Table 1 shows, nearly 14 percent had nothing more than their clothing and bedding, items not counted in assessing wealth.

Official figures, however, do not fully portray the degree of economic jeopardy which threatened many veterans with dependency and which probably led them to see themselves as in need of assistance. Table 1 shows that when applicant-assessed wealth, assets less all debts, is compared with court-assessed wealth, veterans in all wealth categories are further reduced, especially those reporting more than $200 in property. The effect of indebtedness can be seen in other ways. For example, had every claim of debt been deducted from the court-reported assets, average wealth for all applicants would have been cut nearly in half, from $129 to $70. Even this figure is probably high, because the War Department regulation restricting deductions to first mortgages likely discouraged many applicants from reporting debts. Among the 31 percent who ignored regulations by declaring debts of all kinds, average wealth dropped from $253 in court-

Table 1

WEALTH DISTRIBUTION OF ALL APPLICANTS IN THE SAMPLE

Value ($)	Court-Assessed Wealth Cases (N_1)	%	Applicant-Assessed Wealth Cases (N_2)	%	Difference $(N_1 - N_2)/N_1$ (%)
201 and less	...	...	15	1.7	...
-101 to -200	...	...	20	2.3	...
-51 to -100	...	...	22	2.5	...
-1 to -50	...	...	60	6.8	...
Zero	118	13.4	115	13.1	-2.6
1 - 50	406	46.3	362	41.3	-10.9
51-----100	138	15.7	118	13.5	-14.5
101-----200	99	11.3	84	9.6	-15.2
201-----500	62	7.1	44	5.0	-29.1
501 and more	54	6.2	37	4.2	-31.5
Total	877	100.0	877	100.0	...

Table 2

AVERAGE PER HOUSEHOLD AND PER CAPITA WEALTH FOR EACH REGION

Region	Court-Assessed Wealth Average per Applicant Household ($)	Average per Capita	Applicant-Assessed Wealth Average per Applicant Household ($)	Average per Capita
New England	160	47	81	23
Middle Atlantic	95	30	47	15
South	112	35	110	34
West	102	27	53	14

assessed assets to $64 in self-assessed wealth. As some of their testimonies confirm, these veterans probably saw the pension as the means to prevent economic collapse, household dissolution, and dependency.

Whether by court measures or self-assessments, applicants fell far below contemporary standards of wealth. In 1819, for example, each New York State resident had an average of $205 in real and personal property compared with $30 per capita reported by New York State pension applicants.[12] Table 2 shows that, while per capita wealth was lowest for claimants in the west and highest in New England, the differences were minimal. Regardless of the region, these veterans shared a meager portion of the nation's wealth.

Table 3 provides data on household composition and Table 4 shows a connection between household type and economic status. Table 3 indicates that few veterans lived alone and that their household compositions varied greatly, averaging between three and four people. A large number, 25 percent, had five or more members. Only 15 percent of the claimants lived in households classified as solitary. These veterans were widowers, separated from their families, or had never married. Most of these men lived by themselves and only rarely were found in an almshouse. Conjugal households, those composed of only a husband and wife, were reported in more than a quarter of the applications, while nuclear households containing husband, wife, and children were found in nearly half of the claims. Less than 13 percent of the veterans lived in extended households, a figure which falls within the range expected for most Western societies.[13]

Table 3

ANALYSIS OF HOUSEHOLDS

A. N PEOPLE IN APPLICANT'S HOUSEHOLD (Counting the Applicant)

People	N Households	% Households
1	139*	15.8
2	250	28.5
3	142	16.2
4	123	14.0
5	102	11.6
6	54	6.2
7	26	3.0
8	21	2.4
9	13	1.5
10+	7	0.7
Total	877	99.9

Mean= 3.35   Mode= 2.85

B. DISTRIBUTION OF HOUSEHOLD TYPES (All Applicants)

Type of Household	Total N	%
Solitary	132	15.1
Conjugal	233	26.5
Nuclear	400	45.6
Extended:		
Applicant living with kin	21	2.4
Kin living with applicant	78	8.9
Nonrelatives living with applicant	13	1.5
Total	877	100.0

*Of the 139, 132 were later classified as solitary households and seven were part of extended households.

Extended households are usually divided into three categories: (a) "extended up," meaning an older relative was present; (b) "extended down," which indicated the presence of a younger relative other than offspring; and (c) "multiple up and down," which refers to two conjugal or nuclear units bonded into one household. However, because these categories are based solely on composition, they mask distinctive functions performed by the households and important differences among them.

On the one hand, twenty-one applicants, 2.4 percent, reported that they were taken in by kin. These extended households functioned essentially as asylums for the veteran and, in a few instances, included wife and children. On the other hand, 9 percent of the claimants extended their households by creating a refuge for kin such as grandchildren, married children and their spouses, and mothers, while thirteen veterans, 1.5 percent, reported nonrelatives living with them. These three types of extended households were very different. Veterans who took in kin were generally younger than claimants in other kinds of extended households. Table 4 shows that veterans who made their households into refuges for kin had over four times more in court-assessed wealth than veterans who had moved in with kin. For households with nonrelatives the multiplier increases to eight.

Table 4 also illustrates a hierarchy of wealth among all types of households. Solitary veterans were at the lowest level with an average of $20 in court-assessed wealth, ollowed by $64 for applicants living with kin. Nuclear households had an average of $141 in assets, while those at the highest levels were

Table 4

WEALTH DISTRIBUTION BY TYPE OF HOUSEHOLD (Average Wealth)

Type of Household	Court-Assessed Wealth ($)	N
Solitary	20.00	132
Conjugal	105.00	233
Nuclear	141.00	400
Extended		
Applicant living with kin	64.00	21
Kin living with applicant	279.00	78
Nonrelatives living with applicant	500.00	13

Table 5

IMPACT OF DEBT ON HOUSEHOLD COMPOSITION OF NUCLEAR HOUSEHOLDS

	Mean Household N	Size	% Households with Males 15 and over	% Households with Females 15 and over
Debtors	154	4.8	47.4	60.4
Nondebtors	246	4.4	36.0	44.7

Table 6

DISTRIBUTION OF AID RECEIVED BY HOUSEHOLDS PRIOR TO PENSION

Type of Household	Aid Claimed N	%	No Aid Claimed N	%	Total N
Solitary	28	28.8	94	71.2	132
Conjugal	36	15.5	197	84.5	233
Nuclear	52	13.0	348	87.0	400
Extended					
Applicant with kin	19	90.5	2	9.5	21
Kin with applicant	5	6.4	73	93.6	78
Nonrelatives with applicant	2	15.3	11	84.7	13
Total	152	17.3	725	82.7	877 (100)

NOTE.—Contingency coefficient = 0.34

the extended households which functioned as refuges for the veteran's kin or housed nonrelatives. Confirming this pattern, the proportion of veterans reporting any real or personal property increased from 53 percent among solitaries to 76 percent for veterans living with kin, while conjugal, nuclear, and other extended households all surpassed 90 percent.

Important distinctions emerged between nuclear households reporting debts and those that did not. Debtor households were, on the whole, wealthier than nondebtor households. The data show that retention of children was more likely among those households whose little wealth was threatened by debt. As Table 5 illustrates, debtor households contained more males and females fifteen years old and older than nondebtor households. The higher retention of older children suggests that even a small amount of property could have a substantial effect on family composition. Sons and daughters may have remained to preserve their stake in their father's estate, or filial support of parents may have been more readily given when there was danger of slipping into pauperism rather than after such a state had been reached.

In nearly one case in five, applicants claimed dependency. Table 6 gives the proportion of applicants who claimed to have received charity from their family, friends, or town prior to the pension. The table shows a scaling of need among household types which nearly corresponds to the pattern of wealth in Table 4. The percentage claiming aid was highest for solitaries and applicants living with kin. It was lowest for the nuclear households and households where kin were living with the applicant.

Table 7 examines the sources of assistance utilized by households which claimed aid. Sources of aid differed substantially among solitary, conjugal, nuclear, and extended households. Thirteen percent of the aid claimed by solitaries came from their families as compared with 24 to 61 percent for conjugal and nuclear households, respectively. As might be expected, extended households provided high levels of family aid. Town support went mainly to the solitary veterans and impoverished couples.

The overall picture of the applicants drawn from the statistical features underscores their diverse origins and conditions. These claimants were not from a single impoverished class; they came from various levels of social structure. The picture shows a mixture of laborers, farm owners, and businessmen, the geographically mobile and immobile, the literate and illiterate, the very old and middle-aged, debtors and nondebtors, the destitute and those on their way to destitution. No one household type characterized these poor. Most households seemed to be in a process of decomposition, yet in a number of instances household recomposition had occurred, as evidenced among claimants living with kin and veterans taking in kin and nonrelatives. In a number of cases, assistance from kin and friends bolstered a weakened household economy. For others, especially the solitaries, who were also the poorest and oldest group of claimants, town relief had become their main support. Ironically, the poor-law features of the pension act can be credited for categorizing these veterans as an impoverished class.

Table 7

SOURCES OF ASSISTANCE RECEIVED BY HOUSEHOLDS

	Sources						
	Family		Friends		Town		Total
Type of Household	N	%	N	%	N	%	N
Solitary.....................	6	12.5	15	31.2	27	56.3	48
Conjugal....................	11	23.9	17	37.0	18	39.1	46
Nuclear.....................	39	60.9	11	17.2	14	21.9	64
Extended:							
Applicant with kin.........	19	90.5	1	4.3	1	4.3	21
Kin with applicant.........	5	100.0	0	0	0	0	5
Nonrelatives with applicant	1	50.0	0	0	1	50.0	2
Total	82	43.9	44	23.5	61	32.6	187 (100)

NOTE.—The 152 cases reported 187 sources of assistance because a few applicants had received or were receiving help from two sources.

The War Department made the final determination of the veterans' claims. The only official guideline was to accept applicants in the "lowest grade of poverty." To implement this guideline, the department used several criteria. It sorted claimants according to the court-assessed value of their property and the possession of real property. It attempted to determine the veteran's health, ability to work, amount of aid received, the number of people in his family, and the cost of living in his region. In borderline cases, the length of the veteran's service could determine eligibility.[14]

An analysis of accepted and rejected claimants revealed that, while no absolute poverty line emerged, the department awarded pensions in most cases in which the applicant had less than $100 in personal and real property. This line remained fairly constant throughout the program. Nevertheless, discretionary judgments were made when other criteria were weighed. Generally, applicants with $100 or less in court-assessed property who received some charity, lived as solitaries, in conjugal households, or with kin, served for the entire length of the war, lived in the South, and were over seventy years old, were most likely to get the pension. Veterans with over $100 in assessed wealth, including real property, who were still supporting children, had served nine months and who lived in New England, were least likely to get the benefit. Table 8 summarizes these generalizations.

Case Studies

Much more can be learned about these applicants through case studies which amplify the quantitative data with testimonies

Table 8

WEALTH, PROPERTY, AND REGION CATEGORIES OF ACCEPTED AND REJECTED APPLICANTS

A. COURT-ASSESSED WEALTH--CATEGORIES

Applicants	Zero N	%	$1-$50 N	%	$51-$100 N	%	$101 and More N	%	Total N	%
Accepted	117	15.6	399	54.1	132	18.0	102	12.2	750	86.6
Rejected	1	0.9	1	0.9	3	1.7	111	96.5	116	13.4

B. LAND OWNERSHIP

Applicants	Owned Land N	%	Did Not Own Land N	%
Accepted	75	10.0	675	90.0
Rejected	90	77.6	26	22.4

C. REGION

Region	Accepted N	%	Rejected N	%
Northeast	358	82.9	74	17.1
Middle Atlantic	245	90.4	26	9.6
South	67	94.4	4	5.6
West	80	87.0	12	13.0

NOTE.--Eleven cases out of the sample 877 were dropped from the analysis of the War Department's poverty line because they failed to satisfy the military service requirement. Two of the rejected cases with less than $100 in assets had apparently filed incorrect claims. Contingency coefficients: A = 0.63; B = 0.51; C = 0.12.

found in the pension files.[15] Nearly one-third of the veterans volunteered comments about their circumstances. These usually consisted of only a phrase or a few sentences. Occasionally applications were accompanied by affidavits describing unusual conditions facing the veteran. In a few instances, the pension file contained correspondence supporting the applicant's claim. Despite the pleading tone of the testimonies, they add insights into the causes of impoverishment and help explain the claimants' perceptions of the physical and psychological effects of poverty and of the potential impact of the pension on their lives. The following case studies are arranged by household type--solitary, conjugal, nuclear, extended--and include rejected and accepted applicants. Unless otherwise indicated, these veterans received pensions.

Solitary veterans, who by all measures of the data were deeply impoverished, unsurprisingly portrayed themselves as losing the struggle to sustain an existence. The data in Table 9 reveal that most of them were penniless. Tables 6 and 7 show that many grubbed out a living only with the help from their community and friends, rather than from family.

For veterans like Asher Russell and John Waid, beset with infirmity and total destitution, their only choice was to become a pensioner or a town pauper. Until Russell, age sixty-six, received his pension in 1818, he had been supported by the town of Wethersfield, Connecticut, for ten years. He claimed that he would have to return to town rolls if his pension were not continued. Similarly, John Waid, a seventy-two-year-old infirm laborer, told the War Department that he was penniless and unable

Table 9

WEALTH CATEGORIES FOR EACH TYPE OF HOUSEHOLD

	Court-Assessed Wealth							
	Zero		$1-$50		$51-$100		$101 +	
Type of Household	$\underline{N}$	%	$\underline{N}$	%	$\underline{N}$	%	$\underline{N}$	%
Solitary	68	51.5	51	38.6	6	4.5	7	5.3
Conjugal	23	9.9	121	51.9	40	17.2	49	21.0
Nuclear	17	4.4	195	48.7	69	17.2	119	29.7
Extended:								
Applicant living with kin	5	23.8	12	57.1	3	14.3	1	4.8
Kin living with applicant	4	5.1	22	28.2	19	24.4	33	42.3
Nonrelatives living with applicant	1	7.7	5	38.5	1	7.7	6	46.1
Total	118	13.5	406	46.3	138	15.7	215	24.5

NOTE.—Contingency coefficient = 0.49.

to work, and that without the pension "the town would be obliged to support me."[16]

In the cases of Icabod Beckwith and James Graton, town overseers of the poor applied for the pension on their behalf. In 1820, the overseers in Ludlow, Massachusetts, told the War Department that the sixty-nine-year-old Beckwith had no wife, no family, and no property. He was described as "a pauper disabled in body and mind" with no means of support other than from the town and from friends. The overseers of Hartford, New York, described Graton as a seventy-three-year-old insane pauper with four dollars in goods to his name. At the time of the claim, he was living apart from his wife who was also supported by the town.[17]

In Abraham Taylor's case, the fall into extreme poverty had dissolved his family. In 1820 Taylor was living in Montgomery County, New York, sometimes sharing quarters with his brother. His wife and son, age sixteen, were living in Vermont. Taylor told the court that in 1816 his family broke up because he could no longer support them. His wife and son had moved to Vermont to live with friends, and since that time his circumstances had further diminished because he could no longer work because of rheumatism. He reported only a few things in his pension application which totaled $17 in value.[18]

For Henry Buzzell, age sixty-five and living alone, poverty was imminent because of infirmity and the unexpected loss of kin assistance. In 1825 Buzzell, appearing before court in Strafford County, New Hampshire, claimed to be a penniless and disabled farmer who was no longer able to support himself. Buzzell told the court that he had once owned a farm that supported his family, but in 1812 he began getting "feeble." At that time he deeded the farm to his son, Jacob, in return for an agreement that Jacob would maintain his father for life. The son had lived up to his obligation until recently when, Buzzell swore, "Jacob has become poor and wholly unable to support me or contribute to my relief and I am now entirely left destitute." Buzzell claimed to have no other family to turn to and consequently was wholly "dependent on charity." Without the pension, Buzzell would have become a town-supported pauper.[19]

To summarize, the solitary veterans were for the most part at the end of their ability to be self-supporting. For a few, such as Henry Buzzell, impoverishment may have occurred despite careful planning for continued support in retirement or in case of illness. For others, like Abraham Taylor and James Graton, households had been whittled away by poverty and infirmity. For some, poverty in old age was a continuation of the hard times of their youth compounded by the anguish of seeing their children eke out meager existences. Despite various paths to poverty, nearly all, as shown in tables 4, 6, and 7 and as illustrated in Icabod Beckwith's case, claimed that their assets were gone, their health was failing, and that they were without family resources and even family ties. The normal life of independence and kinship was near an end and life as a public ward had either begun or was imminent.

The applications coming from veterans who lived in conjugal households also contained stories of bankruptcy, fractured families, destitution, dependency, and pauperism. Like many of the solitary veterans, a few couples reported being aided by the town (see Tables 6 and 7) before obtaining pensions or being on the verge of becoming town wards if they did not receive pensions. Other veterans told the War Department that support from children was insufficient, uncertain, or impossible because the children were either poor or far removed. Couples held, on an average, five times more in assets than solitary veterans, but 60 percent of them had already slipped under the $50 mark in court-assessed property. (See Table 9.) In addition, 20 percent of the couples held debts as compared with 10 percent of the solitary veterans. The debt figure suggests that a large number of couples were vulnerable to bankruptcy. Many couples appeared close to the condition reported by solitary veterans--loss of assets, broken households, and dependency on friends and the town--which, for a few, could mean spending the remainder of their lives in an almshouse.

The testimonies of Henry Hallowell and Michael Waggoner reflected the fears of other couples who were better off. They saw themselves losing self-sufficiency and dreaded pauperism. When Hallowell, who was refused a pension, appeared before the court in Lynn, Massachusetts, in 1820, he was sixty-five years old, living with his wife (age not given), and had an estate valued at $448.50. His property consisted of three-quarters of an acre of land, "part of a dwelling house...consisting of two back chambers," an "old shop," an "old barn, part of a cellar," and "one-half pew in a Methodist Meeting House." Hallowell had acquired this property in a previous marriage. He acquired additional property through remarriage. His current wife's part interest in a dwelling house, four-fifths of an acre of land, a wood lot, and a salt marsh brought $28 a year in income. In addition, he and his wife received $12 a year by renting rooms in their house and part of the cellar. Hallowell claimed that he still needed to work as a fisherman to support himself and his wife and to aid his two married sons, who were both "very poor and destitute." He noted that one of the sons was receiving help from the town. This precarious network of kin help, supplemented by town aid and income from rent and real property, was near collapse because, in Hallowell's words, he was "weak in body and unable to do much work" and because his wife's health was also poor. Michael Waggoner, who received the benefit, was sixty-six and lived with his wife, fifty-five, on a small farm in Pennsylvania. In 1820 Waggoner told the court that he was "infirm" and in debt, and that his wife was in "bad health." His total estate was valued at nearly $400, about the same as Hallowell's, but Waggoner also reported owing $300 on a first mortgage on his farm. He claimed that the pension was needed to pay off the mortgage; without the benefit he would lose the farm and his means of making a livelihood. War Department regulations allowed the deduction of first mortgages, leaving, in Waggoner's case, $65 in assets, well below the department's unofficial poverty line.[20]

Most couples who included testimony, like Hallowell and Waggoner, portrayed themselves as once self-sufficient tenant farmers, laborers, tradesmen, and landowners who, through failing health, rising debts, old age, and a declining ability to work were on the edge of losing their meager assets. They wanted the pension to retain their status as well as to prevent their being ground down by disability and poverty. Federal policy, however, was intended mainly to aid destitute veterans--as the rejection of Hallowell's claim illustrated. Only if the veteran held a first mortgage, like Waggoner, did federal guidelines favor aid to prevent loss of home and position in the community.

Testimonies from veterans heading nuclear households resembled those provided by couples. These too were poor, indebted, aged, and infirm men who scratched out a living in a desperate effort to sustain their households. While they generally succeeded without aid from kin, friends, or town (see Tables 6 and 7), the struggle for self-sufficiency was difficult. The cases of Joel Atherton, a rejected claimant, and Joseph Craven, who was awarded the pension, illustrate the precariousness of nuclear households containing young and disabled children as well as the War Department's discretionary power to award or withhold assistance.

In 1820, Atherton, age fifty-six, was living on his farm in Portland, Maine, but could do little work because of "rheumatism." His household consisted of his wife, age fifty-four, who was reported to be in "comfortable health and able to do part of the housework," and eight daughters. His two oldest daughters, ages twenty-two and twenty-four, lived at home and were "very feeble." His six other daughters, ages eight to twenty, also lived with him, and all but the youngest were "able in part to support themselves." His property, valued at $210, consisted of forty acres of farm land, a barn and attached half-house, a cow, a yearling, five sheep, farm tools, and household goods. He claimed no income and no collectible money and noted debts amounting to $275. In essence, Atherton told the court that if he did not get the pension he would have to dispose "of all the little property I possess" in order to pay debts. His application was denied.[21]

In the case of Joseph Craven, a sixty-one-year-old baker living in Elizabethtown, New Jersey, the federal poverty line was bent because family tragedy compounded his declining health, deepened his impoverishment, and threatened to dissolve his household. Prior to his court testimony, Craven's son had suddenly gone blind. The boy was sent to a hospital in New York but discharged after a few months because his condition was considered incurable. According to the affidavit received by the court, "The father is now required to take him away, take care of him, that he may no longer be a burden on that institution." The effect produced "very great despondency" in Craven which "rendered him incapable of that exertion, which contributed somewhat to keep him above absolute poverty." Without the pension, Craven faced the likelihood of losing his property ($205) to creditors and his son to the overseers, and possibly finding himself and his wife on the auction block for outdoor relief.[22]

The testimonies from nuclear households leave a general impression of veterans either barely able to keep afloat or else being dragged down by the afflictions of their young. In a few instances, the ability and desire to have and raise children had exceeded the family's capability to maintain them. While healthy girls and boys could and probably did contribute to the household's support by working or helping with chores, as in Joel Atherton's case, they often compounded the veteran's poverty. In these cases, the impact of poverty was not only broader because it included children but also more threatening because the household stood on the verge of ruin and dismemberment should it fail to sustain itself. Nevertheless, the survival of these households revealed the tough, resilient strands connecting family members.

Veterans' testimonies suggest that household ties, once broken, were irreparable. The ex-soldiers realized that they faced not only economic dependency but also changes in family relations. Feeble or handicapped children might be placed out or put into an almshouse. Young men would leave in order to escape the pull of their parents' poverty. Families might end up being supported by the town and thus losing control over their own lives. The veterans were clinging to their property and their family ties for some comfort, security, and status.

Testimonies from veterans who were taken in by kin revealed the character of reformulated family ties. As Table 4 shows, in nearly all of these cases the veterans were completely destitute. In a few instances, their pension helped to keep the household going. The pension forged a link with kin which, if broken, threatened to cast off the applicant to live in circumstances such as those described for the bleakest solitary veterans and couples. The following cases illustrate the variety of circumstances existing among veterans living in reconstituted households.

William Worster was completely dependent upon the kin with whom he lived. In 1820 he told a court in York, Maine, that he was a seventy-five-year-old blacksmith with $20 in property and was suffering from old age, "descreptitude and poverty." He said that he was no longer able to work to support his wife, age seventy-seven, who was still in "tolerable shape." Worster reported that he and his wife were "wholly dependent on the charity and benevolence of my son, Samuel Worster with whom I live."[23]

The Mann and Davis families reestablished ties which made them interdependent and which were mutually beneficial. Nathan Mann, age fifty-eight, his wife, sixty-four, and an unmarried son (no age given) had moved to the farm of another, married son. Mann told the court that he still had to support his own family as well as provide aid to his "feeble" daughter-in-law and her infirm child. He was, however, less able to help with the farm because of rheumatism. Also, he had burdened the household with $119 in debts against $30 in assets. Daniel Davis was a sixty-eight-year-old penniless laborer who could not work because of rheumatism. Davis, his forty-seven-year-old wife, and their three sons, ages seven, eight, and ten--one of whom was an "idiot"--had been taken in by his daughter from an earlier marriage and his son-in-law and received additional help from the daughter's brothers and sisters who lived nearby. While one can only guess at what members of these families thought of each other, it is reasonable to suspect an ethic of filial and parental duty to help kin in need, and a household economy capable of supporting more members, led to the effort to establish new bonds.[24]

Worster, Mann, and Davis worried that their children would no longer be able to support them or that they would become unbearable burdens and be forced to leave. Similarly, James Worren feared that while his sons, ages twenty-four and twenty-eight, could support themselves, they could not maintain Worren himself, fifty-nine, and his wife, sixty, without the pension. The situation was particularly tenuous because Worren could do little to help the household because of an asthmatic condition.[25]

Bartholomew Stevens of Summerset County, Maine, had experienced what Worren feared. He had been forced out of his son's household and had become a town ward. Stevens and his wife, both age seventy-two, were paupers who had lived off the town until he received the pension under the 1818 act. When they got the pension, Stevens and his wife moved in with their son whom they claimed to be "a man with small property" unable on his own to support his parents. Stevens stated that without the pension he and his wife would be forced to leave their son's home and return to being supported by the town.[26] Despite their precarious position, veterans like Worster, Mann, Davis, Worren, and Stevens could count themselves among the lucky few who were able to find refuge among kin.

Claimants who took in kin were the wealthiest group of veterans (see Tables 4 and 9), but they reported a variety of circumstances which taxed their resources, threatened their self-sufficiency, and justified, in their minds, the supplemental support promised by the pension. Veterans heading these households reported burdensome responsibilities such as caring for aged mothers, infirm children and in-laws, grandchildren, daughters deserted by their husbands, widowed daughters and their children, daughters whose husbands were off trying to establish their own homesteads, and young married daughters and sons who could not make a start on their own. But, as the case of Phineas Hamblett demonstrates, federal officials were not inclined to award pensions to these households.

Hamblett was the main link in the chain of his family's support. In 1820 Hamblett was living on his farm in Cheshire County, New Hampshire. His estate was assessed at $777, but he also claimed debts totaling $253. Hamblett's household was a refuge for disabled and aged kin. His wife, sixty-two, was deaf and blind. His daughter, thirty-nine, lived at home because she was too infirm to support herself. In addition, Hamblett's mother-in-law, age ninety-two, lived with them and was totally dependent upon him for support. Hamblett stated that although he was fairly well off and still in good health at age sixty-five, he was no longer able to work much.[27] Hamblett's concern must have been shared by others. What would happen to him and to his property should he cease to be able to keep up his farm and stave off the creditors? Hamblett probably knew of collapsed households such as those of Henry Buzzell and Joseph Craven. The prospects of a similar disaster probably led to his self-assessed claim of indigency. However, his claim was denied.

A "Life-Course" History

A more complete portrait of the veterans, their poverty, and the impact of federal aid requires a life-course study linking application data with public records and local histories.[28] Rufus Burnham was randomly picked for such a study from a list of pensioners in Essex County, Massachusetts. Through study of Burnham's life course, greater insight may be gained into the accuracy of the application data, the causes and conditions of poverty, and the effects of the pension. In Burnham's case these factors were well documented. In 1820 Burnham's claim to continue on the pension rolls was rejected because of excessive wealth.[29] Three years later the pension was restored. Burnham was accepted under a new law which made veterans rejected under the 1820 act eligible for the benefit if they had subsequently become impoverished. Claimants were required to document changes in wealth or other circumstances which had reduced them to "the lowest grade of poverty."[30]

Burnham was born in 1748 in Boxford, Massachusetts, the first of three brothers and sisters, all of whom survived to adulthood.[31] In 1763 Burnham's father was declared insane, and his estate of nearly Ŀ300 was put into trust by the court to be used to support the Burnham family. Rufus Burnham was placed under a court-appointed guardianship. By 1775, the Burnham estate was nearly gone. By 1777, it had been completely used to pay for support of other family members. Rufus Burnham, once the son of a yeoman farmer with good economic prospects, now faced a bleak future as a landless farm laborer. When the war broke out, Burnham joined the militia, fought at Bunker Hill, and was discharged at the end of 1775. He continued to serve short terms in the militia until June 1778, when he enlisted for nine months in a Massachusetts unit of the Continental line. After this duty, Burnham saw no more war except as a host for a Hessian prisoner and his family.

In November 1777, Burnham married and within five years had three children, Sarah, Seth, and Hannah. Between 1784 and 1785 Burnham bought forty-three acres of land with a house and barn for ₤210. He also sold most of that land during these same years for a slight gain, which leads one to believe that he either was speculating or had accrued some debts which had to be paid. For five years Burnham and his family lived on their fourteen-acre farm. In 1790 Burnham sold his property and moved to rented quarters, where he remained until 1822. The reasons for the sale can only be surmised. Boxford's population dropped by 8 percent between 1790 and 1800, possibly indicating an economic constriction that adversely affected the Burnhams. In 1818, when Burnham applied for the pension, his household consisted of his wife and his children, Seth and Sarah. Hannah, his third child, had married in 1804 and was no longer in the community. Burnham received a pension.

The pension made a significant impact on the Burnham household. Within a few months of his father's receipt of the pension Seth, age thirty-six, bought a farm two miles down the road from his father and married Caroline Herrick, age twenty-two, the daughter of a well-to-do neighbor. Most likely, Seth had remained in his father's household to assist his parents while saving money to buy property. The pension released Seth from the need to contribute to his parents' support and enabled him to establish his own household. Within two years of the marriage, Seth and Caroline had their only child, Charlotte. A year later Seth was elected a selectman for Boxford, serving for one year. By 1855, the year he left Boxford, Seth had acquired a taxable estate valued at $2,400.

In 1820 Rufus Burnham reapplied for the pension as required by law. His claim showed that while Seth had moved out, his daughter Hannah had returned home in a sickly condition. Burnham reported that he was seventy-two, infirm, suffering from a hernia, and nearly blind in his right eye. His wife, age seventy-one, was also in poor health. Only their daughter Sarah, age forty, who cared for her parents and presumably for Hannah, was healthy. Burnham had three acres in marshland worth $25, livestock valued at $147, and goods totaling $106. Like many of the veterans cited earlier in the discussion of wealth, Burnham claimed debts--in his case $150. He was dropped from the rolls because "his property amounted to more than any other person whose name has been continued on the list and who served so short a time."[32] For two years Burnham appealed the decision.

Following this loss of support, Burnham and his wife were aided by friends, Sarah, and probably Seth. Sometime between 1820 and 1822, neighbors lent Burnham money to build a house next to his rented quarters. The loan was probably made with the expectation that Burnham would be restored to the rolls and use the pension to repay neighbors. As his neighbors' help demonstrated, Burnham "was much esteemed" by the community and considered "an honest, upright and industrious citizen" deserving assistance. In 1822, Burnham, now a widower and blind, moved to this new house with his two daughters.

The discontinuation of the pension, however, put the Burnham household in severe jeopardy. By 1823, when he reapplied for the pension, Burnham claimed to be penniless and was officially reported as such. In 1821 his real property, three acres of marshland, was conveyed to Sarah to pay off a $50 debt, possibly accrued for his care. His livestock had been either consumed or "sold for expenses of family." For example, he sold six cows and a heifer for $105 to pay rent and taxes. Accompanying testimony from townsmen confirmed Burnham's claim that without the pension he could not support himself "except by public or private charity." Furthermore, impoverishment and infirmity had transformed Burnham's household status. In 1820 he was the head of the household, but in 1823 he was nearly subordinate to his daughters, or as Burnham put it, "two daughters live with me, or rather I live with them." According to Burnham, Sarah and Hannah were too "infirm" and "indigent" to continue to support him.[33] No references were made to Seth's ability to aid his father and sisters.

Restoration of the pension in 1823, which included back payments to 1820, sustained the household and even allowed the Burnhams to build a modest estate. It also meant that the town would not expect Seth to support his father and possibly his sisters. Burnham's household remained intact until 1834, when Hannah died. Two years later, at age eighty-seven, Rufus died. Sarah inherited the house and the remainder of her father's estate, which had increased in value to over $500. In 1842, Sarah, now aged sixty-two, announced her intention to marry a resident of Middleton, Massachusetts. The marriage never occurred. In 1844, she married a neighbor and widower, Joseph Tyler, who then moved to her house. He apparently had little wealth. When she died in 1858, her estate was put in trust for her husband's support, with her brother Seth and his heirs as remaindermen. When Tyler died in 1864, the estate was liquidated by Seth, with the small balance going to Tyler's creditors.

The reconstruction of the Burnham family history provides insight into the variety of conditions which ultimately led 20,000 veterans to declare poverty and into the impact of the pension upon their lives. Burnham was neither the product of a cycle of poverty nor part of a floating class of paupers. He began his life as the son of a yeoman farmer who had a "substantial" estate. When his father became non compos mentis, the town stepped in to place the children under guardianships. In 1768 the father and youngest son were placed with others to live. It is not clear whether the remainder of the family stayed on the farm until it was liquidated for debts in July 1777. Nevertheless, by 1777 Rufus had to start from scratch and seemed to be fairly successful until 1790 when he lost most of his estate. Despite his decline, Burnham appeared to have a solid place in the community. His son married well, acquired wealth, and had a high standing in Boxford. The pension appeared to be instrumental in sustaining his strong family ties, in part because it benefited all of the members of the households. Seth was able to go ahead with his plans to establish his own household. Rufus Burnham's household was maintained without charity and became a refuge for the infirm Hannah. And finally, Sarah eventually acquired an estate that made an attractive dowry and helped to sustain her widowed husband.

Conclusion

As Gerald Grob reminds us, welfare policies seldom are the products of a single motive and a single goal, and they often do not turn out as planned.[34] The 1818 pension act reflected a mixture of motives and conflicting purposes. It appealed to benevolent and patriotic feelings, assuaged guilt for earlier injustices dealt Continental soldiers, and served the nationalistic policies favored by the Monroe administration. The pension act created the largest federal program of direct relief until the New Deal. Ironically, it also produced the first federally defined class of poor by placing thousands of veterans below a national poverty line.

Despite poor-law features, the pension act was not a conventional poor law like that which might be applied to impoverished veterans by their towns. Town aid was reserved for persons who were judged both morally worthy and economically needy. The rate of support varied to meet the need for subsistence, and assets could be encumbered or liquidated by the town to help support the pauper. That need was constantly reviewed by the local overseers and adjusted accordingly. Although most town poor received outdoor relief, that is, supplemental aid while living in their own homes, overseers could also disperse the poor among other families by placing them out or on occasion auctioning them off to the lowest bidder through public auctions.

In contrast to these local practices, the federal poor law assumed, prima facie, that every Continental soldier was worthy of aid, so the only question to be answered was whether he needed it. Once judged in need of aid, the claimant was not granted relief rated to his need but rather awarded a lifetime pension at a rate higher for officers than for ordinary soldiers. By passing the War Department's means test, the veteran was transformed from an alms seeker into an honored pensioner with a guaranteed annual income for life. There was no evidence in federal policy that poverty was perceived as a social problem, or that the poor were feared and needed to be controlled.[35]

The pension act reveals that American social welfare is based not only on Elizabethan poor-law traditions but also on new practices which combine features of a pension plan and poor-law provisions. The distinction is significant because it illuminates the complexity of American social welfare. On the one hand, traditional practices create a net to catch worthy and deserving individuals who are unable to support themselves. While not automatically entitled to aid, they nevertheless have the right to appeal for assistance. On the other hand, as this study illustrates, American welfare includes practices which, in effect, invite individuals to apply for assistance from the nation in recognition of their membership in a group identified with particular cultural ideals. The recognition of cultural value and impoverishment afforded to Revolutionary War veterans led to the first federal policy to provide relief to such a group through a pension.

The 20,000 claims made under the pension act are a rich source of demographic and wealth information which had never been systematically studied. They amount to a national survey of poverty among a large number of elderly poor and their households in the early Republic. The data, case studies, and Burnham's life course show that the poor who applied for the pension represented various sections of society and occupied different economic strata. Poverty, acting somewhat like a press, compacted the strata and forced a number of individuals to lower positions. Poverty not only meant relative economic deprivation but also consisted of a number of interrelated factors such as old age, declining health, reduced self-sufficiency, and household decomposition. According to the veterans, illness, the death of a spouse, departure of children, the burden of handicapped or dependent children, mental anguish, impoverishment of children, and indebtedness accentuated the slide toward poverty and dependency. Sometimes a network of kin and friends formed to halt the slide. Poverty was best combated in households where there were healthy children. They contributed to household support, attracted help from kin, or relieved pressure on the household by leaving. Older veterans who were penniless had to resort to direct support from friends and the town. Conjugal households remained open for the aid of kin but could deteriorate rapidly without support.[36]

Despite the variety in causes and conditions of poverty, the veterans shared common goals--the retention or restoration of self-sufficiency. They wanted to protect meager assets, avoid further losses, and defend their positions as heads of households. They sought to halt the grinding effects of poverty and to prevent household decomposition and a decline in status. The pension helped them meet their goals by enabling them to return to relative independence, by helping to reestablish or sustain households, by contributing to the formulation of networks of kin and friends' support, and by cutting town costs for relief. There were also psychological and social benefits. The lifetime income ended the dread of pauperism and ensured recipients an honored place in their communities as pensioned heroes of the Revolution.

Notes

*Reprinted with permission of The Social Service Review, John P. Resch, and the University of Chicago from The Social Service Review 56 (June 1982): 171-195. Copyright 1982 by The University of Chicago. All rights reserved. Research support for the project was provided by Merrimack Valley College, the Newberry Library, and the National Endowment for the Humanities. In particular I wish to thank John Shy, Robert M. Mennel, David Hackett Fischer, Barbara Hanawalt, and Terry Savage for their contributions to this project. Special thanks go to Robert H. Bremner for his constant support and friendship.

1. Annals of Congress, 15th Cong., 1st sess., 1817-1818, pp. 2518-2519. The House passed the bill "without division," while the Senate voted twenty-three to eight in favor of the bill (Ibid., p. 512, Journal of the Senate, 15th Cong., 1st sess., 1817-1818, p. 200). Amendments, particularly over the exclusion of state militias, created some sectional and partisan divisions.

2. For the debate on the bill in the House and Senate, see Ibid., pp. 140-159, 191-200, 497-499, 505-506, 510-512. For expressions of public sympathy toward the veterans, see Niles' Weekly Register, 23 November 1816, 8 February 1817, and 1 March 1817. For recent discussions on revolutionary values, see Alfred H. Kelly and Richard D. Miles, "Maintenance of Revolutionary Values," Annals 426 (July 1976): 25-52; Jack Greene, "Values and Society in Revolutionary America," Ibid., pp. 53-69. For a detailed and thoughtful treatment of how the revolutionary generation perceived the Continental army within the emerging political culture, see Charles W. Royster, A Revolutionary People

at War: The Continental Army and American Character, 1775-1783 (Durham: University of North Carolina Press, 1980).

3. Annals of Congress, 15th Cong., 1st sess., 1817-1818, p. 1698.

4. Ibid., pp. 191-197.

5. William Glasson, Federal and Military Pensions in the United States (New York: Oxford University Press, 1918), pp. 1-3, 20-53; Robert G. Bodenger, "Soldiers' Bonuses: A History of Veterans' Benefits in the United States, 1776-1967," (Ph.D. diss., Pennsylvania State University, 1971), pp. 27-28. For general discussions of the pension and half-pay controversy, see Royster, pp. 333-351, 373-378; Richard Kohn, Eagle and Sword (New York: Free Press, 1975), pp. 1-53, 277-303. See also John Shy, "American Society and Its War for Independence"; Don Higginbotham, "The American Militia"; and Richard Kohn, "American Generals of the Revolution," all in Reconsiderations of the Revolutionary War, ed. Don Higginbotham (Westport, Ct.: Greenwood Press, 1978), pp. 72-123.

6. Walter I. Trattner has recently observed that the federal government has been little studied in the antebellum period for its social welfare practices because it is generally believed that, except for emergency relief, some land grants, and the Dorothea Dix bill, the national government was not involved in social welfare. Walter I. Trattner, "The Federal Government and Social Welfare in Early Nineteenth-Century America," Social Service Review 50 (June 1976): 243-255. The Dix bill, passed by Congress in 1854, provided 12,225,000 acres of public land to

support institutions for the insane and deaf. President Pierce vetoed it. See Children and Youth in America, ed. Robert H. Bremner, (Cambridge, Ma.: Harvard University Press, 1970), 3 vols., 1, pp. 789-791.

7. Annals of Congress, 16th Cong., 1st sess., 1819-1820, pp. 2614-2615. For comments on the attorney general's opinion that the benefit was intended only for veterans in the "lowest grade of poverty," see The Papers of John C. Calhoun, ed. W. Edwin Hemphill (Columbia: University of South Carolina Press, 1977), 14 vols., 5, p. 265. In 1823, a second amendment was passed to overrule the attorney general's opinion that, because of the silence of the law, the secretary of war was not empowered to grant pensions to claimants who were rejected under the 1820 amended law but who had subsequently become destitute. The 1823 amendment allowed rejected claimants to reapply with a new schedule of property plus a full explanation of why their property had been sold. See Annals of Congress, 17th Cong., 2nd sess., 1822-1823, pp. 1409-1410.

8. Glasson, pp. 95-97; Bodenger, pp. 26-42, 389-390. The figures on the costs and the number of applicants who passed the 1820 means test, the number of people composing their households, and the average number of years veterans received relief are derived from a statistical analysis of a random sample of 877 claims found in "Revolutionary War Pension Files," Record Group 15, National Archives, Washington, D.C.

9. Daniel P. Moynihan, The Politics of a Guaranteed Income: The Nixon Administration and the Family Assistance Plan (New York: Random House, 1973), pp. 113-235.

10. Annals of Congress, 17th Cong., 2d sess., 1822-1823, p. 283.

11. "Revolutionary War Pension Files," Record Group 15. The sample was taken from microfilm publication M805, which consists of 898 reels containing the applications and selected correspondence.

12. Niles' Weekly Register, 26 February 1820.

13. Lawrence Stone, The Family, Sex and Marriage in England, 1500- 1800 (New York: Harper & Row, 1977), pp. 4-10, 21-29, 651-687, 759-781; Peter Laslett and Richard Wall, Household and Family in Past Time (Cambridge: Cambridge University Press, 1972), pp. 1-89; Kenneth W. Wachter, Eugene A. Hammel, and Peter Laslett, Statistical Studies of Historical Social Structure (New York: Academic Press, 1978), pp. 105-111.

14. Annals of Congress, 16th Cong., 1st sess., 1819-1820, pp. 852-854.

15. On the life-course perspective, see Transitions: The Family and Life Course in Historical Perspective, ed. Tamara K. Hareven (New York: Academic Press, 1978), pp. 1-64. The life-course perspective seeks to describe and analyze the interconnections among individual, houshold, and social developments within a historical context. By contrast, cohort and life cycle approaches examine slices of a population which are usually divided by age groups. The data in this study indicated that the age of the applicant--except for those few over seventy-five--had little to do with the circumstances described in the claims, thereby severely limiting the value of either cohort or life

cycle analysis. Life course more closely fitted the data because of its focus on individuals who are in a "continuous interactive process" with their families and community--a process shaped by demographic and economic factors and social values. For an assessment and application of the life-course perspective to the aged which emphasizes the demographic factors in determining individual choices, see Daniel Scott Smith, "The Course, Norms and the Family System of Older Americans in 1900," Journal of Family History 4 (Fall 1979): 285-298.

16. Asher Russell, "Revolutionary War Pension File," S40368 (hereafter cited as Pension File); John Waid, Pension File S35378.

17. Icabod Beckwith, Pension File S34023; James Graton, Pension File R21885.

18. Abraham Taylor, Pension File W26508.

19. Henry Buzzell, Pension File S45529.

20. Henry Hallowell, Pension File S32800; Michael Waggoner, Pension File S40636.

21. Joel Atherton, Pension File W23471.

22. Joseph Craven, Pension File S34612.

23. William Worster, Pension File S35148.

24. Nathan Mann, Pension File W9908; Daniel Davis, Pension File W3519.

25. James Worren, Pension File S45452.

26. Bartholomew Stevens, Pension File W25074.

27. Phineas Hamblett, Pension File S44407.

28. The selection was made from the list of persons who had once or were still receiving benefits as of 1834. The list

amounts to a census of all applicants. See The Pension Roll of 1835 (Baltimore: Genealogical Printing Co., 1968), 1, p. 67. In my monograph (in preparation) on the pensioners, life-course studies are being developed for all the Continental veterans in Boxford and Salem, Massachusetts, and in Peterborough, New Hampshire. This methodology will permit comparison between Continental veterans who did and who did not apply for the pension as well as the development of case histories linking individual veterans with their households and communities. The concentration on one region should provide other historians with a solid basis for similar life-course studies of veterans from other regions.

29. Rufus Burnham, Pension File S34125. Burnham's claim resembled that of many other veterans. He was the head of a nuclear household (45 percent of the cases), one of nearly half of the applicants in their mid-sixties to early seventies. Like most veterans Burnham was infirm and a tenant farmer who had few possessions. Also, he was burdened with debts.

30. See above, note 4. According to the sample data, 16 percent of the applicants in 1820 were rejected, most because of excessive wealth. One-third of these applicants were restored to the rolls under the 1823 amendment.

31. The discussion of Rufus Burnham was composed from a wide range of sources. See Massachusetts Soldiers and Sailors of the War (Boston, 1896), pp. 865-866; Vital Records of Boxford (Topsfield, Mass., 1905), pp. 18, 121; Sidney Perley, The Dwellings of Boxford (Salem, Ma., 1893), pp. 70-71, 227-228;

Sidney Perley, The History of Boxford (Boxford, Ma., 1880) pp. 219, 228-231, 237-238, 283, 384; An Abstract of the Valuation of Real and Personal Property in the Town of Boxford for the Year 1855 (Salem, Ma., 1856), p. 18; Essex, South District Court, Grantee Deeds, Docket 142, 169; Docket 143, 188; Grantor Deeds, Docket 141, 215; Docket 145, 20; Docket 151, 146; South District Court, Probate Court Records, Documents 4155, 4163, 4164, 55942; and Pension File S34125.

    32. Letter, J. L. Edwards, War Department clerk, to Jeremiah Nelson, U. S. representative from Massachusetts, May 7, 1822, in Rufus Burnham, Pension File S34125.

    33. Pension application, April 8, 1823, Rufus Burnham, Pension File S34125.

    34. Gerald Grob, "Reflections on the History of Social Policy in America," Reviews in American History 7 (September 1979): 293-306.

    35. For discussions of poverty and benevolence during this period, see David J. Rothman, The Discovery of the Asylum (Boston: Little, Brown & Co., 1971), pp. xiii-xx, 155-205; Raymond A. Mohl, "Poverty, Pauperism, and Social Order in the Pre-Industrial American City, 1780-1840," Social Science Quarterly 52 (March 1972): 940-944. These two sources develop the social disorder/social maintenance explanation of early nineteenth-century responses to poverty. Lois Banner, "Religious Benevolence as Social Control: A Critique of an Interpretation," Journal of American History 60 (June 1972): 23-41, summarizes the role of religion and the enlightenment in early nineteenth-century philanthropy. See also Paul Goodman, "Ethics and Enter-

prise: The Values of a Boston Elite, 1800-1860," <u>American Quarterly</u> 18 (Fall 1966): 437-450; M. J. Heale, "From City Fathers to Social Critics: Humanitarianism and Government in New York, 1790-1860," <u>Journal of American History</u> 58 (June 1976): 21-41. These two studies argue that civic stewardship was a principal motive initiating and guiding responses to poverty. It should be noted that all of the above studies use local societies, exemplary persons, state practices, or a combination of these to develop their cases. For a recent study of urban poverty and relief, see Priscilla Clement, "The Response to Need, Welfare and Poverty in Philadelphia, 1800 to 1850," (Ph.D. diss., University of Pennsylvania, 1977).

36. For studies dealing with the effect of poverty on family structure and the impact of pensions on family relations, see Michael Anderson, <u>Family Structure in Nineteenth Century Lancashire</u> (Cambridge: Cambridge University Press, 1971), and his "The Impact on the Family Relationships of the Elderly of Changes since Victorian Times in Governmental Income-Maintenance Provision," in <u>Family, Bureaucracy, and the Elderly</u>, ed. Ethel Shanas and Marvin B. Sussman (Durham, N.C.: Duke University Press, 1977), pp. 36-59.

Sarah Josepha Hale, Matron of Victorian Womanhood
by Angela Howard Zophy

The career of Sarah Josepha Hale spanned most of the Victorian era in the United States. She emerged from the New England middle class to become not only a minor national literary figure but an acknowledged and influential spokeswoman for her sex. She served in a breakthrough position as the editor of the major woman's magazine of the antebellum period, <u>Godey's Lady's Book and American Ladies' Magazine</u>. During her forty-year tenure at <u>Godey's</u> from 1837 to 1877, she was known and revered as "Mrs. Hale" by two or more generations of readers. In this powerful position as <u>Godey's</u> editor, Hale participated in the formulation and promulgation of the Victorian definition of Woman's Role in the nineteenth-century United States. She determinedly advanced the causes of women's education and employment as integral aspects of Woman's Sphere. Hale was the matron of Victorian womanhood in two senses, both as a presiding matriarch of the Cult of True Womanhood and as a vigilant custodian of the definition of the limitations of Woman's Sphere.[1]

The traditional woman's role in the nineteenth century was in fact a recent adaptation to accommodate the impact upon women in the middle class family as industrialization and urbanization absorbed and altered the values of the eighteenth-century agrarian society of the United States.[2] By the 1820s scientific and technological progress made possible and, more to the point, profitable the publication and circulation of a genre of literature which targeted a specific audience of white Anglo-Saxon Protestant middle class women who were experiencing the transition from agrarian co-workers in an extended family and producers of crucial household goods and services toward becoming urban homemakers who were economic dependents within the nuclear family and primarily the consumers of the massed-produced goods and services required by their households.[3] Displaced from agrarian economic self-sufficiency, town and city women in the home were charged with managing the Private Sphere which supposedly was comprised solely of their homes and families. These women were expected to create in the middle class home a "haven in a heartless world," a sanctuary for men from the crass competitive commercial marketplace of the Public Sphere.[4]

In the first quarter of the nineteenth century, cash in the form of wages replaced both the barter of goods and the exchange of services in the United States economy. The economic roles of men and women changed accordingly, for in general middle class women were barred from wage employments. Women as a group lost whatever economic parity they had gained in the pre-industrial colonial era. Specialization and professionalization effectively excluded women because skilled trades and the professions of teaching, medicine, the ministry and the law were to be acquired and certified through apprentice systems or by educational institutions which were open to men only.[5] Therefore rural and urban women alike sought and received clarification of the proper Woman's Role from the genre of nineteenth-century women's literature, especially women's magazines.[6]

Twentieth-century historian Barbara Welter discerned within this literature a consistent definition of Victorian womanhood. Welter aptly designated four recurring traits--purity, piety, domesticity, and submission--as these consistently appeared in Victorian literature for women, as fundamental to the nineteenth-century "Cult of True Womanhood." This cult perforce regulated adult women's behavior and personality by focusing women's lives upon marriage and the family, thus limiting women to the domestic circle.[7] Victorian society split into two separate spheres: men were to function as producers and wage-earners, protecting and providing for women and children through their labor in the workforce; women were to perform the unpaid work of household and family care.[8]

As an author of women's books and as the editor of Godey's, Sarah Josepha Hale accepted and applied the current concept of Woman's Sphere. She promoted as uncontestable woman's biological destiny as mother and homemaker to rule the domestic sphere; she supported service to others, in the family and the community, as woman's duty; and she emphasized that women alone could provide the spiritually uplifting home life for men and children to counteract the relentless materialism of the Public Sphere. Woman's Sphere was also a center of women's informal but considerable power to render the domestic circle a citadel from which women might sally forth into the public arena as the agents of True Womanhood, ministering to the needs of society as they did to those of the family. Hale translated the seemingly inescapable maternal role of women into a locus of social power.

As mothers of the white race, middle class women were necessarily both the custodians of domestic virtue and the guardians of the national morality, indeed, of the spiritual consciousness of western civilization. Hale entitled this innate feminine power over others, Woman's Influence, by which the Christ-like example of dutiful and altruistic women gently led men as well as children to do their duty. Woman's Influence applied indirect feminine moral suasion, rather than ethical or logical confrontation, to see that everyone behaved properly. Since Woman's Role as mother of the race was ordained by God and nature, Woman's Influence must likewise spring from those divine and natural sources. Through their use of this romantic and evocative concept, Hale and her literary cohorts elevated public esteem for women's quintessential role of childcare and generated at least lip-service veneration from men for women's non-economic (that is, non-wealth producing) biological function with its attendant power of Woman's Influence in the midst of a masculine commercial culture obsessed with the acquisition of wealth.[9]

As the editor of the American Ladies' Magazine of Boston from 1828 to 1836, and then of Godey's of Philadelphia from 1837 to 1877, Hale used her editorial columns to address politely but directly the issues of women's education and employment, while her views were indirectly represented in the rest of both magazines' contents. In her Godey's column, "The Editors' Table," Hale consistently presented her readers an expanded role for women within the context of Woman's Sphere, one that enhanced women's social position without diminishing women's domestic identification. Hale spoke directly to her readers in "The Editors' Table" and her literary notices which appeared unobtrusively at the "back of the book," among the final pages of Godey's between the crafts instructions and the advertisements. Bolstering women's self and social esteem during a period of decline in women's economic status, Hale played a central role in justifying the propriety as well as the necessity of education and employment opportunities for women in the antebellum period. Mrs. Hale, therefore, participated in the transformation as well as the transmission of the socially acceptable concept of Woman's Sphere and of the equally respectable ideals of True Womanhood.[10]

Godey's was a formidable vehicle to disseminate Hale's opinions. In a working relationship that paralleled the division of labor in the Victorian middle class marriage, publisher Louis A. Godey managed the magazine's finances and circulation, while Hale as editor imprinted her integrity and priorities upon the text of Godey's Lady's Book. Hale brought to Godey's a format of poetry, fiction, features and how-to sections that set the pattern and the trend for women's magazines of the 1840s and 1850s and which survives today. Godey's tasteful embellishments, for which it is largely remembered today, and its respectable literature promoted as traditional the concepts of Woman's Sphere, Woman's Influence and the Cult of True Womanhood. As the editor of one of the most widely circulated women's magazines in the two decades before and after the Civil War, Hale had access to a large readership eager for the printed word. Mr. Godey boasted of more than 150,000 subscribers in 1860 and of 500,000 readers in 1869. The proliferation of books and magazines joined the increased numbers of newspapers and pamphlets, all of which were the principal agents of nineteenth-century commercialized mass culture.[11]

Though denied equal access to education, women were nonetheless part of literate post-Revolutionary audiences in the United States. As literature became big business, writing and editing magazines offered women such as Hale employment as well as an opportunity to educate and entertain other women. Under Hale's direction, Godey's led the periodicals dedicated to "amuse and instruct" the gentle sex. Hale's impact upon public opinion stemmed not only from her prominent position as editor of Godey's, but also from the particular timing of her literary career. Hale was a prototype of the antebellum literary woman: she was self-educated, capable and driven to her career outside the home by economic necessity. Her life and her career ran true to form for the eastern seaboard middle class "scribbling women" (as Hawthorne called them in a fit of pique) who emerged as popular figures in antebellum women's literature. As a widow supporing five children, Hale used her respectable need and her unimpeachable conservatism to undercut any criticism of her support of women's education and employment, implying always that her shared cultural heritage and bourgeois world view validated her role as a proper spokeswoman for Victorian women. To her readers, Mrs. Hale was Emily Post, Dr. Joyce Brothers, Betty Crocker and Heloise all rolled into one authoritative True Woman.[12]

Hale used Godey's not only to reflect conventional wisdom

about woman's proper role but to mold her public's opinion on many issues concerning women, especially education and employment for women. Hale accepted the finite limitations of Woman's Sphere but interpreted the limitations to include any activities necessary for a True Woman to do her duties. Hale perceived that Woman's Sphere included more than the passivity of specie propagation, nurturing service in the home, and receptive worship in the church, although she never denied these as quintessential woman's work. Hale presented her readers an expanded definition of activities that women might and sometimes **must** properly do to fulfill their duty to family, society, nation and God. Reasoning from practical necessity, Hale argued the propriety of women's increased activities beyond the home in benevolent and public service organizations as well as in education and employment.[13]

Hale sought to alter two particular conditions to enable women to become more effective in their proper sphere: women's access to adequate and formal education and women's increased employment possibilities. Hale championed both causes on the grounds of necessity, not sexual equality. She was part of a conservative social movement of domestic feminism which labored to secure improvements in women's education. Lydia Maria Child and Lydia Huntley Sigourney, for example, were also literary women who used their prestige to promote the importance of an adequate education for the cause of True Womanhood.[14] Emma Willard, Catharine Beecher, and Mary Lyon participated directly by establishing private schools for girls which offered more than the superficial curriculum of the "finishing school" which had been the standard schooling available to eighteenth-century middle class women. These new seminaries were endorsed and publicized by Hale as agencies of True Womanhood.[15] Equally significant, Hale shared with all these women a less obvious agenda which tied formal education to an expansion of job opportunities for respectable ladies in financial distress. Hale and her contemporaries supported women's working outside the home on a contingency basis only. Adverse circumstances must require women to become self-supporting, not to engage in a search for self-fulfilment.[16]

Although Hale devised special features to promote women's education in her early years at Godey's, by the 1850s Hale used her two-page editorials, "The Editors' Table," to present her seldom varying argument that in order for women to fulfill their proper role they must be educated.[17] Although Godey's subscribers were assumed to be the ladies of leisure for whom the Cult of True Womanhood delivered all that it promised, Hale promoted education as a safety net for respectable women who might inherit the financial responsibility for their families, lest they be left with the meager employment options of domestic service, sewing for hire, or serving as governesses (all of which were most suited to single women). Hale's commitment to woman's primary function as wife and mother was tempered by her personal experience of having been widowed suddenly with five children under the age of seven to be supported and educated. To facilitate the survival of individual women and of True Womanhood itself despite such crises, Hale endorsed as appropriate any paying job that could be integrated into the limited concept of woman's work. To Hale and other True Women, the service professions of teaching and health care were obviously and appropriately extensions of woman's domestic role in the larger Public Sphere.[18]

Thus Hale was instrumental in expanding the circumference of Woman's Sphere without challenging its fundamental concept of female biological destiny or endorsing social change threatened by the women's movement, much less women's equality. Hale was aware that her own career and life contradicted the ideal of True Womanhood, because she worked outside the home and in fact ceased to have a "home" after her husband died. When she moved to Boston in 1828, Hale "boarded out" because that was more convenient and practical, since four of her five children were in boarding schools. Hale repeatedly justified her career as the means to educate her children as her late husband would have wished, and she justified her lifestyle as appropriate given her circumstances. Such justification was required of all True Women who worked outside the home. She provided a vivid example that wherever True Women went, whatever they did in the workplace, they would always display the purity, piety, domesticity and submission of True Womanhood. Morover throughout her fifty years of editing women's magazines, she maintained that women working outside the home for wages would be, at best, a necessary evil; paid employment was to be available as a temporary or emergency option only for self-supporting women--those married, widowed or single women for whom there were no husbands, fathers or brothers capable of providing for them. A True Woman's presence in the paid labor force in no way challenged the primary and God-given

Woman's Role as wife and mother nor male hegemony in the Public Sphere.[19]

Hale's campaign for institutions to provide women's education on a par with that available for men commenced with her first editorial statement in the <u>Ladies' Magazine</u> in 1828. Until her retirement from <u>Godey's</u> in 1877, Hale's espousal of incremental improvements in women's education in the United States never waned. Her crowning achievement as a proponent of women's education occurred in 1865 with the founding of the first liberal arts college for women, Vassar. Hale participated in the arduous struggle for equitable educational opportunities for women because she believed that woman's capacity and obligation to learn was no less than man's. Interestingly, though a proponent of women's equal intellectual potential, Hale never confronted the inherent contradiction of supporting comparable curricula for women while fettering women's use of that education to serve the limited ends of Woman's Sphere.[20]

The life experience of Sarah Josepha Hale demonstrated how difficult it was for a woman in early nineteenth-century America to get an adequate education, regardless of her aptitude and motivation, and how useful an education could be to a woman's survival in times of family crisis. Her mother had been a noble example of the Republican Mother of the late eighteenth century, a role model of the literate, intelligent woman who taught her children to read before they attended common school. Hale's father was a wounded American Revolution veteran who never succeeded in farming or business, yet encouraged his daughters as well as his sons to learn. Sarah Josepha kept pace with her older brother Horatio in common school, but her sex barred her from following him to Dartmouth. Horatio, however, tutored her during vacations and she read determinedly on her own. As a young woman, she used her informal education to support her father by teaching school after her mother and younger sister died. Two years later, at age twenty-five, she married David Hale, a self-educated lawyer who shared Horatio's commitment to Sarah Josepha's continuing education. The couple used their evenings to pursue home study of classical and contemporary literature, history and natural sciences. Later as a widow, Hale applied her hand-me-down education to achieve some distinction as a writer and thus was recruited by Reverend John Blake to edit the Ladies' Magazine in Boston. Hale understood that her fall from prosperity was not unusual for women in middle class Jacksonian America, but she credited her possession of an education as the means to a successful career which enabled her to restore her family to the comfort and security of the middle class.[21]

Hale did not originate ideas but rather employed contemporary theories and practices regarding women's education to suit her purpose. In her basic strategy, she first established the propriety of women's being educated and of their being professional teachers; then she supported the establishment of quality schools for women; lastly, she worked to assure that the staff and administrative positions within those institutions were reserved for women only, thereby providing jobs for educated women without their having to compete for men's positions.

Throughout her campaign for women's education, Hale challenged an educational double-standard which excluded women from men's schools and colleges yet allowed men to serve as teachers and supervisors in women's schools. Bolstering her argument upon the fundamental Woman's Role of mother of the race and therefore teacher of the children, Hale adapted the self-contained model of Women's Sphere to the area of women's education. Since education was a crucial part of Woman's Sphere, it must be operated for and by women who would serve not only as instructors but as True Woman role models instilling in their students (as men could not) the self-sacrificing traits of purity, piety, domesticity and submission no less than the three "r's." The consequences to the Cult of True Womanhood of exposing young women students to the male model of academic achievement did not bear contemplation: the existence of Margaret Fuller provided the threatening example of an intellectual woman. Fuller had been rigorously educated by her ambitious father to prove his own power to mold even a female mind as much as to acknowledge his daughter's intellectual gifts. The prospect of women's intellectual equality, that spectre of the fearsome female "blue stocking," haunted the domestic feminists' campaign to increase women's access to education.[22] Hale always stressed that education for women served society and the nation and reinforced the value of women in their proper sphere of activities.[23]

Utilizing the gains in women's education established by eighteenth-century educator Benjamin Rush and others, Hale started from a premise that women <u>could</u> learn and it would be wasteful not to realize that potential. Hale deftly appealed to the Yankee trait of thrift, rather than that of social justice, both in her support of women's education and the entry of women into the field of public school teaching. If women were to be educated, the ensuing practical questions of where, in what manner, and by whom followed. The stickiest question of all proved to be, "to what purpose?" Hale neutralized the charge of inherent feminism within the cause of furthering women's education by wedding education to the maternal role of Woman's Sphere. Hale's conservative approach, though laden with contradictions, disarmed the would-be critics of women's education who, after all, were correct in their fears that educated women would be much harder to control and keep in woman's place.[24] As a true believer of True Womanhood, Hale relied on women's sense of duty to keep them anchored within their sphere regardless of their increased educational opportunities or their broadened intellectual horizons. Hale consistently disavowed any feminist intent or result in suuporting women's education: she sought to enhance woman's esteem, not women's rights.[25]

Throughout her editorial career, Hale pursued a systematic campaign to advance women's educational opportunities by targeting one obvious and seemingly innocuous necessity after another. As a general acceptance of one improvement was achieved, Hale pressed on to the next. While editing Ladies' Magazine before she went to Godey's, Hale helped establish the propriety of and need for educating women. At Godey's, she applied her increased editorial clout to supporting institutions which would provide advanced curricula for women. In the early period of Hale's editorship of Godey's from 1837 to 1840, Hale concentrated her support mainly upon the stronger girls' seminaries and "female academies" so prevalent during the first half of the nineteenth century. During Godey's golden decade of the 1840s, Hale turned her readers' attention toward women's schools which provided a rigorous curricula designed to train women formally for the teaching profession. In the next fifteen years of her editorship from 1850 to 1865, she added her voice to the current call for normal schools, public colleges to train teachers, and for establishing private separate liberal arts colleges for women. Hale's support of separate medical schools and certain vocational training schools for women reflected a trend in women's education during the pre-Civil War decade. In the post-war and final years of Hale's editorship from 1865 to her retirement in 1877, she spoke out for the consolidation and expansion of the pre-war gains--lobbying for more women's liberal arts colleges, normal schools and medical schools while advancing the cause of co-education in land grant colleges in the West. The progression of Hale's goals for women's education paralleled the developments in women's education in the United States from the 1820s through the 1870s.[26]

Hale was pragmatic and cautious in her campaign to expand women's educational opportunities. She recognized that the prestigious men's schools and colleges were not inclined to accept female students, so she supported newly created schools for girls and women. Hale acknowledged the improbability that public funds would be allocated to establish and maintain women's schools especially in the East and the South; so she praised and reinforced individual and group efforts to found the more academically sound private schools which were emerging in the 1820s and 1830s. These schools served a dual purpose, in Hale's opinion, by creating administration and teaching positions for women as well as supplying a solid education for the girl students. Hale admonished True Women to apply their Woman's Influence to secure the financial assistance of True Men for these institutions. For those women unable to attend such a school, Hale urged self-study and offered a specific reading program in her "Editors' Table" in addition to the implied suggested readings in her literary notices. Hale fortified all her efforts for women's education with the fact that ignorance was incompatible with and lethal to the exercise of Woman's Influence.[27]

The founding of Vassar College in 1865 achieved Hale's ultimate goal for women's education with its well-endowed facilities, its liberal arts and science curriculum, and, in response to the insistence of Hale and others, half of the nine professorships designated for women. Its dormitory arrangement provided a surrogate "home" with the supervision and protection women students were believed to require. Hale even prevailed in the removal of the qualifier word, "Female," from the college's title. A preponderance of women in all the subordinate staff positions at Vassar completed Hale's vision that all levels of women's education would be directed and controlled by True Women.[28]

By 1865 Hale had progressed from the improvement of the individual woman through self-study and/or formal training to the improvement of society through increasing woman's role in public and private education.[29] Hale equally supported academic and vocational women's schools which would produce a generation of women qualified for the new employments in the mid-nineteenth-century workplace. She assured her readers all these new positions for women were merely modern adaptations of traditional woman's work.[30] After the Civil War, Hale concentrated on institutions of women's education and endorsed the limited concept of co-education being tried in the mid-West, where to avoid the expense of separate institutions women were allowed to attend segregated classes in the land grant colleges. Co-education, Hale noted for her readers' edification, had been implemented abroad especially in a few medical schools. In the antebellum United States, separate medical schools for women had to be founded. Hale supported these institutions and lobbied for medical training to assure women's presence and hegemony in the fields of gynecology, obstetrics, pediatrics as well as in nursing, all of which were obviously part of the healing arts of Woman's Sphere.[31] While Hale countenanced differentiated titles for women academics and professionals, she strenuously opposed any effort to devalue their degrees.[32]

Hale ended her half-century of editing with a sense of satisfaction. She had played a crucial role in acquiring for women commensurate educational opportunities in private and public institutions, both separate and co-educational.[33] She lived not only to see women's education an accomplished fact but women's domination of the teaching professions as well. This emboldened her to broach the issue of equal pay for women as a practical matter without arguing on the basis of women's equality.[34] Hale's daughters' lives demonstrated that the application of women's education was dual. One married and became a society matron and mother of six; the other became a spinster teacher who died at her desk. But both were True Women, each serving her family and the nation in her own True way. Hale's impact as the high priestess of the Cult of True Womanhood upon the women of the nation was no less effective.[35]

As in her editorial support of advances in women's education, Hale consistently endorsed women's entry into the paid labor force on the restricted basis of service and necessity, but with an undercurrent of concern for women's integrity and right to be allowed an opportunity to become self-supporting rather than pitiful objects of public or private charity. Her approach characterized the efforts and the limited goals of domestic feminism. Hale publicized specific professions and jobs as appropriate for women because the job descriptions, at least in the capable hands of Godey's Editor, easily could be proven to be within the recognized Woman's Sphere. From 1837 to 1877, Hale's editorial promotions and informational notes paralleled the trends in nineteenth-century women's employment.[36] Although the literature and lavish illustrations of Godey's presented and elevated the image of woman in the home, Hale's editorial commentary supplied an alternative image of woman in the workplace as well.[37]

Throughout her forty years at Godey's, Hale augmented her view of what properly constituted woman's work in the editor's ladylike but nonetheless opportunistic fashion. If Hale accepted the differences between the sexes, she made the most of those differences when it came to coopting more jobs for needy and qualified True Women. The employments of writing, teaching and garment making were duly noted in Hale's editorials of the 1830s and 1840s and set the pattern for Hale's emphasizing the domestic attributes of jobs she designated as woman's work. In her literary notices, Hale promoted the published works of True Women authors both as sources of appropriate reading matter and from an implied sense of female literati solidarity.[38] Applying the same rationale and tactics which proved successful in establishing women's jobs in public and private education, Hale's editorials of the 1850s designated certain medical and religious occupations into her ever-expanding definition of the work of Woman's Sphere. By the 1860s and 1870s, Hale incorporated many light industrial and commercial jobs that in the twentieth century have become known as traditional women's white and "pink" collar employments.[39] Hale supported all advances in employments on the basis of financial need and public service. The temporary and altruistic nature of women's work outside the home has bequeathed to employed women a legacy of dead-end, low-paying jobs. The concept of the limitations of Woman's Sphere proper has lingered into the twentieth century, restricting women to the jobs of the "pink-collar ghetto" and even in the professions vaguely justifying as acceptable sex discriminatory practices in hiring, pay and promotion of women.[40]

Sarah Josepha Hale led public opinion through her editorial impact upon Godey's and her role as an author of instructional books for women, but she was careful not to push either the cause of women's education or employment beyond her public's sense of what was currently acceptable. Her forty years of Godey's editorials on women's education and women's employment follow the nationwide trends with a spooky concurrence. The ladylike manner of Godey's editor deliberately obscured her role, making it difficult to ascertain whether she was a leader or a follower in either movement. This subtle manipulation was a tactic perfected by Hale to deflect any criticism of her own role or that of her magazine. Godey's policy of avoiding any reference to things political was legendary, for example, the only acknowledgment of the Civil War was found in a postwar humor piece describing the difficulties of a southern subscriber in procuring her copy of Godey's because of the Union blockade. Hale's articulation of the causes of women's education and employment grounded them within Woman's Sphere, thus rendering them respectable and legitimate. As part of Woman's Sphere, education and paid employments for women were necessarily limited and restricted, creating for women the psychological ambivalence of balancing career aspirations against home duties and an additional burden of pervasive and socially acceptable patterns of discrimination against women.[41]

Hale functioned as Matron of Victorian Womanhood in every sense of that term. As a model True Woman, she had served as a matron and matriarch in her own home, a respectable married woman who was a homemaker and a mother; and later, in the workplace, she served as an example of the valiant, productive, self-sacrificing and self-supporting widow. Hale consciously pursued her duty as a True Woman in her capacity as *Godey's* editor. In her relationship with her readers, she functioned simultaneously as the sentry, supervisor, instructor and guard maintaining order and decorum among the inmates within the fortress and prison that constituted Woman's Sphere. Just as pre-literate womanhood had passed on crucial survival information in the oral tradition from generation to generation, Hale used her editorial position to translate into the written word the intergenerational transmission of the essential body of tradition and knowledge that constituted the Cult of True Womanhood for Victorian women. If Hale accepted the existence of the limitations of the concept of Woman's Sphere, she assiduously defined the proper activities of Woman's Sphere to compensate for women's lost social and economic power within the Private Sphere through her ruthless appropriation of modified or newly developed paid employments in the Public Sphere. She identified education as an essential tool for True Women whether in the home or the workforce. She quickly labeled as women's work those activities of production and service to family and community which increasingly were being transferred from the Private Sphere into the Public Sphere throughout the nineteenth century. In her definition of what activities properly constituted women's work, Hale paralleled much of the later scholarship of women's history which would establish the similarities between the pre-industrial sexual division of labor and that of the industrial workplace of the nineteenth century. It is not historically possible to establish that Hale deliberately intended to construct a Woman's Sphere that simultaneously could provide the security of a fortress for the women in it as well as the stability and social control of a prison for a society dependent upon willingly exploited women in both paid and unpaid women's work. However, her abiding sense of the dignity of her sex is as indisputable as Hale's contributions to the advances in women's education and employment in Victorian America.

Notes

1. The author is pleased to contribute this article as a tribute to Professor Robert H. Bremner. This article presents a summary of the detailed inquiry into Hale's use of Godey's in expanding Woman's Sphere found in Angela Howard Zophy, "For the Improvement of My Sex: Sarah Josepha Hale's Editorship of Godey's Lady's Book, 1837-1877," Ph.D. dissertation directed by Professor Robert H. Bremner, Ohio State University, 1978; hereafter cited as Zophy. For the most thorough examination of Hale's literary career and contribution see Isabelle Webb Entrikin, Sarah Josepha Hale and Godey's Lady's Book (Philadelphia: Lancaster Press, 1946). The prevailing biography of Hale remains Ruth E. Finley, The Lady of Godey's (Philadelphia: J. B. Lippincott, 1931). For an example of a more recent analysis of Hale's importance in nineteenth-century U.S. women's history see Nancy Woloch, Women and the American Experience (New York: Alfred A. Knopf, 1984), pp. 97-146.

2. For a general summary of the changes in women's economic status from the eighteenth to the nineteenth century, see Mary P. Ryan, Womanhood in America: From Colonial Times to the Present, 3rd. Ed. (New York: Franklin Watts, 1983), pp. 19-166.

3. The Female Experience: An American Documentary, ed. Gerda Lerner (Indianapolis: Bobbs-Merrill Educational Publishing, 1977), pp. 108ff.

4. Mary Beth Norton, "The Myth of A Golden Age," in Women of America: A History, eds. Carol Ruth Berkin and Mary Beth Norton (Boston: Houghton Mifflin Company, 1979), pp. 37-46.

5. Gerda Lerner, "The Lady and the Mill Girl," in The Majority Finds Its Past: Placing Women in History (New York: Oxford University Press, 1979), pp. 15-30 and Ronald W. Hogeland, "'The Female Appendage': Feminine Life Styles in America, 1820-1860," Our American Sisters: Women in American Life and Thought, eds. Jean E. Friedman and William G. Shade, (Boston: Allyn and Bacon, Inc., 1976), pp. 133-148 for the varied consequences to women of the economic changes occurring during this period.

6. Frank Luther Mott, A History of American Magazines, 3 Vols. (New York: D. Appleton and Company, 1930), I, pp. 351, 332-342 and James P. Wood, Magazines in the United States, 2nd ed. (New York: Ronald Press, 1956), pp. 53-56, 360. See also Anne Firor Scott, The Southern Lady: From Pedestal to Politics, 1830-1930 (Chicago: University of Chicago Press, 1970) for a description of "Ladyhood" for women who were a significant portion of Godey's readers.

7. Barbara Welter, "The Cult of True Womanhood," American Quarterly 18 (1966): 151-174.

8. For a description of the regional and social background of the New England women of whom Hale is an example see Nancy F. Cott, The Bonds of Womanhood: "Woman's Sphere" in New England, 1780-1835 (New Haven: Yale University Press, 1977).

9. Ann Douglas, The Feminization of American Culture (New York: Alfred A. Knopf, 1977), p. 353.

10. Catherine Clinton, The Other Civil War: American Women in the Nineteenth Century (New York: Hill and Wang, 1984), pp. 40-42; see also Zophy, pp. 48-49.

11. See Godey's Lady's Book and American Ladies' Magazine 20 (1840): 48; 38 (1844): 200; 40 (1850): 294-295; 53 (1856): 279; 60 (1860): 85; 78 (1869): 99; hereafter cited as Godey's. For an assessment of Hale and Godey's role in creating public opinion on True Womanhood see Helen Woodward, The Lady Persuaders (New York: Farrar, Straus, and Young, 1953), pp. 13-31 and Mott, I, p. 351, II, p. 11, and III, p. 6. For data on Godey's subscribers see Zophy, pp. 49-50.

12. Ann Douglas Wood, "The 'Scribbling Women' and Fanny Fern: Why Women Wrote," American Quarterly 23 (1971): 3-24 and Ann D. Gordon, "The Young Ladies Academy of Philadelphia," Women of America, eds. Berkin and Norton, pp. 68-87. For a summary of Hale's life and literary career see Zophy, pp. 14-39.

13. Editor, "The Conversazione," Godey's 14 (1837): 1-5; for a comparison of this editorial policy statement for Godey's with that of Hale's statement for her previous magazine see "Introduction," American Ladies' Magazine, 1 (1828): 1-3. For a general description and analysis of Hale's civic activism see Alice Felt Tyler, Freedom's Ferment (1944; New York: Harper, 1962), esp. pp. 436-438; Keith Melder, "Ladies Bountiful: Organized Women's Benevolence in Early Nineteenth Century America," New York History 68 (1967): 231-254; Carroll Smith-Rosenberg, "Beauty, The Beast, and The Militant Woman: A Case Study of Sex Roles and Social Stress in Jacksonian America," American Quarterly 23 (1971): 562-584. For additional editorial statements of support of women's civic, benevolent, and patriotic organizations and activities see Godey's 20 (1840): 95, 190, 142, 163 and 17 (1838): 47.

14. Godey's 14 (1837): 279; 17 (1838): 191; 15 (1837): 47; and Clinton, p. 41.

15. Godey's 22 (1841): 142. Hale's opinion reflected the influence of Benjamin Rush, see Thomas Woody, A History of Women's Education in the United States, 2 vols. (New York: The Scientific Press, 1924), I, p. 328. For information regarding the persistence of the "finishing school version of education," see Eleanor Wolf Thompson, Education for Ladies, 1830-1860: Ideas on Education in Magazines for Women (Morningside Heights, N. Y.: King's Crown Press, 1947), p. 33.

16. Godey's 14 (1837): 45, 288 and 31 (1845): 178. See also Woody, I, pp. 309, 320, 104. For some perspective on Hale's contemporaries' efforts on behalf of women's education, see Katheryn Kish Sklar, Catharine Beecher: A Study in American Domesticity (New Haven: Yale University Press, 1973) and Arthur C. Cole, A Hundred Years of Mount Holyoke College (New Haven: Yale University Press, 1940).

17. "Ladies' Mentor," Godey's 14 (1837): 45-48 and 15 (1837): 93. The concept for this feature and its successor, "The Progress of Society," Godey's 18 (1839): 95, was implemented initially in a similar series earlier in Hale's Ladies' Magazine.

18. "The Progress of Society," Godey's 17 (1838): 140 and Godey's 71 (1865): 360; 60 (1860): 468; 72 (1866): 87; 82 (1871): 288; and Hale's valedectory editorial which appeared in her last issue as editor, 95 (1877): 522.

19. Godey's 38 (1849): 294-295, 366 and 71 (1865): 536. However, Hale defended the True Womanhood of those women who

never married: Godey's 29 (1844): 238 and 50 (1855): 559-560; 52 (1856): 506-507; 57 (1858): 68; 68 (1864): p. 379.

20. See note 13 above; Woody, I, p. 108 and II, pp. 470, 200. Regarding Vassar, see Godey's 68 (1864): 488-489, 577, 594; 69 (1864): 84-85; 70 (1865): 95-96. Regarding Vassar's curriculum and charter fresh(wo)man class see 71 (1865): 360. The Hale-Vassar correspondence is in the Vassar College Library.

21. Sarah Josepha Hale, Woman's Record, or, Sketches of All Distinguished Women from "the Beginning" till A.D. 1850. Arranged in Four Eras. With Selections From Female Writers of Every Age (New York: Harper & Brothers, 1853), p. 686 and Zophy, p. 39.

22. Susan P. Conrad, Perish the Thought: Intellectual Women in Romantic America, 1830-1860 (New York: Oxford University Press, 1976), pp. 38-41, 43-44, and 45-92.

23. Hale's "Conversazione," note 13 above and Godey's 40 (1850): 75; "Ladies' Mentor," Godey's 14 (1837): 45-48 and 280-281; 15 (1837): 93; 14 (1837): 185-186 and 15 (1837): 46; and 44 (1852): 88 and 68 (1864): 199-200.

24. Godey's 44 (1852): 88; 38 (1849): 294-295, 366. While Hale early on urged hiring women teachers because they worked for less, she later advocated equal pay seen in Godey's 45 (1852): 194; 59 (1859) 370; 71 (1865): 84.

25. Godey's 95 (1877): 522.

26. Hale's opinions regarding women's curriculum issues appear in Godey's 39 (1847): 202; 36 (1848): 247; regarding coeducation see 69 (1864): 354; 77 (1868): 542; 84 (1872): 287; 88 (1874): 563.

27. Godey's 71 (1866): 537 and Zophy, pp. 64 and 67.

28. Finley, p. 205 ff.

29. A series of home-study features ran from December 1846 through 1847 in Godey's 33 (1846): 294; 34 (1847): 269; 35 (1847): 213.

30. Godey's 44 (1852): 288; 48 (1854): 463; 49 (1854): 80. See also Leslie Parker Hume and Karen M. Offen, "Introduction" to "Part III, The Adult Woman: Work," in Victorian Women: A Documentary Account of Women's Lives in Nineteenth-Century England, France, and the United States, eds. Olafson Hellerstein, Leslie Parker Hume, Karen M. Offen (Stanford, Ca.: Stanford University Press, 1981), pp. 272-291.

31. Godey's 72 (1866): 92; 73 (1866): 263; 89 (1874): 187; 80 (1870): 382; 90 (1875): 185-186; 95 (1877): 436.

32. Godey's 69 (1864): 85 and 79 (1869): 565-566.

33. Godey's 33 (1846): 235-236.

34. Godey's 45 (1852): 194; 59 (1859): 370; 71 (1865): 84.

35. Godey's 29 (1844): 238.

36. Gerda Lerner, The Woman in American History (Menlo Park, Ca.: Addison-Wesley Publishing Company, 1971), p. 93 and Ryan, p. 122.

37. Godey's 46 (1853): 380; 66 (1863): 579; 45 (1852): 293; 47 (1853): 84 and Marion Harland, "Phemi Roland," Godey's 76 (1868): 133-141.

38. Zophy, p. 68.

39. For Hale's references to paid positions which she deemed appropriate for True Women see Godey's 46 (1853): 380; 66

(1863): 579; 45 (1852): 293; 47 (1853): 84 and 178; 49 (1854): 273; 65 (1862): 401, and 71 (1865): 466; 47 (1853): 178-79 and 66 (1863): 306. Hale also proposed women as strike breakers in Godey's 48 (1854): 271; 49 (1854): 367 and 553; 68 (1864); 442. Hale asserted that women's entry into such jobs did not violate the concept of Woman's Sphere in Godey's 71 (1865): 537. See also Zophy, pp. 174-176; and Elizabeth Faulkner Baker, Technology and Woman's Work, 2nd ed. (New York: Columbia University Press, 1866), pp. 70-74 for women's entry into women's white collar jobs. See also Louise Kapp Howe, Pink Collar Workers: Inside the World of Women's Work (New York: G.P. Putnam's Sons, 1977) for the consequences of the concept of "women's work."

40. Ryan, pp. 195, 341 and 278-290 and Female Experience, ed. Lerner, pp. 257-258. See also Group for the Advancement of Psychiatry Committee on the College Student, The Educated Woman: Prospects and Problems (New York: Charles Scribner's Sons, 1975) for the twentieth-century impact of nineteenthcentury attitudes and practices regarding women's education.

41. See Godey's 23 (1841): 293-295 for Hale's editorial policy of eschewing political issues; and in the same volume, p. 141, for the publisher's statement of that basic Godey's policy. For the postwar feature article mentioned see Elzey Hay of Georgia, "Dress Under Difficulties; or, Passages from the Blocade [sic] Experience of Rebel Women," Godey's 73 (1866): 32-33. However, for all her circumspection, Hale did endorse women's legal rights in Editor, "Rights of Married Women," Godey's 14 (1837): 213-214; 32 (1846): 44-45; 45 (1852): 542-548; 52 (1856): 79-82; 70 (1865): 278; 81 (1870): 86; 82 (1871): 477. For

reference to her publications beyond Godey's which dealt with political issues, see Zophy, pp. 90 and 96.

Origins of Welfare in the States:

Albert G. Byers and the Ohio Board of State Charities

by Robert M. Mennel and Stephen Spackman*

For the past fifteen years, government programs to aid poor and dependent people have been attacked by both liberals and conservatives. In the 1960s, a coalition of academics and social workers formed the welfare rights movement to criticize the inadequacy of New Deal and Great Society programs and to propose various strategies to bring about a guaranteed national income. Because welfare rights advocates were unable or unwilling to form alliances with moderate groups, the guaranteed income never materialized. An alliance of liberals and conservatives defeated President Nixon's welfare reform plan in 1969 while the liberal agenda itself was decisively rejected in the presidential elections of 1972 and 1980. Ronald Reagan's election signified the ascendancy of conservative criticisms that welfare programs have been too generous, going well beyond assistance to the "truly needy" and encouraging able-bodied people not to work. Conservative plans to trim benefits and eliminate programs appear more likely to succeed than the liberal effort to secure a guaranteed national income. The question remains whether either apporach contributes to the stability of the polity.[1]

To gain perspective on the tendency of debate to polarize and moderate policies to founder, we have sought a vantage point removed from contemporary controversies yet related to them. A case study analysis on the development of welfare as a state responsibility in the nineteenth century fulfills our purpose. Compared with current federal programs, early state welfare had a narrower scope and authority. Inspection of local and state institutions was often contested while non-institutional aid and services were non-existent at the state level and amounted to little more than sporadic handouts in local jurisdictions. But we share with our ancestors a belief that poverty is a problem amenable to reduction if not elimination. Like us, they had a range of choices to make and, in developing their responses, they often rejected moderate courses of action. The comparison is worthwhile.

Recent work on the history of social welfare in the United States has tended to assume a national persective, either in the interests of coverage or because the authors have been convinced that a unified point of view toward social issues existed among those nineteenth-century Americans who were willing and able to take action.[2] While not disputing the value of these studies, we hope to illuminate the subject more fully by examining the early years of public welfare in Ohio. We shall focus particularly on the career of Albert Gallatin Byers (1826-1890), who served as the first Secretary of the Ohio Board of State Charities (BOSC) from 1867 until his death.[3]

Several factors governed our choice of Ohio. The state's diversified population and economy seemed a suitable example of northern and midwestern conditions.[4] Moreover, there survives an excellent combination of materials describing the topic in the state documents, which outline the structure of public finance and inspection, in the BOSC reports (written by Byers), which graphically portray conditions in the institutions and conflicts between local governments and the state authorities, and in Albert Byer's own diaries and a brief but interesting file of letters sent to him in his official capacity.[5] When these materials are used in conjunction with the annual reports of the National Conference of Charities and Correction, it becomes possible to reconstruct what we think is an illustrative portrait of the formative period of state welfare.

The bill creating the Ohio Board of State Charities in 1867 was advocated by Republican Party reformers who controlled state politics for the better part of two decades, beginning in 1855 with Salmon P. Chase's election as governor.[6] Three-time governor, and later President, Rutherford B. Hayes was the other major figure in this group. The reform faith that the state should encourage education, relieve disease, reform the wayward and aid the victims of war had produced a substantial number of institutions by the end of the Civil War. Three insane asylums, a penitentiary, a blind asylum, a reform school for boys, a deaf and dumb asylum, and an institution for the "idiotic" were in operation while a fourth insane asylum, a soldiers' home, and a soldiers and sailors' orphans home were about to open. There was active discussion on the need for a girls' reform school and an "intermediate" reformatory for male first offenders. In addition, the state paid annual subsidies to the Longview Insane Asylum (Cincinnati), Miami University and Ohio University, while further expenditures were likely as Civil War veterans aged and as the state responded to the Morrill Act, which granted to states the proceeds of federal land sales for the establishment of public colleges and universities. It must be added that although these institutions were created by one political faction, their incorporation, like that of the BOSC, received broad bipartisan legislative support.[7]

But why was it necessary to create a state authority to inspect public institutions? Two reasons stand out. First, legislators, pressured by local philanthropic groups, had been forced to take cognizance of the generally dreadful conditions of county and municipal jails and infirmaries (almshouses). As the incorporator of these governments, the state had a legal obligation to inspect their institutions and to prevent cruel treatment and neglect. Second, and of greater concern, legislators felt increasingly unable to control costs and monitor conditions in the state institutions. A state board of charity would, it was hoped, bring local institutions up to minimal standards, whittle down the budgetary requests of the various state institution trustee boards and root out corruption wherever found.[8]

A brief analysis of the financial and governmental structure of late nineteenth-century Ohio provides pertinent background information on these problems and thus the means for explaining why the mission of BOSC was substantially compromised from the outset. We begin with two generalizations: First, local government (that is, counties, townships, municipalities and school districts) raised and spent most of the public monies. Second, though state expenditures were therefore relatively small, a significant and growing proportion of its budget was devoted to education and welfare expenses. Both of these points require development.

Table 1, a summary of taxes collected by local and state government from 1860 to 1880, indicates the local predominance.[9] In 1860 county and municipal taxes were twice as high as state taxes and the difference increased during the decade. County taxes increased at an average annual rate of 23 percent, while the municipal increase was nearly 20 percent. County and municipal taxation combined to account for over 80 percent of all public levies by 1870, a proportion which held steady in 1880 (and even into the twentieth century).[10] For state taxes the average annual increase during the 1860s was less than 7 percent, and the state percentage of all taxation shrank from 32 to 20 percent, a share that declined further by 1880. The municipal burden remained the most substantial, increasing during the 1870s on both a total and a per capita basis, while state and county taxes decreased in both categories.

Table 2, Ohio Public Debt from 1860 to 1880, emphasizes the stress on municipalities. The figures clearly show debt declining at the state and county level while climbing sharply in the towns and cities.[11] This was due, on the one hand, to the retirement of state canal bonds and the completion of county jails and infirmaries, and on the other hand, to the capital expenditures for the schools and public works needed to meet the demands of an urbanizing population.[12]

Although state taxation and debt were declining in relation to local burdens, welfare spending was creating pressure upon

Table 1

Ohio Taxes, 1860-1880

Year	State Total/Per Capita	County Total/Per Capita	Municipal Total/Per Capita	All State/State Local Government Total/Per Capita	Municipal/ Taxation (%)	County Taxation (%)
1860	2,839,575/1.22	1,970,870/0.84	4,205,281/1.80	9,611,021/3.86	31.6	68.4
1870	4,727,318/1.77	6,501,941/2.43	12,297,289/4.61	23,526,548/8.84	20.1	79.9
1880	4,480,489/1.40	6,131,502/1.92	15,144,667/4.74	25,756,659/8.06	17.4	82.6

Source: U.S. Census Reports, 1860-1880. See note 9.

Table 2

Ohio Public Debts, 1860-1880

Year	State	County	Municipal	All State and Local Government
	Total/Per Capita	Total/Per Capita	Total/Per Capita	Total/Per Capita
1860	16,927,834/7.24	--/--	--/--	--/--
1870	9,732,078/3.64	4,237,543/1.59	8,272,367/3.10	22,241,988/8.33
1880	5,735,000/1.79	2,962,649/0.93	40,058,805/12.52	48,756,454/15.24

Source: U.S. Census, Report on Valuation, 1880.

Table 3

Ohio State Accounts, 1867

Fund	Receipts	%	Disbursements	%
Sinking	2,243,276.73	36.2	1,865,084.12	34.0
General Revenue	1,999,421.22	32.4	1,777,264.17	32.3
Common School	1,525,325.79	24.8	1,469,436.00	26.6
All Other	408,911.39	6.6	386,680.05	7.1
Total	6,176,955.13	100.0	5,498,964.34	100.0
Balance	--	--	677,990.79	--

Source: Ohio, Annual Report of the Treasurer of the State, 1867.

available revenue. The structure of state finance is illustrated in Table 3; 1867 is an apt year since the BOSC was established then. Of a series of separate funds, whose income and expenditure were kept independent from each other, the three most important were the Sinking Fund, the General Revenue Fund, and the Common School Fund. In 1867, these funds accounted for more than 90 percent of both receipts and disbursements.[13]

General revenue was the crucial account. Representing about a third of the total budget, it was supported by a general property tax and met the day-to-day running expenses of the state government. Its major commitments were salaries, legislative costs, and the expenses of the state institutions. Institutional costs, outlined in Table 4, made a decisive impact upon the state budget. In 1867, institutional building and operating expenses accounted for 53 percent of disbursements from the General Revenue Fund--that is, more than half the everyday operating costs of the state government--and 17 percent of disbursements from all funds.[14] More important, these costs could not be controlled as easily as the state's other major obligations, the Sinking Fund and the Common School Fund. Although these two funds accounted for 60 percent of total disbursements in 1867, the Sinking Fund was declining in importance as the canal bonds were paid off while school expenses were curtailed by the requirement that localities bear the brunt of costs. By contrast, legislators were annually beseiged for funds by institutional trustees with costs escalating to the point that several delegates to the State Constitutional Convention of 1873 feared state insolvency.[15]

Table 4

Cost of Ohio State Institutions, 1867

Salaries	50,196.00
Expenses	398,861.12
Buildings	400,262.67
Miscellaneous	102,890.90
Total	942,210.69

Source: Ohio, Annual Report of the Treasurer of the State, 1867. See note 14.

The situation was further complicated by the fact that appointment of institutional trusteeships represented one of the few sources of patronage for the state's chief executive. The state constitution denied the governor a veto and allowed him only a few appointments. Even the trustee appointments had to be confirmed by the state senate. Thus, with each change of administration, "reorganization" of trustee boards was always a possibility. Institutional trusteeships were highly priced even though unpaid. Not much could be made from per diem expenses, but the offices conferred or recognized status, carried their own appointing power over institution staff, and even though trustees were barred from direct commercial connection with their institutions, they did determine the placing of contracts. The net effect was to create support for the institutions and their programs in both the legislative and executive branches and thus dilute the impact of cost cutting and efficiency campaigns.[16]

Given both the preponderance of local government and the political power of state institutions, it was no surprise that in debate on the bill to set up the Board of State Charities, legislators weakened the draft in order to protect their own financial and political interests, to cut costs and to leave patronage undisturbed. The original bill provided the board with the services of a modestly paid executive secretary who was empowered to:

> investigate and supervise the whole system of the public charitable and correctional institutions of the state, and counties, and shall recommend such changes and additional provision as they may deem necessary for their economical and efficient administration.[17]

In the legislative give and take, however, the words "supervise" and "counties" were deleted, leaving trustee boards unchallenged and the localities subject to discretionary rather than mandatory visits. The power to inspect technically remained because the state chartered local government and occasionally subsidized local institutions, but with the additional removal of the provision for a paid secretary the likelihood of regular inspections appeared remote.

The law that emerged from debate, then, confined the Board of State Charities (whose members were to draw only expenses) to visitation and the gathering of information. In this respect, the BOSC was treated only slightly worse than other state agencies. The Gas Commissioner and the Inspector of Steam Boilers had to use their salaries and personal funds to purchase testing equipment, while the Inspector of Mines pleaded in vain for one assistant to help him conduct inspections.[18] In short, these early boards and commissioners were armed mainly with the weapon of publicity. Personal conviction and administrative skill would be the ingredients of whatever success they might achieve.

The first trustees of the Board of State Charities suitably represented the reform wing of the Republican Party. Foremost among Governor Jacob Cox's appointees in 1867 was Joseph Perkins, a Cleveland banker, philanthropist and railroad founder. Robert W. Steele of Dayton helped organize the first state agricultural fair and tirelessly promoted public libraries and higher education. Douglas Putnam of Marietta had a distinguished Civil War record and, like the others, had formed his allegiance to the

Republican Party in the anti-Nebraska agitation of the mid-1850s. The other major figure of the early board was John W. Andrews, a Columbus lawyer who was appointed by Governor Rutherford B. Hayes in 1870. Representing different parts of the state, these men were united in belief--as Protestants (Presbyterians or Congregationalists) valuing good works as a path to salvation and as Republicans who saw their party as symbolizing God's blessing of the American people.[19]

The trustees, defined their primary task as soliciting funds from "private but influential citizens" in order to pay the salary of an agent or executive secretary. This position had been deleted by the legislature but there could be little objection since no state funds were involved, at least initially. Practical but also socioeconomic reasons explained their course of action. Because the trustees had extensive business interests, they could plausibly claim that they would be unable to fulfill the law's requirement of substantive inspection of the state's institutions. But they also knew that the law's high moral intent had been substantially compromised by legislators who had gutted the power of the board to enforce its findings. Therefore, the hiring of an agent would not only save them time but also allow them to express their displeasure at institutional conditions without suffering directly the opprobrium of being unable to effect change. What they required was a person of some repute who would view the position as a promotion.[20]

Albert Gallatin Byers fulfilled their needs. In 1867 he was serving as minister of the Third Avenue Methodist Church in

Columbus and also as chaplain at the Ohio Penitentiary. In the latter capacity he had made a reputation as a persistent critic of the corruption and cruelty dominating the institution. Penitentiary trustees may have been glad to loan his services. Certainly, the BOSC trustees hired him because of his zeal although their esteem was measured because he was poor. Years later, John Andrews pityingly remarked upon Byers's threadbare life when recommending him for other jobs.[21]

Since Byers would more than repay the trustees for their confidence, it is worth knowing more about him. He was born in Uniontown, Pennsylvania, in 1826 of Scotch-Irish parents. He and his brother and sister received a strict Presbyterian upbringing, although Albert became an accomplished humorist and storyteller who proudly emphasized his Irish heritage. After his father's death, the family moved to Portsmouth, Ohio, where Byers began to study medicine. In 1849, however, he was enticed by the Argonauts, a party of gold-hunters heading for California. He nearly starved to death on the trek but stayed a year until news of his mother's death called him home. Soon thereafter, he decided "at his mother's grave" to become a Methodist circuit rider. Throughout the 1850s, he served with great success in several of the impoverished counties of southern Ohio. Byers was a small slender man with startlingly white skin. His high cheekbones and animated expression made people think that he was an actor, and indeed he had a reputation as a performer in the pulpit. In 1852 he married Mary Rathbun of Cheshire, and the first of their seven children was born in 1854.[22]

Byers's Civil War experience initiated a process of self-questioning which was to last for the rest of his life. From 1861 to 1863 he served as chaplain of a Portsmouth volunteer company that fought at Chickamauga and Lookout Mountain. He returned exhausted from comforting and treating the wounded but nevertheless viewed his ministerial role as somewhat confining even in the larger town of Columbus. By the 1860s, Methodism in Ohio and elsewhere had become an established middle class denomination. Primarily concerned with promoting temperance, Methodists were experiencing ideological confinement as Free Methodists and pentecostal sects captured the revivalistic audience while the Arminian wing drifted toward various secular causes such as civil service and charity reform. Byers inclined strongly toward good works and thus eagerly seized the Penitentiary chaplaincy and the offer to be secretary of the BOSC. In 1867 he also stood as Republican candidate for the state senate from Franklin County. That election was bitterly fought over the issue of black voting rights, with Democrats throughout the state charging that Republican support of manhood suffrage would inevitably lead to legislated social equality between the races. In heavily Democractic Franklin County, Byers lost by a large margin.[23]

Byers's militancy was counterbalanced by his doubt that he, as a minister, could effect change. He once wrote Rutherford Hayes urging a "flinging dirt" campaign against a local Democratic candidate and then discounting his own advice, "I find myself, preacherlike, dabbling in politics." Also, he was loyal to a fault to his benefactors. Pleading with Hayes to run for governor in 1875, Byers addressed him, "not... as a Republican. I appeal to you as a citizen for the sake of the state. As a man for the sake of humanity. As a Christian for the sake of truth and benevolence... [in the hope that] under God you may be triumphantly elected." Thus, his willingness to confront the opponents of charity inspection, combined with his eagerness to serve the reform wing of the Republican Party, made him an ideal choice for secretary of the BOSC.[24]

Byers's first report was decisive in tone and emphasis. He skimmed over state operations with ritualistic criticism of the Penitentiary and praise for the other "large and noble Benevolent Institutions." By contrast, he found the county jails and infirmaries "not only deplorable but a disgrace to the state and a sin against humanity."[25] In reaching his judgment he drew upon his years of experience as a ministerial visitor as well as his initial inspections for the Board. He was keenly aware that local politicians and their appointees would resent his visits and try to get him dismissed if he made critical remarks, but his reports show why he took the risk.

Albert Byers discovered appalling conditions in jails as he traveled about the state. "Fairfield County Jail--Rathole," reads one entry in his diary. That one in Trumbull County was "utterly, indescribably mean," while the jail in Washington County was "dark, poorly ventilated and miserably kept." Byers also discovered that the Sheriff of Union County was using his jail as a brothel. Filth, vermin and spittle permeated most of the institutions visited.[26]

Perhaps conditions like this were only to be expected in

jails, but in the Richland County infirmary Byers found a man whose feet had frozen off during the previous winter. In Jefferson County seven naked insane people crouched together in one cold damp cell. A man in the Pike County infirmary was covered with flies. A Ross County woman had been so contorted by chains that she could hardly be distinguished from a pile of rags on the floor. In Columbiana County a couple fornicated in the courtyard, while in Lucas County, a nymphomaniac entertained a group of insane men. In none of these places was there a superintendent present when Byers made his inspection.[27]

Byers was particularly incensed by the plight of children in these infirmaries. He warned of "the harvest not only to the individual life of the child, but the state, which must be gathered sooner or later from such sowing." After visiting the Hamilton County (Cincinnati) almshouse he reported that he was "unable to give the numbers of little, half-clad, filthy and squalid children that seemed fairly to swarm in the midst of these scenes of unmitigated misery."[28]

The county spoils system was a major reason for the cool reception Byers often received. Elected directors appointed superintendents at a derisory salary, or let the office to the lowest bidder (a literal case of farming, given the nature of the institutions), who then padded his salary through a judicious choice of institutional contractors and suppliers. As the county commissioners and infirmary directors usually took their cut, inmate care was bound to suffer. Byers directly attacked the responsible individuals. "Quite inferior men" were often chosen as directors, he said, while most superintendents were "notoriously lazy in habits, selfish in nature, socially, intellectually and morally unfit."[29]

Byers recognized, however, that while corruption accounted for much of the inmate neglect, fear and ignorance also underlay the hostility that greeted him. A Jefferson County infirmary director agreed to a joint tour provided that he did not have to accompany Byers inside the building. In Noble County, inmates had their own keys, locked themselves in at night and, Byers concluded, plausibly considered themselves "an independent community because of the distance and remoteness of the superintendent's house." The infirmaries were in fact not institutions but poor homes, often as decrepit as any in the county. "How are your buildings ventilated?" asked Byers in an early questionnaire. "By air coming in at doors and broken panes of glass," replied one superintendent. "Have you any facilities for bathing?" "The Ohio River is not far off," answered another.[30]

Byers took the humor and pathos of these episodes as evidence of popular receptivity to the idea of benevolent authority. To encourage this sentiment, he believed that it was necessary not only to insist upon his own right of inspection but also to seek ways of broadening the impact of his ideas. On his own powers, Byers minced no words: "Let it be understood that all public institutions are liable to visitation and examination at the most unexpected times, and that abuses will be unsparingly exposed." To increase this influence, Byers effectively utilized women's church and temperance groups. One of his principal allies was the Springfield crusader Mrs. E. D. "Mother" Stewart, known throughout the state for her militance and determination. After a visit to the Clark County infirmary, she dryly reported to him that her reception "lacked a little of that cordiality necessary to establish confidence between parties coming together under such circumstances." Undeterred, Mrs. Stewart journeyed to the neighboring Champaign County infirmary where she initiated the removal of three children to the Soldiers' Orphans Home in Xenia. In Ross County, three ladies, delegated by Byers, started a press campaign against the infirmary director.[31]

To capitalize on the sense of shame evoked by the inspections, Byers provided specific plans for improving conditions. These suggestions ranged from particular ways of improving sanitary conditions to model plans for an entirely new jail or infirmary. Furthermore, he vigorously promoted the efforts of counties and voluntary organizations to establish, either singly or in cooperative groups, separate homes for orphaned and neglected children.[32]

Before long, Byers could point to signs of progress. In 1870 Hardin County opened a model infirmary and the McIntyre Children's Home in Zanesville began its work. More important, local officials became more receptive to advice. The Clinton County superintendent wrote Byers thanking him for suggestions, while the directors of the Green County infirmary cooperated at the cost of "the severest public criticism."[33]

Betterment, however, had a price and Byers had to pay it. By 1870 opposition to his criticism was mounting especially in the urban counties. He had singled out the institutions in

Cuyahoga, Lucas and Hamilton counties because he believed that, compared with many of the rural areas, they had more than enough wealth and knowledge to provide decent care. Thus, the Cuyahoga jail was "an offense, wholly out of character with the general intelligence and moral sense of the community where it is tolerated." In Athens County, Byers's report sparked a local investigation that disputed his conclusions and demanded an official rebuke. From the beginning, the BOSC trustees were aware that Byers was ruffling feathers. They understood the necessity of critical inspections, but they also knew that the position of executive secretary was politically fragile. They urged Byers to spend some time inspecting state institutions and, in an effort to sooth relations with the counties, wrote a letter to him that was printed in the 1870 BOSC report. The passage regarding county visitations read as follows: "You will impress upon the officers who you meet, that you come as a co-worker with them, and to aid them by your suggestions, and not in a hostile, carping, criticizing spirit..." The Board endorsed Byers's ideas of using "good citizens--both men and women" as visitors but forbade him from invoking state authority to gain compliance with his suggestions.[34]

Byers was willing to focus on state problems. He bitterly castigated the lax management and corrupt building contracts at the Central Insane Asylum (Columbus) that had led to a fire killing many inmates; he vigorously promoted the establishment of an intermediate penitentiary for first time offenders; but he would not relent in his criticism of county jails and infirmaries. Indeed, in 1871 he stepped up his attack on cronyism in the election of infirmary directors in the larger counties.[35]

When the legislature next met, Byers's job was in jeopardy. The politicians' strategy was appropriately devious. Rather than confront Byers directly, they eliminated the entire BOSC without formal explanation; but it was well understood that the protest from the major counties was responsible, and analysis of the vote on elimination confirms the fact. The Senate vote was 24-10; in the House of Representatives it was 69-22. Byers's support came almost entirely from Democrats representing sparsely populated rural areas. Twenty of the twenty-two representatives who voted to retain the Board were Democrats and Mansfield was the largest town in the area favoring Byers. The delegations from Cincinnati, Cleveland, Columbus, Dayton and Toledo, all heavily Republican except Columbus, voted unanimously in favor of elimination.[36]

Some of the counties favoring Byers, for example Pike and Ross, had also been severely censured by him. Unlike the urban counties, however, these areas took his advice and improved their treatment and facilities. Their amenability may be explained by the fact that rural almshouses were often little more than shacks and could easily be renovated or replaced. By the same token, a change in superintendents could work wonders in Circleville, but have less impact in Cleveland where other indolent and negligent officers might be retained. The irony of the situation lay in the fact that the Democrats who listened to Byers and followed his advice represented that portion of the electorate which had rejected his vision of a just society at the polls in 1867.

The abolition of the Board hurt him deeply. "From here on no heart or time for diaries," he wrote. "Period of 4 years and 2 months on his own."[37] Though physically ill as well as sick at heart, he remained undaunted. In later years he remarked that the legislature might abolish the Board, but they could not abolish him. Clearly, he had come to view charity inspection as his vocation. Preaching an occasional sermon but seeking no new congregation, he worked for several years, perhaps as a salesman. He used his spare time to seek allies who shared his views, above all his belief that "partizan purposes" [sic] should not be a factor in the selection of jail wardens and infirmary directors. Foremost among these friends were John Jay Janney and Roeliff Brinkerhoff. Janney, a Virginia-born Quaker and former member of the Republican state committee and Columbus City council, was also well-connected in philanthropic circles and known for his passionate advocacy of prison reform. Brinkerhoff, a lawyer-banker from Mansfield, was a leading figure in the Democratic Party and greatly interested in both penology and the reform of public charity.[38]

With Janney's assistance, Byers organized the Prison Reform and Children's Aid Association of Ohio in August, 1874. As executive secretary of the society, Byers resumed his visitations, although the voluntary character of the association gave these a somewhat different emphasis. He continued to inspect jails and infirmaries, with the usual mixed reception, but placed special emphasis on encouraging voluntary groups to establish homes for orphaned and dependent children. The twelve homes that had been established before the Civil War were all privately organized and usually served particular groups. In 1850, Cincinnati, for example, had five asylums--two Catholic, one Protestant, one German Protestant, and one for "colored orphans." Byers sought to encourage a tolerant approach regarding admissions in order to establish a population base sufficient enough to support an institution even in rural areas. By the early twentieth century there were fifty county homes for dependent children, and at least as many private refuges.[39]

Byers did not envision converting his Children's Aid Association into a charity organization society similar to those forming in Ohio and other states. One of the main concerns of charity organization societies was to control the expenditures of outdoor or home relief, the suspicion being that "unworthy" individuals and families avoided work by applying for food and fuel from the various charities of the town or country. The charity societies did not give aid themselves but coordinated existing agencies and required all applicants to submit to a stringent means test before gaining any relief. Byers, however, was more interested in positive achievements, such as the children's homes.[40]

Byers hoped that his group would revive interest in the BOSC. He defended the voluntary approach, in a letter to Hayes, because, "the politicians could be set at defiance and a popular sympathy awakened that does not ordinarily respond to work--however charitable--done by law." But with Hayes once again in the governor's chair in 1876, Byers's advocacy of voluntarism evaporated. The Board was necessary, he contended, not only because "good people" supported it but because it could challenge the power of "the preachers" who had often opposed the "appeals for material aid" of the Children's Aid Association.[41]

Certainly, Ohio's welfare problems had not disappeared with Byers's dismissal. Indeed, they had intensified. The recession of the early 1870s made a decisive impact on the infirmaries and the administration of poor relief. In 1872 the number seeking admission to county infirmaries increased by 34 per cent, while the number supported by county outdoor relief nearly tripled. Meanwhile, the disarray of the state institutions was becoming more apparent, with another insane asylum fire and widespread concern over operational costs. The 1873-1874 State Constitutional Convention denounced the waste and inefficiency in state institutions and desired to revive the Board of State Charities. The main point of contention in its extensive debates on the subject was not whether there should be a new board, but whether it should be appointed or popularly elected.[42]

The Convention changed nothing, however, because its proposed Constitution was rejected at the polls, leaving intact the old 1851 charter. This granted permanent state support only to institutions for the insane, blind, and deaf and dumb, although it did not specifically exclude other state welfare activity. The way was open, therefore, for the rebirth of the Board of State Charities, and Hayes's election provided the occasion. With his encouragement, the legislature voted by a wide margin to reestablish the agency.[43]

The new board differed significantly from its predecessor.

As secretary, Byers received a stipulated annual salary of 1,200 dollars. The governor was made ex-officio president, with the power to appoint six trustees, three from each party, to staggered terms. In this way, Roeliff Brinkerhoff became a trustee, joining John Andrews and Joseph Perkins from the old board. More important, the BOSC received the right to at least comment upon "all plans of public buildings." Byers regarded his complete lack of power on this question the most significant defect of the first board.[44]

Byers was the obvious choice to be secretary of the new board. He resumed his duties with enthusiasm and renewed his attack upon deficient county institutions. Eventually, he secured passage of a law providing that county probate courts appoint a board of visitors (three of the five members to be women) to inspect and report on local institutions to the BOSC. This formalized the means by which he had extended his influence in the 1860s. Also, Byers began to pay more attention to conditions in the state institutions. In 1880, for example, he uncovered the efforts of authorities at the boys' reform school to hide the fact that a black inmate had died because of an overseer's beating. At the behest of local officials, he encouraged asylum superintendents to be more communicative about their admissions procedures, and he tried to prevent state institutions from remanding difficult cases back to the counties.[45]

One measure of Byers's success may be found in the file of letters addressed to him during the period 1884-1885. Besides calming disputes between state and local officials, he provided a reference service for institutions seeking to employ able people and information for citizens from other states searching for ideas on charity and prison reform. Among other communications, Byers received an anonymous letter offering information on "the sanitary condition" of the girls' reform school and a petition from inmates of the Knox County infirmary asking the directors to provide indoor washing for older inmates and to delouse the house. The courteous tone of the letters and the cordial response of most superintendents and directors to Byers's inquiries marked a significant change from the early days.[46]

Despite these successes, life remained hard for Albert Byers. He supplemented his meager salary with itinerant preaching and sought repeatedly but unsuccessfully to gain a position with various national prison reform groups. Commenting upon his efforts, John Andrews wrote, "it is probably in his interest to make the change to a position that promises greater permanence, with less turmoil and personal bitterness, than his present post which has brought him necessarily into collision with the local authorities of many counties and all over the state." It was not to be. After Frederick Wines blocked his appointment as Secretary of the National Prison Association, Byers resigned from the group, bitterly lamenting the frustration of "the one great and all absorbing ambition of my life."[47]

Byers did acquire a national reputation as an expert on public charity. In 1889 he addressed the National Conference of Charities and Correction (NCCC) on the role of the state boards. Beginning with Hastings Hart's definition of the board as "a balance wheel to steady the motion of the charitable machinery,"

Byers elaborated on the faith animating the movement:

> No community in any state throughout this nation will ever complain of the cost of meeting the actual demands of the dependent. They may not approve of extravagance, but they will not knowingly tolerate the withholding of that which is needful. Stealing of public money may be condemned, malfeasance or misfeasance may be forgiven; but to stint the poor is, to the American conception of public duty, an unpardonable sin.

State boards, he concluded, performed an "indispensable" service by checking both "stint" and "extravagance," and thereby encouraging that state itself to be "at once merciful and just, as near like God as any state may be."[48]

Byers's health was already failing when he gave this speech. He was chosen to head the NCCC in 1890, but collapsed while conducting the closing ceremonies. He recovered enough to attend an autumn charity meeting in a wheelchair. Greeting Hastings Hart, he said:

> This has been a beautiful world. It has been a joy to live in it, and I have delighted in the friends I have had. At first it seemed to me as if I would not bear to go out of the world, as if I had a work to do that is not done; but that feeling is gone and I look forward to the future with as much joy and peace and delight as I have ever had in my life.

A few weeks later he died at home. Andrew Elmore delivered the eulogy at the next NCCC meeting, concluding: "Many a man is a nice, good man in a Conference like this, who is a tyrant at home. Dr. Byers was a charming man in his own family. It was there I loved him best."[49]

Albert Byers's life and his career on the Ohio Board of State Charities recall a world in which the relief of human suffering was regarded not as a problem to be solved by the state, but as an obligation to common humanity undertaken by religious and public-spirited people. There is little evidence in Byers's career of a commitment to the expansion of state activity or authority for its own sake. Indeed, for all his work with state and local institutions, he remained convinced that private charities "are far more efficient and satisfactory, as a general rule, than public charities can be." He always relied on the interpenetration of public and private agencies, as his Prison Reform and Children's Aid Association, his local visiting committees, and the close links between the Board of State Charities and NCCC demonstrate. Members of the National Conference of Charities and Correction referred to their organization as the "church of divine fragments." As postmillenarian and Arminian Protestants, they viewed their work as necessary actions to ensure the reign of peace and justice before Christ's second coming and the final judgment. Since intolerable conditions and treatment were still evident in many places, Byers warned, the millenium was "not so much at hand as some of us would wish." The main hope was to sustain practical efforts and moral pressure.[50]

This faith has apppeared insufficient or even ominous to the modern age. Advocates of the welfare state regard care as a constitutional entitlement. During the 1960s and 1970s, they influenced the expansion of the number and variety of public programs under which people of all ages and conditions may qualify. At the same time, they have continued to criticize the capitalistic system for its niggardliness. The conservative reaction, now regnant, not only questions the concept of entitlement but, as a self-proclaimed moral majority, has inaugurated crusades against day care, school lunch, and abortion programs that serve poor and dependent people. Though presented positively, as part of a "pro-family" agenda, the Moral Majority resonates coerciveness and meanness perhaps not unlike that encountered by Albert Byers in the 1870s.

Historians have contributed less than they imagine to contemporary debate. They have appeared for the most part as witnesses for liberal points of view. Thus, nineteenth-century charity reform is portrayed as a threatening development. Individuals like Byers are viewed as agents for dominant social groups who were intolerant of Catholics and immigrants and anxious to achieve control by harsh and parsimonious public policy. A slightly different scenario has benevolent workers appearing as the direct ancestors of contemporary advice-givers and social workers who supposedly use therapeutic jargon to make themselves more secure and their audiences more expert-dependent. In this way, capitalism has purportedly shattered both individual self-confidence and the integrity of the family.[51]

Without disputing the arrogance of conservatism, either new or old, we insist that the historical record is more complex. Certainly, Protestant charity reformers had their share of prejudices. The National Conference proceedings abound with unflattering remarks on immigrants. Many NCCC members were enthusiastic about eugenics, a "science" that they would eventually link to the politics of immigrant restriction. However, the activities of these reformers were principally motivated by the foul institutions and inhumane treatment that they personally uncovered. And, more often than not, the poor conditions were the responsibility of native-born Protestants like themselves. Albert Byers, though relatively free of the prejudices of the day, was not a perfect man. He regularly denounced political spoils but used his influence to secure for his son a position as personal secretary to Governor "Calico Charlie" Foster. He sermonized on brotherhood and reconciliation, yet enthusiastically supported the Grand Army of the Republic which helped to keep alive the animosities of the Civil War. Nevertheless, these imperfections seem less important than his principal accomplishment--the reformation of public welfare through vigilance, compassion and suggestion. In this endeavor, he sought to comfort the afflicted rather than to cultivate a client population.[52]

Albert Byers's experience is meaningful because he was necessarily cautious about state power but relentless in pursuing abuse. The Ohio Board of State Charities was a weak organization, even in comparison with the other state boards of the day. Byers could not control the appointment of trustees and superintendents of state institutions; nor could he monitor their expenditures or audit their books. At the local level, publicity remained his main weapon.[53] Nonetheless, the people of Ohio responded to his fervor. They cleansed their jails and almshouses and provided separate homes for dependent and neglected children. And even though relapses occurred, we believe that Byers' accomplishment has a modern echo. Glenn Tinder has recently written:

> The welfare state is a relatively humble spiritualization of the public order. It symbolizes the idea that government should serve justice and kindness. If we give up trying to invest our politics with that modest amount of spiritual significance--if fiscal responsibility comes in effect to be our understanding of the highest good--what will remain in our public life to command respect?[54]

In an age that glorifies self-aggrandizement and inequality, the conviction that doing good is its own reward may serve us well. By linking us to moderate but active people of an age gone by, it encourages us to persist until a new commonwealth philosophy takes shape. For there is little hope of coping with the future without recognizing that our obligations to each other are rooted in the past.

Notes

*Reprinted with permission from Ohio History 92 (1983): 72-95. Robert M. Mennel is Professor of History, University of New Hampshire. Stephen Spackman is Lecturer in Modern History, University of St. Andrews, Scotland. The authors wish to acknowledge support from the Central University Research Fund of the University of New Hampshire, the British Academy and the Carnegie Trust for the Universities of Scotland, and the assistance of Larry Gwozdz and Frank Levstik, formerly of the Ohio State Archives. This article is dedicated to Robert H. Bremner, Professor Emeritus, The Ohio State University, whose scholarship in social welfare history continues to enlighten us all.

1. The literature on this subject is immense, but see especially Frances Fox Piven and Richard Cloward, Regulating the Poor: The Function of Public Welfare (New York, 1971) for the welfare rights point of view and Martin Anderson, Welfare: The Political Economy of Welfare Reform in the United States (Stanford, 1978) for the conservative rejoinder. Anderson heads President Reagan's Domestic Policy staff. See also Daniel P. Moynihan, The Politics of a Guaranteed Income: The Nixon Administration and the Family Assistance Plan (New York, 1973) and Christopher Leman, The Collapse of Welfare Reform: Political Institutions, Policy, and the Poor in Canada and the United States (Cambridge, Mass, 1980).

2. For the survey approach, see James Leiby, A History of Social Welfare and Social Work in the United States (New York, 1978). David Rothman, The Discovery of the Asylum: Social Order

and Disorder in the New Republic (Boston, 1971) and Conscience and Convenience: The Asylum and Its Alternatives in Progressive America (Boston, 1980) epitomize interpretations portraying reformers as if they were of one mind. Examples of more focused studies are Richard W. Fox, So Far Disordered in Mind: Insanity in California 1870-1930 (Berkeley, 1978) and Gerald N. Grob, The State and the Mentally Ill: A History of the Worcester State Hospital in Massachusetts, 1830-1920 (Chapel Hill, 1966). Older studies recapitulate laws and administrative policies and pay little attention to social context. See Francis Cahn and Valeska Bary, Welfare Activites of Federal, State, and Local Governments in California, 1850-1934 (Berkeley, 1936); David Schneider and Albert Deutsch, A History of Public Welfare in New York State, 1867-1940 (Chicago, 1941).

    3. Gerald N. Grob, "Reflections on the History of Social Policy in America," Reviews in American History 7 (September 1979): 293-305 has proposed case studies as a means to shed new light on the subject.

    4. Few southern states created charity inspection authorities before 1900, largely because the number of institutions to inspect was so small. By the late 1920s, however, with southern urbanization and industrialization well underway, Sophonisba P. Breckinridge reported, "central supervisory authority" in all but three states (Mississippi, Nevada and Utah) and everywhere a trend toward increasing the coercive power of this authority. See Sophonisba P. Breckinridge, "Frontiers of Control in Public Welfare Administration," Social Service Review 1 (1927): 84-99.

For further evidence of Ohio's typicality see Robert H. Bremner, ed., <u>Children and Youth in America</u>, (Cambridge, Ma., 1970), I, pp. 639-650 and II, pp. 250-258; Sophonisba P. Breckinridge, ed., <u>Public Welfare Administration in the United States: Selected Documents</u>, Second Edition (Chicago, 1938), pp. 237-364.

5. A series of diaries belonging to Byers are in box 5 of the Janney Family Papers, Ohio Historical Society (OHS), Columbus, Ohio. He seems to have used them as an aide-memoire and they consist largely of brief factual entries and a meticulous detailing of expenses. Subsequently, some of them were used for other purposes, the 1864 volume, for example, for press clippings from 1868. These in turn have been annotated, probably much later to judge from the hand. See also notes 21 and 37.

6. Ohio, <u>Laws</u>, 64 (1867): 257-258; Ohio, <u>House Journal</u> (1867): 624. Ohio was the third state to establish a charity board, following Massachusetts (1863) and New York (earlier in 1867). Seven other states (North Carolina, Illinois, Rhode Island, Wisconsin, Michigan, Connecticut and Kansas) followed suit by 1873. For an excellent summary of the various circumstances shaping the development of these boards, see Gerald N. Grob, <u>Mental Institutions in America: Social Policy to 1875</u> (New York, 1973), pp. 270-292.

7. For an example of legislative approval of institutions, see Robert M. Mennel, "'The Family System of Common Farmers': The Origins of Ohio's Reform Farm, 1840-58," <u>Ohio History</u> 89 (Spring 1980): 131-134.

8. Ohio, <u>House Journal</u> (1867): 204-235, 624 and appendix, 235-237. An analysis of corruption at the state level is John P.

Resch, "The Ohio Adult Penal System, 1850-1900: A Case Study in the Failure of Institutional Reform," Ohio History 81 (Autumn 1972): 236-263.

9. Table 1 drawn from the following sources: U.S. Census, Statistics of the United States in 1860. Mortality and Miscellaneous Statistics (Washington, D.C., 1866), p. 511; U.S. Census, Eighth Census, The Statistics of Wealth and Industry of the United States (Washington, D.C., 1872), pp. 11, 51; U.S. Census, Ninth Census, Report on Valuation, Taxation, and Public Indebtedness in the United States (Washington, D.C., 1884), p. 25.

10. U.S. Census Bureau, Wealth, Debt and Taxation (Washington, D.C., 1907), pp. 767, 967-969. Ohio law allowed county commissioners to hire "tax inquisitors" to pursue evaders. The inquisitors were paid a percentage of the amount they enabled the government to recover.

11. U.S. Census, Ninth Census, Report on Valuation..., pp. 284-285, 612-613. County and municipal figures are unavailable for 1860.

12. These taxation and spending patterns followed national trends. See U.S. Census Bureau, Wealth, Debt and Taxation, 1913 (Washington, D.C., 1915). On the impact of canal building on Ohio finance see Harry Scheiber, Ohio Canal Era; A Case Study of Government and the Economy, 1820-1861 (Athens, Ohio, 1969)

13. Ohio, Annual Report of the Treasurer of State (1867), p. 9.

14. Figures recombined from the detailed list of disbursements from the General Revenue fund, Annual Report of the

Treasurer of State (1867), pp. 12-15. This detailed listing gives a total differing from that of the summary recapitulation reproduced as Table 3. The recombination here has used the detailed listing.

15. Ohio, Official Report of the Proceedings and Debates of the Third Constitutional Convention, I, part 3 (Cleveland, 1873-1874), pp. 200-238.

16. Most of the surviving Governors' Correspondence for this period in the Ohio State Archives is closely concerned with patronage. Though fragmentary and damaged by fire, these files are a mine of tantalizing information.

17. Ohio, Senate Journal (1867): 624.

18. Ohio, Docs. I (1867): 247-256; Ibid. I (1870): 579, 583, Ibid. II (1876): 81-82.

19. Elroy M. Avery, A History of Cleveland and its Environs, (Chicago, 1918), I, pp. 252, 337; The History of Montgomery County, Ohio (Chicago, 1882), pp. 244-245; History of Washington County, Ohio (Marietta, 1881), pp. 382, 483-485; History of Franklin and Pickaway Counties (1880), pp. 68, 563, 566. These trustee positions were renewable, and Perkins in fact served for over twenty years.

20. Ohio, Docs. II (1868): 634. In 1868 Rutherford Hayes gave the Board $500 from the governor's contingency fund and the following year the position of secretary was officially recognized and modestly funded by the legislature. See Hayes to Joseph Perkins, August 8, 1868, Governor's Papers, Box 8, The Papers of Rutherford B. Hayes, Hayes Mmemorial Library, Fremont, Ohio; Ohio, Docs. II (1870): 371.

21. Andrews to Hayes, December 5, 1883, and January 8, 1885, Hayes MS. See also Albert G. Byers diary, March 15, 18; April 1; May 1, 31; November 28, 1865, Byers Family Papers, Ohio Historical Society (OHS), Columbus, Ohio.

22. Ohio State Journal, 11 November 1890; National Conference of Charities and Correction (NCCC), Proceedings (1891): 243-253.

23. Nelson W. Evans and Emmons B. Strivers, A History of Adams County, Ohio (West Union, Ohio, 1900), pp. 342-42; John Marshall Barker, History of Ohio Methodism (Cincinnati, 1898), pp. 74-75, 123-128; Walter W. Benjamin, "The Methodist Episcopal Church in the Postwar Era" in Emory S. Bucke, ed., The History of American Methodism (New York, 1964), II, pp. 320-360; William Warren Sweet, Methodism in American History (New York, 1961), pp. 341-345; NCCC, Proceedings (1891): 243-244; Ohio, Docs. I (1867): 318.

24. Byers to Hayes, July 6, 1875 and April 19, 1875, Hayes MS.

25. Ohio, Docs. (1867): 235-268. Infirmaries were the county almshouses, usually attached to a farm of about 200 acres which was the prime inducement in attracting a superintendent and his main interest when in office.

26. Byers Diary, Byers MS; Ohio, Docs. I (1868): 1226-1241; Ohio, Report of...Third Constitutional Convention, I, part 3, pp. 200-235.

27. Ohio, Docs. I (1868): 674-677 and II (1869): 803, 831-834.

28. Ohio, Docs. II (1867): 268 and II (1868): 672.

29. Ohio, Docs. II (1869): 791-793.

30. Ohio, Docs. II (1870): 406, 415-416 and I (1888): 1226-1229.

31. Ohio, Docs. II (1868): 652 and II (1870): 385-389, 417; A Biographical Record of Clark County Ohio (New York, 1902), pp. 86-93; Barker, History of Ohio Methodism, pp. 191-219.

32. Ohio, Docs. (1868): 627-631; II (1869): 849-852; and II (1870): 426-434.

33. Ohio, Docs. II (1870): 359-360, 389-390, 414-415.

34. Ohio, Docs. II (1868): 652-660, 672-677; II (1869): 817-820; II (1870): 317, 376-382, 400; II (1871): 48-49, 60; Byers Diary (1870), Byers MS.

35. Ohio, Docs. II (1867): 235-250; II (1869): 766-770; II (1871): 34-35.

36. Ohio, Senate Journal (1872): 114, 120, 160; Ohio, House Journal (1872): 213-214; Ohio, Laws 69 (1872): 10.

37. Byers Diary (Feb. 15, 1872), Byers MS. This volume is different in format from the pocket diaries that Byers carried about with him. The entries for Feb. 15, including another "Board of State Charities Law repealed," are in a much heavier pencil and in a larger hand. These look like later annotations, perhaps, in view of the use of the third person, entered by his wife or his son Joseph Perkins Byers who took over as Secretary of the BOSC following Byers's death.

38. NCCC, Proceedings (1891): 246; Ohio, Docs. II (1871): 92-93. Byers's obituary says only that he was "earning his bread in his own way." The Diary entry for August 5, 1872, reads

"canvassing," but it is unclear whether this refers to selling, seeking allies, or political work. See also John Fyfe to Byers, June 7, 1876, Hayes MS.

39. Hayes MS; Box 21, Janney Family Papers, OHS; Nelson L. Bossing, "History of Educational Legislation, 1851 to 1925," Ohio Archaelogical and Historical Publications 39 (1930): 285-291; Charles Cist, Sketches and Statistics of Cincinnati in 1851 (Cincinnati, 1851), pp. 150-155; Samuel P. Orth, The Centralization of Administration in Ohio (New York, 1903).

40. Box 21, Janney MS, OHS.

41. Byers to Hayes, November 12, 1875, Hayes MS.

42. Ohio, Docs. I (1872): 287-288; Ohio, Official Report of the...Constitutional Convention, I, XXX, pp. 200-238. Another concern about state institutions, their power to incarcerate an individual against his or her will, surfaced at the Convention, with a reference to Wilkie Collins's The Woman in White (New York, 1860), a popular novel of the day treating this theme. An 1869 case involving the custodial authority of the Illinois insane asylum was one reason for the establishment of a charity board in that state. See Grob, Mental Institutions in America, p. 278.

43. Ohio, Senate Journal (1876): 312-313; Ohio, House Journal (1876): 641-642; Ohio, Docs. I (1876): 764; Ohio, Laws 73 (1876): 165-166.

44. Ohio, Docs. I (1876) and III (1877): 92. The bipartisan clause as well as the requirement of mandatory submission of plans were amendments added in 1880. See Ohio, Laws 77 (1880):

227-228.

45. H. A. Millis, "The Law Relating to the Relief and Care of Dependents," American Journal of Sociology 4 (1898-1899): 185; Ohio, Docs. I (1880): 608-610; Incoming Letters (1884-1885), Papers of the Board of State Charities, Ohio Historical Society. See also Ohio, Docs. I (1876): 776.

46. Letter File, Byers MS. 1884-1885 is the only year for which the incoming letter file has survived, and there is no way of knowing whether the total of 183 items is complete, or whether, if complete, it is typical. Nevertheless, 36 percent of the letters deal with the Board's contacts with other states and such organizations as the NCCC, 20 percent deal with Ohio state institutions, 18 percent with administration and visiting, 11 percent with personal cases, 10 percent with jobs, and 5 percent with requests for speeches and sermons.

47. Andrews to Hayes, December 5, 1883 and Byers to Hayes, November, 1889, Hayes MS.

48. NCCC, Proceedings (1889): 89-102.

49. Ibid., (1891): 253.

50. Ohio, Docs. II (1870): 354; NCCC, Proceedings, (1891): 247 and (1889): 99-102. See also Timothy P. Weber, Living in the Shadow of the Second Coming: American Premillennialism, 1875-1975 (New York, 1979), p. 3-12, 168-169.

51. In addition to Rothman, Discovery of the Asylum and Conscience and Convenience, see Clifford S. Griffin, Their Brothers' Keepers: Moral Stewardship in the United States, 1800-1865 (New Brunswick, N.J., 1960) and Christopher Lasch, Haven in a Heartless World: The Family Besieged (New York, 1977).

52. Charles Forster to Roeliff Brinkerhoff, December 22, 1879, The Papers of Roeliff Brinkerhoff, OHS, Columbus, Ohio; Ohio, Docs. II (1870): 355.

53. Orth, Centralization of Administration in Ohio, p. 177; NCCC, Proceedings (1889): 89-97 and (1893): 33-51.

54. The New Republic, March 10, 1979, pp. 21-23.

J. Sterling Morton and the Conservative: Jeffersonianism on Trial
by Ronald Lora

The burgeoning urban populations, the giant corporations, and the rise of numerous movements protesting traditional economic and political assumptions in late nineteenth-century America tried the patience of political and intellectual leaders who had long called themselves Jeffersonians. One such person was J. Sterling Morton, the distinguished Nebraska statesman who served the Territory as editor, boomer, and political leader, and later the state and nation as conservationist, U.S. Secretary of Agriculture, and once again as editor of a journal of discussion titled the Conservative. Rooted in rural, small-town America, Morton placed the Conservative, which he edited and published on the west bank of the Missouri River from 1898 until his death in April 1902, at the service of Jeffersonianism as it was generally understood before political philosophers of the twentieth century harnessed the great Virginian to their dreams of social democracy. In the last eloquent effort of his life, Morton hoped "to do a large missionary work among the economic savages of the Western country."[1]

Born in New York in 1832 and raised in Michigan, Sterling Morton on the October day of his wedding in 1854 set out with his bride to make his fortune in the Nebraska Territory. Traveling to Chicago and then south to St. Louis by rail, the Mortons took a steamer to St. Joseph, arrived at Council Bluffs by stage, and settled in Bellevue during the first winter. Shortly after arriving in Nebraska, Morton paid two hundred dollars for a quarter section of land west of Nebraska City from the man who had preempted it from the government. Living in a small log house, he supervised the construction of a four-room frame house. Several remodelings through the decades produced Arbor Lodge, the stately mansion which stands today on that same parcel of land on the subhumid prairie, a monument to one of our most devoted conservationists.

In 1854, however, Nebraska was not yet a white man's land. Herds of buffalo still roamed the lower Platte, while the footstep of the Indian sounded in the near distance. Although few whites, save for trappers, hunters, and settlers who could go no farther, lived in the Territory, there was much activity. The Platte Valley was a major highway to the West. Gold seekers and Mormons, missionaries and migrants filled the overland trails before the Civil War. As the land yielded to permanent settlement, young Morton saw with his own eyes the process of civilization of which Frederick Jackson Turner was to write so eloquently. Nebraska City, Morton's adopted town, was a favored location in prairie country. It became a shipping center, supplying the settlers who passed through and the military outposts established in part to protect them. There, at 933' altitude, the undulating land is rich, the water good. The silty loess soils are fertile and deep, yielding easily to the plow. Nebraska City was hot in summer and cold in winter, but enjoyed fairly dependable rainfall. As one moved beyond Kearney, however, just 180 miles west and 2100 feet above sea level, and on out to Scottsbluff, where at 3900 feet the annual rainfall averaged sixteen inches, the land was far more resistant to settlers' dreams.

Five months after entering Nebraska, Morton agreed to edit the <u>Nebraska City News</u>, the only newspaper both published and printed in Nebraska at the time. That decision marked the beginning of his rise to eminence, for frontier editors wielded considerable power. Their newspapers educated citizens and molded opinion. Other than letters from home and the welcome conversation of travelers, they often were the sole source of news and link to a larger world. Battles for political power and economic development were fought in the newspapers as well as in the sometimes raucous legislatures. Not surprisingly, an impressive number of early political leaders emerged from the ranks of journalism. In this motley world where rancorous debate flourished, where life was often at risk, and versatility conferred fitness in the struggle for existence, young Morton made his way with an eye to the main chance.[2]

His literary and forensic talents soon brought him into politics. President Buchanan appointed him Secretary of the Territory of Nebraska, during which time he served a brief stint as Acting Governor. In succeeding years he sought office repeatedly, usually to be turned aside. Meanwhile, the young editor from Otoe County used his position in newspapering and politics to spread his agricultural and tree planting convictions across the Territory. It was his resolution that in 1872 established Arbor Day in Nebraska. Years later, when the holiday was recognized throughout the country, his birthday, April 22, would become the official date of recognition. Morton's work in agriculture, arboriculture, and horticulture, together with his hard money views, made him a worthy candidate to head the young U.S. Department of Agriculture. He served at President Cleveland's request from 1893 to 1897, the first person from west of the Missouri River to hold a cabinet position. Some believed that the Secretary of Agriculture, whose courage and moral integrity were not in doubt, would have made an excellent president, but he was in fact too independent and contemptuous of the crowd and popular vagaries to have been an effective candidate.[3]

When William McKinley defeated William Jennings Bryan in their first encounter, Secretary Morton at sixty-four was not ready to retire. Casting about for a creative outlet to harness his energies, he found his four sons, already successful and desirous of keeping their father occupied near home, ready to help. Together they raised the needed capital, incorporated the Morton Printing Company, and the former agriculture secretary again became an editor, this time of a new weekly called the Conservative. The statement of purpose printed in the first number on July 14, 1898, informed readers that the Conservative would publish "in the interest of the conservation of all that is deemed desirable in the social, industrial and political life of the United States." It would defend the rights of individuals and the rights of labor as well as respect the rights of capital. The gold standard would with all vigor be extolled as the measure of honesty and justice in political economy. Because all are "laborers," no attempts to divide Americans into classes could be recognized. Frugality at all levels of government deserved support, as did the civil service merit system. Finally, the Conservative hoped to become "useful as a truthteller, and influential as a militant exponent of everything... which the experience of one hundred and twenty-two years of national independence has proved to be worth conserving." As the nation was entering the Progressive era, Morton wrote a correspondent that as editor he hoped to protect individuals against the group by preaching the message of economic freedom to "the free silver sinners of this country."[4]

Morton's journal of discussion appeared every Thursday. Its typography was extremely neat. In approximately sixteen pages with three columns per page, the Conservative covered a wide range of topics including trusts, sound money, politics, trees and conservation, railroads, and William Jennings Bryan, whose activities appeared under the heading "Bryanarchy."[5] The arguments against overseas expansion were thoroughly aired. The editor wrote much for his own weekly, but solicited articles from persons he thought would make competent contributors and frequently reprinted articles and speeches that interested him.[6] William Graham Sumner appeared, with the first number carrying an extract from "What the Social Classes Owe to Each Other." So did Edward Atkinson, advocate of hard currency and one of the founders of the Nation, whose western counterpart the Conservative hoped to become. Other contributors included Carl Schurz, University of Chicago economist J. Laurence Laughlin, Dr. George L. Miller, editor of the Omaha Daily and Weekly Herald and old friend, and Professor Arthur Latham Perry of Williams

College, author of Principles of Political Economy. The majority of contributors, however, were lesser-known persons, local leaders, businessmen, Western history enthusiasts. All were treated equally, regardless of reputation; no contributor received payment for his thoughts.

Occasionally, entire numbers were devoted to single themes, or to symposiums on education and the chances for success of young men in the United States. "American Miscellany" sections appeared regularly, as did "Scientific Miscellany," "Current Comment," and peppery comments on politics. In a column of "Conservatisms," contributors at times submitted apothegms such as

>   -Imposed obligations are slavery.
>   -Conservatism is the acme of intellient self-preservation, individual or national.
>   -There is nothing higher or nobler than intelligent self-control.
>   -No man is responsible for the acts of another unless he assumes the obligation.
>   -Wars inaugurated for any other purpose than national preservation are usurpation of power by the government.
>   -The true conservative thinks. The true conservative reads. The true conservative thinks again.[7]

Although Morton involved himself in the business affairs of the Conservative, day-to-day responsibility fell to John Nordhouse, who doubled as private secretary, a position he held while the editor had been U.S. Secretary of Agriculture. Subscribers received the weekly for the modest charge of $1.50 per year, payable in advance. When important events loomed in the near future, such as the presidential election of 1900, readers were offered a three-month subscription for thirty cents.[8] Advertisements became an increasingly important source of revenue, filling three pages at first and growing to nine or ten during the last year of publication. A thousand dollars bought a full-page advertisement for a year. Wanting desperately for the operation to pay for itself, Morton conducted a voluminous correspondence to drum up support from all manner of businesses, the railroads, and local banks.[9] The subscription list varied from five to fifteen thousand, with a middle number the normal printing. Special issues, however, called for larger printings, up to eighteen thousand, a good number ninety years ago.[10] The Conservative was in competent hands in both an editorial and business way, but was so integrally connected with Morton's political and intellectual interests that it ceased publication with the editor's death.

In assessing the intellectual thrust of the Conservative, it is important to note that the editor took pride in being a Jeffersonian. Morton venerated the Sage of Monticello, whose works he owned, and Monticello loomed in the background as he remodeled Arbor Lodge. By Jeffersonian, Morton meant a believer in limited government, the strict construction of the Constitution, religious toleration, the love of liberty, and the practice of individual freedoms. Especially did he insist with William Graham Sumner that the federal government not direct the economic life of society, pass protective tariffs, grant subsidies to special interest groups, or perform tasks normally undertaken by families. He held to the primacy of the individual over the government in time and in moral authority. The government protected life, liberty, and property; all else was oppression.[11] This seems clear enough, yet contradictions remained. When thinking of the vast social and economic transformations that attended the industrial process, the intellectual writing privately remembered another Jefferson who held that intelligent citizens of a republic could through a process of reasoning better determine the nature of appropriate government actions than by slavishly following tradition: "Each man must do his own thinking and each age determines its own social and political problems for itself. The Past cannot prescribe with accuracy for the Present."[12]

In Morton's estimate, however, the powerful currents of political and economic protest that swirled about in the 1890s, calling for a more just America, forced this Jeffersonian principle to yield to others with more dogmatic import. Again and again, the themes of self-reliance and self-denial echoed from the Conservative as the keys to individual success or failure. As he had staked all on the future of the West, so might other risk takers find success in the twentieth century. Morton's faith in golden America found support in a symposium published on the young man's chances for success under existing economic conditions. The fifteen participants were self-made men representing the legal, railroad, educational, ministerial, and journalistic fields. A pronounced optimism that the road to success had never been more easily travelled suffused the symposium columns. Diligent work was required, and loyalty and fidelity, too, but effort would be noticed and in time rewarded. "To say that the young man who has the greatest talent or natural aptitude for the work will get to the top, is to state a truism that applies to every... profession," wrote the editor of the Chicago Record-Herald.[13]

Men in the full swing of their careers cannot be expected to appear as detached intellectuals, but few symposiums have been so lacking in detachment and objectivity. The Horatio Alger stories popular at the time often displayed greater realism. Contributors recognized, as Alger did not, that success under modern conditions required technological skill and organizational know-how. Unlike the popular writer of boys' stories, however, none assigned a role to luck. Chance meant opportunity, not good fortune. The symposium closed with lines that defined the stance of the symposium participants:

> "There's little in life but labor;
> And tomorrow may find that a dream;
> Success is the bride of endeavor,
> And luck but a meteor's gleam."

The Alger hero succeeded in life, to be sure, but not merely because he mixed work with ability. He willingly accepted help from friends as he kept watch for fortune to smile. Symposium contributors on the other hand argued that the successful created their opportunities. Gone was the humility, benevolence, and sense of creaturehood in a circle of friends that readers found endearing in Alger.

Several readers complained that contributors, "selected from the hirelings of plutocracy," saw success on a one-dimensional and morally hazardous plane of money and material accumulation. The charge was just. Only one had expressed doubts about the morality of those who owned and operated society. The president of small Defiance College (Ohio) had warned against the young men who in the "hurry up" age of turn-of-the-century America neglected their education in pursuit of the Big Money: "The mercenary spirit of our age is... the greatest foe of education and religion. In our hurry to get rich we have scarcely time to become either learned or pious." The celebration of America found a large audience, however, as demand exceeded the week's printing of 17,500. Other newspapers reprinted portions of the "Young Man's Chances" and Morton did likewise in the following month.[14]

What the Conservative feared above all else from its vantage point in the West was the decline of individuality in the face of a coming collectivism. Herbert Spencer's dictum that no government can be better than the people who staff it and George Washington's warning sounded in his Farewell Address that men beware of "that love of power and proneness to abuse it, which predominate in the human heart" were common themes. The "polishing processes of modern civilization seem to grind away all of the sharp corners of individuality," wrote one contributor; concentrated urban centers "grind away and erase independence." The once-proud individual melts into the crowd, and civilization itself weakens before the onslaught of deracinating massness and concentration. In the presence of the clamor that "government shall run railroads, telegraphs, farms, and warehouses, or confronted by combined and arrogant avarice, commanding that taxes shall be laid upon all to make incomes for a few," only educated citizens, themselves re-dedicated to defend the limited powers doctrine in the American constitutional tradition, could effectively conserve the Republic.[15]

Morton's administration of the Department of Agriculture faithfully reflected his views on government. He had proved himself a forceful taskmaster, establishing the civil service system and repeatedly insisting that department personnel practice efficiency and frugality in the use of public funds. Not long after assuming office, he wrote the Chief of the Weather Bureau complaining of "luxurious extravagance" and recommending cutbacks and job terminations. To the Superintendent of the Veterinary Experiment Station in Washington, D.C., the new secretary bluntly declared his seriousness of purpose: "I wish it distinctly understood that wherever there is an opportunity to economize, it should be embraced with alacrity, and that if you do not economize someone will be put in your place who will." No money would be spent to eradicate weeds, sell seeds, advertise for farm groups, subsidize starch plants, push for tariff support, or inspect meat. Indeed, he vigorously opposed the passage of pure food laws. What good would food investigations do? Citizens concerned for their own health would check food themselves. There was little doubt that President Cleveland had found a serious follower of the Jeffersonian gospel in government. During Morton's tenure in office, the Department of Agriculture returned to the Treasury a little more than $2 million, about 18.5 percent of what had been appropriated.[16]

Among the creative achievements for which Sterling Morton is best known, insofar as he is known at all beyond the plains country, was his crusade to plant trees. Nothing expressed better his forward-looking self. There is a quiet drama in seeing the conservative take a grand risk, leaving settled society for a largely treeless section of the old Louisiana Purchase with few signs of successful settlement, preparing to improve the environment for future generations. Having played in the Michigan woods as a child, the pioneer settler stood aghast at the barrenness of the prairies. Although he came to love the expanse of the western horizon, there were moments in the early years when it was touch and go whether the psychological and aesthetic losses occasioned by the wind-swept landscape would drive him to heed his father's advice and return home. From the beginning, he had trees sent to him from the East, not only shade and forest trees but several varieties of fruit trees. Together he and his young wife made plans for an orchard. Meanwhile, he championed the planting and preservation of trees to all who read the Nebraska City News and promoted the cause in his political work. There were many in the prairie states who cared deeply about trees and forests, and territorial legislatures added their encouragement. But it was Morton's resolution the Nebraska legislature accepted, establishing that one day each year be devoted to tree planting. On that first Arbor Day in April 1872, a splendid moment in American conservation history, Nebraskans planted a million trees.[17]

On the occasion of the first tree planting celebration in Nebraska, Morton wrote in the Omaha Daily Herald:

> Trees grow in time. The poorest landowner... has just as large a fortune, of time, secured to him, as has the richest. And the rain and sunshine and seasons will be his partners, just as genially and gently as they will be those of any millionaire, and will make the trees planted by the poor man grow just as grandly

and beautifully as those planted by the opulent.... There is a true triumph in the unswerving integrity and genuine democracy of trees, for they refuse to be influenced by money or social position and thus tower morally, as well as physically, high above Congressmen and many other patriots of this dollaring age.[18]

Behind the poetry, the founder of Arbor Day had a solid grip on the economic and political necessity of trees. From the Dakotas to Texas, wood and water were scarce, an unfortunate fact that provoked bitter complaints from the overlanders and early settlers. This more than pioneer hardships and hostile Indians kept settlers from the prairie plains before the Civil War. Wood was needed for fuel, construction, fencing, and even to bring rain, some believed.[19] With a vigorous tree planting campaign, barren Nebraska in its competition with other states could place its claim on the future: timber would lure settlers and settlers would bring the railroads, statehood, and economic prosperity. His several positions as Acting Territorial Governor and legislator, newspaper editor, and railroad agent, provided Morton with an ideal base from which to promote trees, ever mindful of what the publicity would do for Nebraska as a center of environmental improvement.

It was predictable that the Conservative would become one more vehicle for Morton's crusade. Nearly every number of the Conservative carried word of forestry, conservation, and horticulture. A special Arbor Day edition, opening with the admonition to "Plant Trees," reminded readers of other uses of trees. They provided railroad ties, telegraph and telephone poles; they provided shade, sheltered wildlife, and protected against winter blasts, retained water and soil and protected river banks, provided wood for wagons, implements, and furniture. The aesthetic dimension of finely planted groves enhanced the spirit against the bleakness of winter.[20] City dwellers learned that trees and parks would benefit them by tempering the heat reflected from brick and asphalt and by helping to purify the air of noxious fumes. Articles pertaining to woodland management on farms were more common, however. Several called for planning on a large scale. Unless inducements in the form of reduced taxes were offered, private capital would not flow into forest management. Private forests (95 percent of the woodlands in the United States) would vanish. Sounding a more sentimental theme, various writers proffered farm beautification as one means of keeping sons and daughters at home, a plea that resonated less and less in an urbanizing society. Create a farm home environment that is "rich in cultivating influences, a live inspiration, a perennial joy to the farmer, his wife and children," so that if children head for the city "they will never fully rest till they come back to the old farmstead." In a triumph of hope over reality, E. Benjamin Andrews of the University of Nebraska told the National Farmers' Congress at Sioux Falls, South Dakota: "You can have this so if you will."[21]

There is a poignancy in this awareness in agrarian America that husbands and fathers must somehow surmount their cash-poor status so as to enrich and to lighten the burdens shouldered by their wives and daughters: "the dreary sameness of their experience, rare breaks or pauses in work that can never end, the treadmill, the plodding, the ever-abiding shadow."[22] For too many, the years of toil and hardship had smothered the sweet affirmations of womanhood.

As Morton entered the evening of his life, nothing save the loss of a family member caused him such bereavement as the destruction of fruit or forest which he would never see replaced in size and character. He was quite prepared to write obituaries to trees downed by a storm.[23] This sentimental identity with nature's bounty colored too his views of Christmas which he shared with readers of the New York World in December 1901. As the seasonal pomp and display of worldly wealth ill fits the teachings of the man from Nazareth, so "cutting down symmetrical and beautiful young conifers to hang toys upon is rank treason to posterity, whose lumber and timber are thus wantonly wasted. Christmas trees... are the destruction of a necessity for coming generations, to merely please the children of this generation. The Christmas tree ought to be abolished."[24]

More central to the political objectives of the Conservative was its campaign for sound money. Nearly every issue carried at least a short plea for the virtues of the gold standard. Quotations abounded from Jefferson, Paine, Adams, and Webster, all against the issuing of paper money. The conservative Nebraska Democrat had given much thought to money and had not trimmed on the matter when it would have been politically expedient to do so. He refused to truck with farmers of the South and West who had long protested the unprofitableness of their vocation. Nor would he recognize that the Populist search for a cheaper currency grew not out of agrarian radicalism but out of the farm depressions of the late nineteenth century. With silver readily available, Populists asked, why not enter it into the national currency to increase its volume and presumably stir new economic activity? Substantial amounts would almost certainly have had an inflating effect, precisely what farmers wanted. Nebraska villagers and farmers split on this issue as they struggled for political power. Morton, a long-settled pioneer who had never been a dirt farmer, was the leading Gold Democrat in Nebraska to stand against the silver tide. Coin must have intrinsic value, he argued. Silver dollars minted at a sixteen to one ratio with gold would cheapen the dollar since sixteen ounces of silver would not, in a free market, buy an ounce of gold. Why subsidize the silver miners while robbing workers of part of their earnings? Sooner or later his countrymen must reckon with the truth that individual welfare rested not on easy money, but on exertion and frugality.[25] Whatever the shortcomings of Populist economic theory, Morton had evaded rather than solved the problem of the nation's serious money shortage.

The money issue lay behind a related theme that brought an incandescent glow to the pages of the Conservative, namely, Morton's campaign against William Jennings Bryan. The vitriol poured on "The Commoner" suggests that a personal element was at work, for Bryan had replaced Morton as Mr. Democrat in Nebraska. Although Morton had long carried the flag for the Democracy, he had also demonstrated a notable talent for losing elections. His campaign for Congress in 1860 brought defeat. Nominated for the governorship in 1866, he lost, and then lost again in that year's congressional race. Three subsequent races for the governorship brought no change. Although Nebraska was a Republican state after the Civil War, as were most in the North for the remainder of the century, Morton undermined his various candidacies by his outspoken honesty and known sympathy for large corporations.

Bryan's willingness to cooperate with Populists and to accept the silver issue as his own made a break between the two Democrats inevitable. How difficult Morton found it to read references to the "peerless" leader, the "matchless orator," the "friend of the masses," and "the great commoner." Readers of the Conservative prior to the 1900 election were schooled in "Bryanarchy," which Morton eagerly defined: "The difference between anarchy and Bryanarchy is that the former believes in no government at all, and the latter believes in no government without Bryan. No government is bad enough, and why any sane citizen should yearn for anything worse, is beyond comprehension." Bryan was not unlike Populist demagogues "who turn furrows with their tongues and raise crops by resolutions." All were scamps, out to "farm the farmers."[26]

By election time, Morton had had more than enough and committed the Conservative to the victory of McKinley, the lesser of two evils. McKinley would approve an equitable arrangement for the Filipinos, or if not, at least could be depended upon "to preserve the present financial fabric." In a post-election analysis, the Conservative editor told his readers to rejoice in the triumph of American citizenship over "anarchistic tendencies" and "demagogic appeals to class prejudices." Meanwhile, his correspondence brimmed with admonition for the Democrats to eliminate Bryanarchy or adjourn sine die.[27]

Doubting the will of the Democracy to cleanse itself of its free silver heresies, yet unwilling to commit to the imperialistic policies of the Republicans, the conservative Gold Democrat renewed efforts to organize a new national organization to be called the Conservative party. He had pursued this intermittently since 1896, hoping that the best elements of the existing parties, especially conservative Democrats and Republicans at odds with their president over Cuba and the Philippines, could gather in Philadelphia's Independence Hall to support sound money and a tariff for revenue only, and to propose an alternative to the imperialistic venturings of President McKinley. His extensive correspondence and frequent appeals in the Conservative won attention but moved no one to undertake the needed organizational chores. Most doubted that success would come. Approaching seventy years of age and unwilling to leave Arbor Lodge for extended periods, the editor had tried to accomplish with his pen what only foot soldiers could do and had to acknowledge defeat.[28]

Sound money, individualism and self-reliance, limited government, conservation, arboriculture, opposition to Bryanism at home and imperialism abroad--these were salient themes of the Conservative, leaving one to be added. The Conservative occasionally read as if it were printed in Railroad, U.S.A. No one should have been surprised. When the railroads built westward in the 1860s and 1870s, they enjoyed close relations with the territorial and state governments. The settlers, too, coveted railroads for their communities and as enticements voted bonds for their construction. To isolated communities, the whistle of the locomotive promised markets and prosperity and brought softer whispers of a place in the national community. Once the railroads were built, a task that had furnished food and provisioning, questions arose over their operation. High freight and passenger rates, in the context of drought, insufficient markets, and falling agricultural prices produced some of the most critical political battles of the era.

The editor of the <u>Conservative</u>, however, never wavered in his conviction that the West required railroads to prosper. An energetic booster of Nebraska while editor of the <u>Nebraska City News</u>, Morton had worked assiduously to entice railroads to the Territory. Competition among them to obtain settlers was stiff, and when Morton sold his newspaper in 1870, the Chicago, Burlington & Quincy Railroad hired the gifted editor to speak and write on its behalf, to promote the sale of its bonds in Iowa and Nebraska, and to serve as a lobbyist in Washington, D.C.[29] He was handsomely rewarded. The Burlington paid him $5,000 per year, plus expenses. Some years saw his income swell to double that figure--that at a time when a factory worker might earn $300 for a year's work. In 1875 Morton wrote to George Pullman, offering his services to the Pullman Corporation, again for $5,000 per year. For a Nebraskan with political ambitions, it was ill-advised to hire out his talents to railroad corporations even as they were coming under popular attack. The question is not one of integrity, for Morton saw little hope for the western economy without a well-developed transportation system. Nevertheless, it would be accurate to describe Arbor Lodge as the house the railroads built.[30]

Years later, wanting to place the Conservative on a firm financial base, Morton found it natural to turn to old friends such as Charles Perkins, once the land commissioner and later the president of the Burlington and Missouri. Additional letters went out to the president or general manager of the Union Pacific, the Atchison, Topeka, and Santa Fe Railroad System, the Chicago & Northwestern, the Illinois Central Railroad Company, asking them to take from 500 to 1,000 subscriptions at the regular rate of $1.50 per year.[31]

His message was blunt: the railroads must pay for an articulate voice on their behalf. "In this way," wrote Morton, "a public sentiment may be founded on right premises. The American people are going to be educated either to a regard for the rights of property, or to a communism. The teachers of the latter seem to be far more active than the instructors in the former." It helped that three of his sons at one time or another had worked for the railroads, with Paul then serving as Vice-President of the Atchison, Topeka, and Santa Fe. In a letter to Kidder-Peabody & Company, Morton appealed to non-railroad corporations as well: the Conservative "must be sustained... by conservative citizens who think it important that the American people continue steadfast to the gold standard. Therefore, I look for advertising patronage from banks, insurance, manufacturing, and railroad companies all over the country."[32]

The railroads responded generously, providing the financial base Morton coveted. Each railroad enclosed with its order a list of persons along its lines who were to receive the weekly without cost. Later Morton would suggest that the need to counter Bryan's paper, the Commoner, should be sufficient to open the coffers on behalf of his journal. He harbored some hope of pushing circulation to 100,000, in part by getting the Conservative into all the rural barbershops in Nebraska, Iowa, and Kansas.[33]

Not surprisingly, the Conservative published studies on the benefits railroads brought to the western states, the positive impact on land values, travel, and geographical mobility. Nor did it fail to demonstrate that freight charges on agricultural commodities had declined significantly over the years.[34] He was able to score points with the data published, but in the public mind he was linked forever to the interests of the wealthy and powerful.

How frustrating it was to find one's self-image so at odds with reality. He deemed himself an apostle of Thomas Jefferson. But which Jefferson? In an age of reform, the question mattered. The third president has been claimed by the faithful among anti-statists, states'-righters, agrarians, rationalists, civil libertarians, constitutional democrats, and isolationists. Seven Jeffersons.[35] A case can be made that J. Sterling Morton, when it suited him, found comfort in each of these houses. Both Jefferson and Morton harbored a deep faith that free individuals could better themselves and society without government help. Freedom meant the warding off of public control, not the harnessing of collective intelligence to effect social change. Both believed that men of the soil were the chosen people of God, that large cities were dens of iniquity. One can easily imagine

Jefferson sharing Morton's tolerance of Mormons and dislike of the prohibition movement.

Yet important differences existed, too. Jefferson believed that good government was founded on public opinion; Morton believed it was based on sound money and credit. Jefferson, whose passion was liberty, feared oppression; Morton, a self-made man, feared attacks on property. Jefferson exhibited a serene confidence that men when not oppressed would exercise good sense; Morton feared that prejudice and passion often accompanied the casting of a ballot.[36] We cannot know whether Jefferson would have been a progressive in the mode of Senator LaFollette and President Wilson. It is conceivable, however, that the president who concluded the Louisiana Purchase, imposed a hurtful embargo, and fought a small war against the Barbary pirates, would in the twentieth century have advised with Herbert Croly the occasional use of Hamiltonian means to achieve the promise of American life. Morton's Jefferson, the agrarian, anti-statist, states'-righter, and isolationist, was one Jefferson. In the social and economic matrix of the late nineteenth century, this Jeffersonianism buttressed the conservative defense of privilege. Morton's enemies had an equally valid claim on the rationalist Jefferson, the civil libertarian, constitutional democrat and revolutionary leader who took his stand with the men of good hope.

At first glance it is curious that a community builder who worked so diligently, often in concert with others, to bring civilization to his corner of the world, saw so little that could be done to shape the larger national society. Part of the reason lies in the age of rapid western expansion and industrial development in which Morton lived. The new manufacturing, transportation, and communication technologies pulled the semi-autonomous island communities into a national market and national policy that taken together constitute the most profound transformation in American history. Private individuals lay at the center of that process. In Morton's early years the land could be tamed and communities built under traditional forms of social and economic life. That was his experience, his truth. The new urban-industrial order, however, would require professionalism, bureaucratic decision-making, and large-scale organization to rationalize the tumultuous process of social and economic change.[37]

Having won success in frontier America, Morton saw little need to square his inherited moral standards and ideology with the economic factors that gave rise to numerous protest movements. The spirit of reform we associate with Progressivism that arose at the time he founded the Conservative held few charms for the conservative Democrat from Otoe County. Having opposed the land-based Populist movement, Morton could hardly be expected to support a reform movement stemming largely from the urban middle class, particularly one that found the solution to overweening corporate power and human suffering in the expansion of governmental authority. Even when reform meant new rules of the game rather than the enlargement of government power, Morton held firm. The initiative and referendum that brought voters more fully into the political process were "absolutely against all the principles of representative government," wrote Morton. "We delegate the power to make laws to legislative bodies. A referendum is an assault upon this system."[38] Like many of his time, Morton took the Jefferson who responded to historical conditions and froze his responses into absolutes. A strong central government had been a danger--and Jefferson feared it. Government had been by the rich--and Jefferson opposed it. Morton, doing likewise a century later, made the <u>Conservative</u> a spokesman for laissez-faire conservatism.

Notes

1. J. Sterling Morton to John J. Valentine, 31 May 1899, Roll 67, J. Sterling Morton Papers, Nebraska State Historical Society, Lincoln, Nebraska.

2. Everett Dick, The Sod-House Frontier (Lincoln, Neb.: Johnson Publishing Company, 1954), especially pp. 417-434 and 459-479, provides an arresting portrait of frontier newspapers and county politics.

3. Charles Dabney, "The Presidency and Secretary Morton," Atlantic Monthly 77 (March 1896): 388-394.

4. Conservative, 14 July 1898, p. 1 and Morton to H.H. Porter, 29 August 1898, Roll 66, Morton Papers.

5. "Bryanarchy," Conservative, 31 August 1899, pp. 2-3; 7 September 1899, p. 5; 28 September 1899, p. 8.

6. Morton to George L. Miller, 20 July 1898; Morton to John DeVitt Warner, 21 July 1898; Morton to Gov. R.W. Furnas, 22 July 1898; Morton to Edward Atkinson, 29 July 1898, Roll 66, Morton Papers.

7. Conservative, 12 September 1899, p. 11; 5 October 1899, p. 11; 10 October 1901, p. 5.

8. Conservative, 13 September 1900, p. 15.

9. Typical of the companies advertising in the Conservative were The Morton Printing Company; Deere & Co. (Illinois); Jay Morton & Co. (Illinois); Merchants National Bank (Nebraska); Union Pacific Railroad; Springfield Fire and Marine Insurance Co. (Massachusetts); National Starch Co. (Nebraska); and the Atchison, Topeka & Santa Fe Railway Co.

10. After a year of publication, circulation figures for the Conservative amounted to approximately 7,000 as noted in Morton to Henry G. Smith, 5 October 1899, Roll 67, Morton Papers.

11. Morton to John W. Lewis, 17 October 1898, Roll 66 and Morton to Douglas I. Hobbs, 22 June 1901, Roll 69, Morton Papers.

12. Morton to A.S. Phelps, 15 July 1901, Roll 69, Morton Papers.

13. "What Are the Young Man's Chances?--A Symposium," Conservative, 15 August 1901, p. 2.

14. Conservative, 15 August 1901, p. 9; 19 September 1901; and Charlotte (N.C.) Observer, 26 August 1901 reprinted in Conservative, 5 September 1901, pp. 2-3.

15. Conservative, 26 September 1901, pp. 1-2.

16. Morton to Mark Harrington, 16 May 1893; Morton to F.L. Kibourne, 20 May 1893; Morton to A.J. Wedderburn, 26 June 1893, Roll 51, Morton Papers and James C. Olson, J. Sterling Morton (Lincoln: University of Nebraska Press, 1942), p. 362.

17. James C. Olson, "Arbor Day--A Pioneer Expression of Concern for Environment," Nebraska History 53 (Spring 1972): 10.

18. Cited in Olson, J. Sterling Morton, p. 165.

19. Edward Everett Dale, "Wood and Water: Twin Problems of the Prairie Plains," Nebraska History 29 (June 1948): 87-104.

20. Conservative, 11 April 1901.

21. Louis Windmuller, "A Plea for Trees and Parks in Cities," Conservative, 10 May 1900, pp. 8-9; C.A. Schenck, "The Capitalist and Forestry," Conservative, 18 January 1900, pp. 10-11; E. Benjamin Andrews, "The Farmstead Beautiful," Conservative

17 October 1901, pp. 6-7.

22. Andrews, "The Farmstead Beautiful," p. 7. For Morton, anything was better than living in cities, however. He told readers of the Conservative that "it is better, much better, to live in a small and healthful town in the West, than in one of the great, rancid, furious, smothering, diseased masses, crawling with deformed and unnatural human animals, that we call world-cities. Boys may grow up to be good men in those surroundings, but there are terrible chances against them. And we do not believe it is wholly infection or example that causes the harm. There can be no normal life in a city; the existence is unnatural." Conservative, 10 October 1901, p. 5.

23. Conservative, 14 July 1898, p. 8.

24. "For N.Y. World," Roll 69, Morton Papers.

25. Conservative, 14 July 1898, p. 4; 28 July 1898, pp. 1-2; 4 August 1898, pp. 2-3; and 13 April 1899, pp. 4-5; Edward Atkinson, "Force Bills on the Money Question," Conservative, 15 September 1898, pp. 6-9; Hon. J.M. Carey, "The Gold Standard From the Standpoint of the Western States," Conservative, 13 October 1898, pp. 10-13; Morton to James A. Cherry, 18 May 1895, Roll 47, Morton Papers. In 1897, Morton became a vice-president of the newly formed National Sound Money League and was elected president the following year. Not much came of this position. Republican victories diminished the threat of the silver crusade and the group disbanded in 1900. It does indicate, however, the degree to which Morton had committed to a strong currency.

26. Morton to Paul Morton, 21 September 1899, Roll 67 and Morton to Edward Campbell, Jr., 8 November 1900, Roll 68, Morton

Papers; Conservative, 21 September 1899, pp. 8-9; 3 May 1900, p. 2; 19 July 1900, pp. 2-3; 6 September 1900, pp. 6-11; 1 November 1900, pp. 1-2; William Allen White, "W.J. Bryan," Conservative, 12 July 1900, pp. 8-9.

27. Conservative, 25 October 1900 p. 4 and 15 November 1900, pp. 1-2; Morton to S.B. Evans, 24 November 1900, Roll 68, Morton Papers.

28. Conservative, 10 November 1898, p. 2; 28 November 1898, p. 11; 6 April 1899, p. 1; and Morton to John W. Lewis, 17 November 1898, Roll 66; Morton to A.J. Sawyer, 10 November 1900, Roll 68, Morton Papers.

29. For two fine articles that demonstrate the effective role railroads played in the settling of the Great Plains see John D. Unruh, Jr., "The Burlington and Missouri River Railroad Brings the Mennonites to Nebraska, 1873-1878," Parts I and II, Nebraska History 45 (March 1964): 3-30 and (June 1964): 177-206. J. Sterling Morton served as a commissioner for the railroad in the 1870s.

30. Rolls 5, 6, and 71 of the Morton Papers document Morton's work for the Burlington railroad. For an example of money received for services see frame 078965 (1875), Roll 71 and Morton to George M. Pullman, 24 June 1875, Roll 47, Morton Papers.

31. See, for example, Morton to R.R. Cable, 30 June 1898; Morton to Paul Morton, 3 July 1898; and Morton to J.C. Stubbs, 18 July 1898, Roll 66; Morton to E.P. Ripley, 10 June 1899; Morton to T.P. Shonts, 11 August 1899; Morton to Stuyvesant Fish, 19

August 1899, Roll 67; Stuyvesant Fish to Morton, 10 August 1900, Roll 44, Morton Papers.

32. Morton to H.H. Porter, 30 August 1898 and Morton to C.W.H. Strongman, 16 August 1898, Roll 66, Morton Papers.

33. Morton to Stuyvesant Fish, 17 December 1900 and Morton to Horace G. Burt, 17 December 1900, Roll 68, Morton Papers.

34. H.T. Newcomb, "Railroad Rates and Competition," Conservative, 8 September 1898, p. 5; "Passenger and Freight Rates on American Railways," Conservative, 18 August 1898, pp. 5-7; "Railroads and Politics," Conservative, 30 January 1902, pp. 6-8.

35. Seven Jeffersons is an arbitrary number. See Clinton Rossiter, "Which Jefferson Do You Quote?" Reporter, 15 December 1955, pp. 33-36.

36. Morton to John M. Carson, 27 October 1900, Roll 68, Morton Papers.

37. Cf. Robert H. Wiebe, The Search for Order, 1877-1920 (New York: Hill and Wang, 1967).

38. Morton to S.B. Evans, 17 December 1900, Roll 68, Morton Papers.

Populism's Stepchildren: The National Farmers' Union
and Agriculture's Welfare in Twentieth-Century America

by Roy T. Wortman*

> You are the lifeblood of the universe
> With the veins of commerce in your hand
>
> You can fill your pockets with Wall St.'s purse
> And be the monarch of the land
>
> So join together a band of brothers
> Unfurl your flag of justice on the topmost towers
>
> And you'll soon be seen by the business world
> And be known as the king of earthly power.
>
> --T.M. Davis, Farmers Union organizer, ca. 1910

> I have often said that if the Farmers Union cannot serve agriculture for this country we will all become serfs and peons, as farmers are in many foreign countries.
>
> --a ninety-five year old Kansas NFU member, 1939[1]

Joseph Fichter, president emeritus of the Ohio Farmers Union was six years old in 1900--old enough to break into tears when his father told him that William Jennings Bryan lost to McKinley. Fichter understood the fate of the small family farmer in moral terms. "There are virtues of farm life--the Farmers Union emphasized this: the integrity, the quality of life about the small family farm." Fichter, who joined the National Farmers' Union in 1915, quoted the Bible on the current status of family farming: "You cannot serve God and Mammon at the same time." For Fichter, as for others in the Farmers Union, preserving family farms was the mission and an active federal government was the means. "If you don't have a family farm, what you've got is a situation that existed years ago in Europe's feudal system where a few wealthy people owned the land and operated it by hired labor, and if we don't have the family farm that's what's going to happen here. Corporations will handle it; we're going to have a few corporations handle these things and the rest of the people will be hired labor."[2]

Joseph Fichter expressed well the sentiments and the ideals of the National Farmers Union. And even as Fichter's understanding of the plight of the American farmer did not change throughout his life, so the commitment of the National Farmers Union has remained undiminished throughout its over eighty-year history. As a voluntary organization the NFU mobilized its traditional and land-owning constituency in support of social and economic programs consistent with the welfare state that emerged in the 1930s under the leadership of Franklin Roosevelt. The National Farmers Union acted as a significant member of the New Deal coalition as it faithfully spoke on behalf of the small American farmer. Founded in 1902, the Farmers Union was an offshoot of the defeated Populist movement and as such insisted that the federal government was the only agency capable of preserving the family farm in the United States. So, too, the NFU contained the tensions of populism. For about half a decade, from 1930 to 1936, the National Farmers Union briefly indulged in what can only be described as paranoid and fundamentally bigoted rhetoric which uncomfortably resembled extremist movements in Europe and the United States. But by 1936 the NFU returned to its democratic, cooperative tradition as it came out in support of Franklin Roosevelt, organized labor, and the welfare state in general. Unlike the large farmer-dominated and market-oriented American Farm Bureau Federation, the National Farmers Union, since the mid-1930s, has identified unequivocally with the political left. The small farmers who made up the NFU have viewed government as a necessary bulwark against the vicissitudes of the weather and the marketplace. According to the NFU, only a strong and active federal government could save the small, capital-poor American farmer.

The National Farmers Union first emerged in the South, specifically in Texas, a state with a history of agrarian radicalism. In the last quarter of the nineteenth century the Farmers' Alliance and its offshoot, the Populist Party, raised important questions for impoverished farmers. Who controls the economy and government? Where was justice and equity for the farmer? Populists tried to gain equity for small farmers through political action in the national elections of 1892 and 1896. They stressed anti-monopoly themes and sought federal intervention on behalf of small land owners. Unfortunately for farmers, by 1896 the "democratic promise" of the Populists failed as a political movement.[3]

After World War II, a technological revolution forced many Americans off the farm as it enabled fewer farmers to produce more food. In the process, America's "first majority" became our "last minority."[4] Yet one organization, the Farmers Educational and Cooperative Society of North America, known by its more common name, the National Farmers Union, staunchly represented rural America and the family-owned farm. Historically, the National Farmers Union dedicated itself to the well-being of the small family farmer, but it also championed other disadvantaged groups in the United States. Since 1902 the NFU represented mainly small farmers who affirmed traditional American religion and cultural values during a period of great stress and change. Yet neither issues nor grievances had disappeared.

Founded in Raines County, Texas, the National Farmers Union arose from the wreckage of the Farmers' Alliance and the Populist movements. In the 1880s chief organizer Newt Gresham, a Texas journalist intensely concerned with the plight of poor farmers who would later form the NFU, served as an Alliance organizer in the South. Gresham later supported the Populists in their attempt for national power in 1892. In 1896 he backed William Jennings Bryan, who lost to the Republican candidate, William McKinley. When Gresham and his colleagues founded the National Farmers Union, some Southern farmers hoped for a resurgence of the Populist Party. But Gresham knew better. He feared that the NFU would fall victim to partisan politics as had the Populists. The NFU thus proclaimed itself a non-partisan organization, thereby hoping to avoid the pitfalls of third-party movements.

In 1902, Gresham established the platform for a non-partisan farmers' group emphasizing mutual self-help, education, and cooperatives. The Union shared the Populists' disdain for bankers, middlemen and commodity speculators. Through a program of self-help, the Union tried to break the financial stranglehold which Southern merchants and planters held over small farmers. Farm cooperation offered small farmers the capital and organization to circumvent the monopolisitc practices and capital scarcity that then characterized Southern agriculture.[5]

The National Farmers Union was also influenced by the traveling lecturers of the Equitable Society of Rochdale Pioneers. This group, an outgrowth of British Chartism, was formed in 1844 by destitute weavers of Toad's Lane, Rochdale, England. The Rochdale Pioneers advocated self-help and cooperation, and supported a policy of open membership in cooperative societies for all except "capitalists," by which they meant bankers, merchants, lawyers, or anyone who through interest or continued scarcity seemed to profit from another person's labor. They emphasized democratic practices and improvement for their members through education. Their cooperatives returned profits directly to the members. Ownership and control of the cooperatives always remained in the hands of members, each of whom had one vote regardless of the amount of trade he generated. Their "travellers" established links with Southern agrarian democrats. A Texan, Owen Dornblazer (1850?-1936), helped introduce the Farmers Union to the Rochdale principles.[6]

While the Union was understandably concerned with the well-being of small family farmers, it also advocated equity for all Americans. The NFU believed that if fairly governed, the world could be free from poverty and want. The Union emphasized the commonalty of the human condition and the dignity of labor. "Truth, Honesty, Sobriety, and Brotherly Love," declared the

Union ritual, are values consonant with "Our noble order's principles of Equity, Justice, and the Golden Rule." These "fruits of life," read the Union's ritual guide in 1910, were vital for a sturdy, virtuous membership. "It must follow as the night the day, Thou canst not be false to any man." Honesty, citizenship, sobriety, and fraternal love were inextricably bound up with "the great God who gave... life and watches over you, whether you are revelling in the sins of the world, sitting around the fireside with your family... or peacefully in your downy bed, lost in pleasant dreams." Members were urged to call each other "Brother" and the Union tried to weld a common bond of historical identification through the suffering of its farmers.[7]

In the years before World War I, NFU membership was predominantly Southern. The Union expanded from Texas to Alabama, Georgia, Mississippi, Louisiana, Arkansas, North Carolina, South Carolina, Tennessee, Virginia, Kentucky, and Oklahoma. In 1906 Charles Simon Barrett, a self-proclaimed "Georgia cracker," was elected president of the Union, an office he maintained until 1928. Barrett's problems--low dues income, the lack of forceful legislative programs, and the inability of Southern cooperatives to function in sound, business-like ways--led to a shift in the locus of NFU regional strength. Southern locals lost members, while membership in the high plains Midwest grew in vitality.[8] In 1908 Southern states claimed 111,022 farm families. In 1914 that number declined to 61,817, and by 1919 fell to 28,135. By contrast, Midwestern family membership showed steady growth. From 14,044 farm families in 1908, the NFU's Midwestern membership grew to 29,738 in 1914, and 93,029 in 1919.[9]

Midwestern states carried on the Southern heritage of NFU ideology and added an element of Scandinavian immigrant social democracy. Although fraternal rhetoric of the Southern NFU diminished in the Midwest, the substance behind the fraternal ideal of the Union did not erode. If anything, it simply took on a newer meaning. The NFU emphasized the idea of fraternity not only between its own members but also for organized labor and minority groups. A concept of organic wholeness between all producers evolved in Farmers Union rhetoric and practice. After eighty years the NFU, representing approximately one million persons in twenty-three states, still emphasizes the basic commitments as set forth by its founders in its early years.[10]

The Union always regarded itself as more progressive than its more conservative rival, the American Farm Bureau Federation (AFBF). The NFU has consistently viewed the AFBF as an appendage of large-scale commercial agriculture, agribusiness, and big business. Founded in 1920, the AFBF disavowed the militant and populistic approach to the welfare of farmers. V. O. Key aptly summarized the sensibilities of the AFBF: its leadership "rests far more easily when the Republican party controls the national governement.[11] In its rhetoric, the NFU at times saw the AFBF in simplistic terms. Where the NFU asserted family farming as a way of life, the AFBF emphasized farming as a commercial venture. The NFU historically sought strict regulation of business and strong federal involvement in agricultural policy. The AFBF, by contrast, especially after 1943, maintained that governmental regulation and social planning were undesirable. Where the AFBF argued that "bigger is better" in commercial farming, the NFU upheld the family farm as an holistic unit. For the AFBF, increased productivity and farm income should be the cornerstones of farm policy. For the NFU, the continued vitality of small family farmers should be the central concern of government farm policy. Significantly, NFU membership consists almost entirely of family farmers, while the AFBF accepts farmers, merchants, manufacturers, educators, salesmen, and persons from other occupations to swell its ranks. In a word, by NFU standards the AFBF is a "capitalistic" rather than a farmer organization.[12]

By the 1920s, the Farmers Union viewed family farming and rural life as something more than a mere commercial enterprise. Unlike the AFBF, the NFU saw small farmers pitted against "plutocracy" in a drama involving vast but not insurmountable odds. Agrarians, argued the Texas Farmers Union in 1920, produced the wealth of the world but had been robbed for years by manufacturers and speculators. The Texans elaborated on this theme by noting that the tension of farmer against manufacturer and speculator created a cultural division between countryside and city. "In the cities are the miserably low and beastly rich," the Union declared, "the genius and the degenerate, the slave and the master, the helpless and the powerful. We have no such [classes] in the country and laws adapted to the cities will not suffice for the country."[13] The NFU defined itself as a special group. Urban society, with its rapid social changes had, by 1920, included over 50 percent of the American population. A sense of isolation complicated the rural outlook of the Farmers

Union during the 1920s and 1930s. Inherent in rural life, as the Union saw the course of events, was the potential for a society which could give equity, encourage cooperation rather than competition, and flourish free from the complexities of urban life. In reviewing the history of farm protest movements in the nineteenth century, James Patton, president of the Union, in 1952 alluded to the power "money merchants" had over the American economy. Twenty-six years later, Patton, now president emeritus, received thunderous applause at a special meeting for young Farmers Union couples during his speech that outlined the state of America. What needed to be done, Patton argued, was to reverse the tables and socialize the corporations.[14]

By contrast, in 1909 the remarks of Charles S. Barrett indicated that the NFU had been more sedate in its earlier days than in its last fifty years. "Temperamentally," said Barrett, "the farmer is slow to think, slow to anger, slow to see that he is the unconscious instrument of selfish men. But after a while he thinks and sees that he... has been wronged." If the farmer were "permanently organized into helpful bodies he at last becomes a conservative. The pangs of sudden anger, righteous anger, do not come upon him." Barrett emphasized the process of becoming "conservative" not in a simplistic left-right dichotomy but rather in the sense of becoming more practical as it organized for effective action.[15] As small landowners, members of the NFU were militant insofar as tangible political action gained short-term results. Nonetheless, they accepted the desirability of privately owned and managed agriculture backed by a sympathetic and helpful government. The idealism and cooperative impulse in the Southern Farmers Union was weakened by economic setbacks in the 1920s which forced the Union to become more prudential and practical. The Union learned from its past mistakes. Southern activists promised too much in the teens and failed to deliver on their promises. Foreign markets for Southern commodities collapsed, and with them fell the Southern cooperative movement which was inadequately structured to cope with speculative cotton trade. To avoid repeating this failure, the NFU took up one of Barrett's suggestions: effective organization geared to moderate change within a market-oriented economy.[16]

Yet this was easier said than done in the 1920s. The decade was a difficult one for American agriculture. As prices declined, so did the purchasing power of American farmers. Increased costs of machinery, fertilizer and the introduction of the tractor placed small farmers at a serious disadvantage with large farms and corporations. Forced to borrow in order to keep up, they found themselves facing never ending mortgage payments. Even the weather seemed to work against them. If there was drought, too much rain or insect infestation, they might lose an entire year's income and be thrown on the mercy of bankers. But even good weather and abundant crops might spell disaster as "good years" invariably led to overproduction, a flooded market and disastrous drops in prices. Consequently, a federal government which took a "hands off" policy towards agriculture, allowing the weather and the market to sift out the inefficient, in effect aided and abetted the destruction of the small, capital-poor farmers. Without a federal policy which considered the preservation of small farmers as well as productivity equally important, the days of the small farmer in America were numbered.

For this reason, the NFU regarded Presidents Coolidge and Hoover as insensitive to the small farmer and the tools of large, corporate enterprise. C. E. Huff, a Kansan who succeeded Barrett from 1928 to 1930 as president of the NFU, urged small farmers to help themselves through the Rochdale principles. Huff recognized the necessity of supplementing the cooperative approach by pooling the bargaining power of farmers to offset the advantages of corporate power. While he encouraged cooperation, especially in Minnesota and North Dakota, where Union co-ops were derisively called "red squares," he also set up legislative pressure groups to influence agricultural policy at local, state and federal levels. Even so, non-partisanship was the hallmark of the Union. In returning to politics in the twenties under Huff, the NFU steered clear of single issue, third parties.[17]

In the early thirties under the leadership of the fourth Farmers Union president, John Simpson (1930-1934), the NFU broke its tradition as it disavowed the Rochdale principles and ignored its earlier cooperative policies. Frustrated by the Great Depression, Simpson and his followers sounded the farmers' plight in simple, angry terms. The NFU's militant rhetoric brought that plight to Congress and the public. In its view, invisible conspiratorial groups dominated, exploited, taxed, and cheated the small farmer. Under Simpson, the Union pushed for an inflationary monetary policy in opposition to both the Republican and Democratic parties. Simpson conjured up ghosts of Greenbackers and Bryan free silverites as the Union moved back to late nineteenth-century tactics and panaceas and away from the bread and butter politics as represented by Roosevelt's New Deal. Simpson advocated a "cost of production" scheme which involved averaging all expenses used for production of a commodity, including the farmer's labor, to determine a "fair price" divorced from marketplace whims. Theoretically, this would allow farmers a fair or earned profit for their commodity. Neither this nor Simpson's free silver ideas were taken seriously by the Roosevelt administration. Instead, the New Deal offered farmers crop limitations, parity payments, and such sympathetic and potentially radical programs as the Resettlement Administration. Yet under Simpson and his followers, there was no consensus in the Farmers Union. Until 1936, the NFU suffered from internal strife. Some members endorsed anti-democratic and pro-fascist policies and backed Father Charles Coughlin's National Union for Social Justice. Moderate elements in the Union, while disappointed in Roosevelt's agricultural policies, preferred the New Deal to the vitriolic views of the Right. The die was cast for a battle.[18]

Simpson epitomized a new impulse for change, one which was at once broad, angry, intemperate, and popular with a large segment of the Union. His small farmer militancy evoked the rhetoric of Populism but often lapsed into conspiratorial theory and even bigotry. He failed to recognize the ethnic diversity of the United States and increasing urbanization which left farmers as only one of several interest groups. While the Roosevelt administration was anxious to help small farmers and even offered a few, poorly funded, almost utopian programs, it had no intention of reversing the changes of the twentieth century. For this reason, Simpson gained sympathy and publicity from right-wing political groups as he promised to "keep things hot, even for the Democrats."[19]

From 1933 to 1936, the Union was rent with faction. During these debates the paradoxical legacy of Populism was exposed. One segment preferred the practical, pragmatic character and inclination of Populism which had advocated rural free delivery, the federal reserve banking system, crop supports, and commodity savings banks, while the other segment seemed mesmerized by visions of a mythic yeoman republic of small farmers free from the machinations of politicians, bankers, merchants, and "alien" influences.

Governor William Langer of North Dakota responded to both of these impulses as he endorsed a wheat embargo--in effect a strike of commodities--to be used unless farmers received cost of production supports and mortgage relief through the then pending Frazier-Lemke refinancing bill. At the same time, Langer made it clear that if legal means failed, he felt no obligation to enforce the law against farmers. He told the Union at its 1933 convention that he would never call up the militia to fight farmers in his state, and that he would use the militia to shoot any sheriff who foreclosed on a North Dakota farm.[20] In the turbulent era of the Depression, such rhetoric was popular in the thirty-one states organized by the NFU, from the high plains to Michigan, Indiana, Illinois, Ohio, Pennsylvania, and Maryland.

Simpson too embodied the paradox of NFU radicalism as he opposed moderation and the New Deal. He declared that the Roosevelt administration was "today just as despicable a bunch in the Department of Agriculture as they were under Herbert Hoover."[21] But the anger of rightists in the Union was not limited to politicians and bureaucrats as they also opposed the recruitment of 4000 Jewish poultry and truck garden farmers into the New Jersey Farmers Union. Their bigotry had so distorted their vision, that they seemed to equate Jewish farmers with "international conspiracies" of "Jewish bankers."[22] Under Simpson "scapegoatism" had triumphed over idealism and practical policy.

Following Simpson's death in 1934, rightists in the Union became even more conspiratorial and bigoted. President E. H. Everson and Secretary E. E. Kennedy set the tone for the NFU from 1934 to 1936. What Simpson began in naive anger was more knowingly completed by Everson, Kennedy, and their followers in the Union. At the 1934 convention, one "Brother Rogers" chastized the federal government for its agricultural policies, suggesting that until farmers receive justice "it would be best to move the National Capitol to the middle west where we farmers can look better after our own interests."[23] The message was clear. The New Deal was mistrusted and older attitudes-- suspicion of cities, industry, commerce, and ethnic minorities-- came to the fore. Such a tension-ridden atmosphere in American agriculture in 1934 allowed Milo Reno of the Iowa Farmers Union and the Farmers Holiday Association to state with impunity that change for farmers would never be attained "until farmers take the gun to their shoulder." In a vein similar to "Brother Rogers," Reno told delegates at the 1934 convention that "there are some fair and honest men in Washington but they are outvoted by the East,"[24] a veiled allusion to alleged mysterious forces, economic as well as ethnic, which subordinated farmers' welfare to other groups.

At the 1934 convention, Congressman William Lemke and Milo Reno lashed out at the federal government, blaming it for numerous ills. Reno epitomized the frustration and despair of farmers when he criticized Henry A. Wallace's attempt "to lead us out of the wilderness." Reno noted that "the government in Washington should be sent to the pen for ten times ten thousand years." For the angry Right, which sought simple solutions to complicated problems, the plight of the small family farmers, in the words of a Kansas delegate, was such that "The only hope... in the situation is the hopelessness of the situation."[25] Following the dictum of "the worse, the better," right-wingers hoped for eventual victory after abject defeat.

In the same 1934 convention in which Reno and Lemke had attacked the New Deal, a North Dakota Farmers Union junior delegate, Marion Hakenson, in his prize-winning essay, "The Machine Age," offered a more complex analysis. Hakenson emphasized the conflict between man and political economy in a depersonalized machine age. He explained that the industrial revolution created an age in which craftsmen were replaced by technicians and producers by middlemen and speculators who prevented fair profits. Hakenson argued that "one of the greatest evils in the present economic system is that it makes allowances for production only, and not for consumption." Machines, he cautioned, must produce solely for production, not for profit. Change and welfare for the laboring people would come only if "the capitalists" no longer "control our nation." For as long as they do, "the voice of the common people" will not be heard. He concluded, "We must not let the machine control us! Policy makers must begin to recognize the American economy so that once more producers received a just return on their labor."[26]

Still, Hakenson's vision offered no specific solutions to the immediate plight of farmers in the thirties. Since the Roosevelt administration also did little to ameliorate the problems of small farmers, protest groups such as Reno's Farmers Holiday Association attracted large followings including many NFU members. Reno's vitriolic anger sought social, political, and economic changes for farmers, but his solutions--withholding actions and physical force--failed to come to grips with the problems of twentieth-century American agriculture. Anger alone, even if righteous, hardly served the interests of small farmers. If anything, it made it all the easier for critics to dismiss them as disaffected and irrational anachronisms.[27]

In 1934, moderates in the Union, committed to democratic due process and disdainful of anti-New Deal and pro-Coughlin factions, opposed the programs of Simpson, Everson and Kennedy. In 1934, Nebraska farmers went so far as to withhold payment of national dues until they had investigated Union policies. Other members objected to the Union endorsement of national radio broadcasts which castigated Roosevelt and the New Deal.[28]

Militant action by the Farmers Holiday Association and tirades against Roosevelt gained the approval of Farmers Union Secretary E. E. Kennedy. Equally revealing of Kennedy's views was his remark to the secretary of the Louisiana Farmers Union: "You produced a Huey Long and he certainly had the Farmers Union spirit in his heart."[29] Just as the anger of an earlier Populist, Tom Watson, helped destroy the integrity and decency of agrarian protest, so the search for new scapegoats and miraculous solutions besmirched the Farmers Union in the mid-thirties. Radio attacks on alleged conspiracies by bankers, the quest for financial panaceas epitomized by free silver plans, and attacks on Harry Hopkins and the Works Progress Administration all pushed the Union away from the mainstream of moderate political thought.

The last straw for moderates was the right wing's endorsement, at the 1936 convention, of the Lemke-Coughlin presidential slate on the National Union Party ticket. Those who had backed the cooperative movement in the late 1920s bitterly resented the push toward the politics of extremism. Inclining toward moderation, many pro-New Deal members of the NFU resented being linked to Lemke and Coughlin. Moreover, Secretary Kennedy and Coughlinites in the NFU alienated more prudent members who resented the angry tirades and blatant partisanship that characterized the 1936 convention.

Out of desperation, moderates gained control of the 1937 convention. Everson, Kennedy and their ilk were voted out of office by a narrow margin, after which they faded into obscurity in their new and short-lived group, the Farmers Guild. Proponents of cooperatives and of moderate political action now controlled the NFU as represented by a new president, a Kansan, John Vesecky (1937-1940). Vesecky heralded a return to economic self-help and legislative lobbying along with the cooperative principles of Rochdale.[30]

In 1938, Vesecky courted social democratic elements in the labor movement. Labor's Non-Partisan League, an independent body, joined with the National Farmers Union in seeking an end to domination of America's economic life by a few corporate giants. The Non-Partisan League and the NFU argued that "Modern corporations are really governmental in character and should be judged by the same standards that American people apply yearly to their state governments." Because corporations, as "economic governments," violated the basic precepts of political democracy, urged the NFU, they must be changed.[31] Accordingly, monopoly capitalism was viewed as a new behemoth. It destroyed economic autonomy of farmers, hampered labor unions, and impersonally and callously controlled the lives of American consumers. Political democracy existed, but economic democracy was thwarted by corporate monopolies.

After 1936, the paranoid and retrogressive vision of the Union's right wing gave way to the recognition of "the pathetic and glorious story of mankind, made increasingly difficult by our complex life." F. R. Lennox, a Union member from Ohio, recognized that "that age of abundance is here," and posed the crucial question: "Will the human mind... be able to apply its usage to the service of humanity on a plane of equality for all? Or will the law of the jungle prevail, when might was right?" To emphasize the cooperative philosophy, Lennox, in a nation-wide radio address, delineated between "acquisitive" and "service" concepts. The former applied the incentive of selfishness, while the latter allowed "a natural and fair exchange in all transactions."[32] Thus, after a moratorium under Simpson, Kennedy and Everson, the NFU resurrected the Rochdale principles. The Union pushed for political pressure and economic justice through support of organized labor, a rejection of the Simpson-Everson years. The Farmers Union once again asserted itself as a "militant, constructive and democratic organization."[33] It opposed fascist governments and sought neutrality for the United States. It lobbied against conscription and pleaded that American arm solely for self-defense. It promoted education for world peace and symbolically boycotted the weapons of war.[34]

By the end of 1938, a tone was clearly set in the NFU, one in which traditional principles of cooperation and democracy were affirmed in a world of "authoritarian political control," dominated by the "blood lust twins, Stalin and Hitler."[35] In 1940, the NFU warned against "the ravages of political and selfish demagogues" and cautioned members to consider a "more advanced tolerant membership loyal to the principles of education and cooperation."[36] As Unionists cherished cooperative principles, they grew ever more skeptical of single-issue panaceas. They warned against simple cures such as cost of production schemes or free silver. In a sensibility reminiscent of other New Deal voluntary groups, Ohio Union members affirmed the necessity to organize farmers "the same as any other trade group." In a cautious vein, Ohio Union members questioned the wisdom of becoming a politicized group. The same ghost which had haunted Newt Gresham in 1902 disturbed Union farmers in Ohio: Populism failed once; never again should an agrarian group try to become a third party. Ohio Union members opted for "critically studying all proposals with a purely educational objective that our members may more intelligently use their established democratic prerogatives."[37]

NFU policy statements at state and national levels castigated fascism but declared that the United States should not become involved in a world war. Peace, coupled with a strong anti-military bias, became the cornerstone of Farmers Union policy. The NFU's anti-military stance stemmed not simply from a tradition of isolation in the Midwest but as well from a fear that the federal government might use the draft to destroy organized labor and other political dissidents. For the NFU, conscription was symptomatic of militaristic, authoritarian societies. It seemed antithetical to a free and democratic United States. Collective action, while lauded for cooperative and national planning, was to be used to enlarge personal freedom instead of restraining it.

In opposing conscription legislation in 1940, the NFU litany systematically berated the draft for disrupting the individual farmer's right to make a living. Low wages in the military were bad enough, said the Union, but even worse, labor's right--and agriculture's right--to organize and bargain collectively might be disrupted should the government decide to draft activists. An army, while necessary, must be based solely on voluntary enlistments spurred by better military pay. In this way, the rational and democratic freedom of choice would invite more recruits. Were conscription enforced, continued the Farmers Union, "a long step forward toward the propagation of foreign dictatorship" would result. Finally, argued the NFU as it sought a peaceful world, conscription grated against the soul of democracy. The totalitarian methods of Germany and Italy, which included conscription, would, if practiced, erode liberty in the United States.[38]

Yet there were those in the NFU who envisioned the struggle between democratic and fascistic governments as an issue greater than that of domestic conscription. To preserve peace and progress in the world at large, America had to choose between true and false prophets. After December 7, 1941, that choice was easily made. During World War II, conscription was no longer an issue for the NFU as it whole-heartedly endorsed the war policies of the Roosevelt administration. Still, the NFU was determined that American involvement in the war not work to the detriment of American farmers as had occurred after World War I under the Harding and Coolidge administrations.

War impelled the Union to act in decisive ways. The lack of skilled staff for the NFU during the war forced it to pay greater attention to organizational skills. Farmers had to be taught the necessity of group action in cooperative, legislative, and educational work. Union leaders employed the analogue of war thesis in an attempt to mobilize social change on the home front. "We have the problem," said President James Patton, "of fighting a battle with a coalition of processors, large vested business interests, banks, insurance companies, and those speaking for the big farmers and plantation operators. Their coalition," continued Patton, "is not only engaged in building up a fascist hatred of organized labor and working people, but also engaged in a very serious attempt to build an agricultural policy of corporatism, absentee owners, and landless serfs." With equal vigor, the Union fought attempts to "enslave the small farmer, tenant, or sharecropper." Throughout the war, it fought profiteering and was the only national farm group to fight the discriminatory poll tax.[39]

Racism and the anti-labor positions of Germany and Italy also set the stage for NFU involvement in public education. With a financial grant from the Anti-Defamation League, the Union developed a program stressing toleration of all racial, religious and nationality groups. Moreover, in 1942 the Farmers Union boasted that it was the only national farm organization which actively sought cooperation from organized labor through the establishment of an NFU labor relations department. In return for its endorsement of labor, the NFU received support from unions for the Farm Security Administration, the New Deal's innovative agency for small farm policy planning, until a conservative Congress in 1943 refused to fund the FSA, regarding its planning policies as too "radical." Although the NFU was hurt by this action, it quickly regrouped and launched an aggressive educational campaign supporting racial justice, the United Nations, and agricultural cooperative ventures.[40]

Axis actions were responsible for the Union's turn toward

internationalism. The NFU at all levels withdrew from its earlier isolationism and Patton, an internationalist, coupled domestic NFU policy with American war aims. Peace, he said, will come in the valleys of the Rhine, Po, Dneiper and Rhone; it must also be secured in the Mississippi Valley. To secure a just social order, said Patton, in reference to the isolationists of the thirties, hangovers of reaction must not be allowed to flourish in the NFU. A constant stream of public information to farm and labor groups conveyed the NFU's message of international cooperation and domestic reform.[41]

In contrast to its stance in the early thirties, the NFU proudly and consciously disassociated itself from the policies of Simpson, Everson and Kennedy. By 1943, the Union asserted that it "should interest itself wherever possible in the liberal movement." For this the NFU had virtually complete support from its membership. The Union clearly linked itself to liberal coalition pressure groups working on issues "arising during the war years and in preparation for the post-war situation."[42]

Toward this end, the NFU supported the National Resources Planning Board, a federal agency concerned with long-range planning and conservation of human and natural resources. When the Board was abolished in 1943 along with the Farm Security Administration, the NFU vigorously protested. President Patton and other Union officials spoke for their family farm constituencies when they attacked Republicans and conservative Southern Democrats in Congress who "exalted private selfishness above public good." The NFU, to attain social change through planning, minced no words in chastising the enemies of national planning.

"Special interests in America which demanded and obtained the abolition of the National Resources Planning Board are now making their own postwar peace plans for America. They are assembling a handpicked coterie of special interests, so organized so that people's organizations may be invited but submerged within the group, and so powerful that the people's government may be intimidated into accepting their dictation." Patton feared that "democratic government in the United States will be set aside and the foundation of government will be undermined."[43]

Disillusioned by Roosevelt's employment of a "trickle down" philosophy, as represented by Bernard Baruch, Patton was equally disappointed with some of FDR's appointments to federal office. Patton sent a strongly-worded telegram to Roosevelt:

> On behalf of the National Farmers Union I must protest the "trickle down" philosophy.... The clear meaning is that we are headed back toward Harding "Normalcy" with the government turning over [to] the monopolies the lion's share of $15 billion in war plants and facilities and $50 billion in surplus war materials.... They offer farmers nothing and to labor not jobs but only an employment service. The Baruch recommendations and subsequent appointments will strengthen Congressional reaction in dealing with reconversion and post-war problems. Ground has been steadily lost since the National Resources Planning Board was put to death. We who believed this is a people's war for a people's peace now see the peace won by the money-changers. We urge you to review immediately the domestic fronts in this war and see that the peace is not delivered to corporatists. My organization will support you with all its vigor in an all-out fight to win the peace for common men.[44]

Deeply concerned with post-war planning, Patton wanted Roosevelt to commit the federal government to planning and social reconstruction. The NFU had reluctantly accepted the New Deal. But under Patton's leadership the NFU made it clear that its own vision of a democratic and just society went well beyond the patchwork program and political compromises of the New Deal. Yet more than politics was involved in the NFU vision of the post-war world. Two years after the war's end Patton wrote, "Application of the Christian ethic--and its counterpart in other religions--remains the only course by which men's yearning for decent human relationships in a society freed from want can be answered."[45]

Several NFU state charters symbolically stated the Union's moral and agrarian vision in their post-war membership requirements reminiscent of Populism. Industrious people who believe in a Supreme Being exemplified piety and moral character. Only those people who were "farmers, country mechanics, school teachers, ministers of the gospel, or an employee of a Farmers Union cooperative" were eligible for membership. Specifically excluded from membership were the occupations of "Banking, Merchandising, Practicing Law, or belonging to any trust or combine that is for the purpose of speculating in any kind of agricultural products, or the necessities of life, or anything else injuriously affecting agricultural interest."[46] The NFU's symbolic commitment championed yeoman virtue in an ever-diminishing rural United States.

Against this almost nostalgic affirmation of nineteenth-century Populism was the NFU's commitment to post-war plans. It actively supported the United Nations, and it lobbied on behalf of an expanded welfare state. In 1948, the NFU linked up with the Americans for Democratic Action to use pressure group tactics for more governmental intervention on behalf of Americans. At state and local chapter levels a democratic faith, support for UN relief efforts, and respect for ethnic, religious, and cultural diversity were taught to Farmers Union children by NFU education officers. These programs emphasized the necessity for cooperation in a diverse, changing world. The education programs emphasized respect for nature, conservation, and the family farm.[47]

In addition to education, NFU members held the deeply rooted belief that an artificially created economy of scarcity was dangerous and even immoral. Patton spoke for NFU membership when he asserted that agricultural policy must be based on abundance rather than on scarcity. Abundance had corollaries: full consumption, full employment, and high wages. But Patton cautioned that if the conservative "Farm Bureau-Chamber of Commerce wins, America will have taken the last step toward complete monopoly and the corporative state. Scarcity forces in industry, labor, and agriculture teamed with our military bureaucracy could control the lives of our people, while all the time yelling about regulation." All depressions were "farm fed and farm bred" and had to be halted through progressive policy emphasizing state intervention.[48] Although the NFU was theoretically non-partisan and had a bipartisan constituency, it balked at Republican policies and backed the Truman administration's policy of full production without restrictions. While Patton did not support Truman in 1946 and 1947, he and the Union endorsed Truman in 1948. Republicans in the 1948 presidential election were ruled out as too conservative and business-oriented. On the surface, Henry Wallace's Progressive Party seemed more appealing, but it was not politically expedient for the NFU to back Wallace.

Moreover, concerned with communist association with the Progressive Party, Patton, a cold warrior, steered the NFU clear of what he perceived as trouble. The NFU's disdain for the Progressive Party epitomized its position on communism. Patton and the Union joined the cold war and purged the NFU of pro-communist elements in much the same way that the CIO purged its ranks in the postwar years. The NFU revoked the charters of its Eastern division and of its Iowa group. Patton saw to it that the American Communist Party had no berth in the National Farmers Union and its programs.[49] Its long-range plans included social programs for abolition of poverty, strict federal control of large corporations, justice for minorities and labor, and individual ownership of farms. In sum, the NFU by 1948 was a liberal, cold war organization.

Liberals in the NFU, satisfied with Truman, reluctantly accepted Republican victory in the 1952 presidential election. While still affirming non-partisanship, the Union continued to push for parity programs which were anathema to Republicans. The Union supported increased federal supports of school lunch programs, crop insurance, conservation, and the strengthening of the Farmers Home Administration. During the Eisenhower years, the Union endorsed an unbalanced budget in hopes of raising farm incomes and creating full employment. To gain these ends Union leaders urged a "legislated economy." The NFU regarded itself as the only agricultural organization capable of pressuring for a "legislated economy" of social and economic planning. It saw the AFBF as wedded to big business, while the Grange, once militant in the 1870s, had evolved into a sedate, rural, social organization.[50]

The NFU responded to the political challenge of the 1950s by vigorously organizing membership campaigns in Indiana, Illinois, Ohio, Pennsylvania, and Virginia. It hoped to increase membership at a time when the "farm bloc" still had political clout. With a substantial increase in membership in the fifties, the NFU sought to counter the more conservative, Republican-oriented AFBF. The NFU strengthened its economic base through well-managed investments in the processing and distribution of fertilizer and in casualty and life insurance. By the 1950s, membership increases and prudent fiscal management allowed the NFU to staff its headquarters in Denver with efficient personnel for field services, insurance, education, and lobbying. Under Patton, the NFU also placed tighter checks on state and local units. Streamlining the Union for organizational efficiency made it more effective in an increasingly complex and bureaucratic managerial society.[51]

Ironically, despite its open opposition to communism, the Farmers Union became a target of anti-communists in the early fifties. The executive secretary of the Farm Bureau in Utah accused Democratic Congressman W. K. Granger of favoring the "Communist-dominated" Farmers Union. Granger aroused the ire of the Farm Bureau by criticizing its close ties with Agricultural Extension Services throughout the United States as too strong. He proposed that the relationship between the Farm Bureau and the Extension Service be severed. The Farm Bureau strongly opposed Granger's legislation, while the NFU endorsed it.

Republican Senator Styles Bridges of New Hampshire joined the fray by endorsing the Farm Bureau's accusation. In response, the NFU filed a quarter of a million dollar lawsuit against the Farm Bureau (Bridges was protected from prosecution by senatorial immunity). A federal judge called the allegations against the NFU "ridiculous" and awarded the Union twenty-five thousand dollars in damages.[52] The Farmers Union also suffered from innuendo by the American Legion during the cold war years. Such charges of "communism" were totally false. In fact, the Union endorsed--although not without debate--the Korean War. Reluctant though Union leaders were to endorse American involvement in Korea, they opposed the draft. The Farmers Union declared that conscription would create a permanent standing army and strip farms of manpower. From the point of view of the NFU, government should use its powers to control the economy but not to violate individual rights.[53] As a consequence, NFU energies in the cold war years were in part spent defending its reputation from smear campaigns.

But the Union also went on the offensive. In the sixties, it opposed both conscription and American involvement in Vietnam. It attacked right-wing groups as "narrow minded bigots searching for a superior moral justification for their shortsighted egomania and selfishness." In public and private pronouncements, the NFU criticized the John Birch Society as an enemy of freedom. Affirming its support of internationalism and the UN, the NFU countered extreme rightist isolationism through an educational campaign which warned members of right-wing groups. The NFU asserted that such groups eroded progress by attacking labor unions, minorities, and immigrants. It also condemned rightist paramilitary groups which might take over local school boards, intimidate clergy, nullify recent social legislation, and question the loyalty of those who disagreed with them. The real battles for social change and against the radical Right, said Reuben Johnson of the NFU, must take place at the local level. Only then could bigots and right-wing fundamentalists be discredited.[54]

At the same time, but with a lesser sense of urgency, the NFU condemned totalitarian Marxism. Patton endorsed Lyndon Johnson and Hubert Humphrey because they were liberals and had farmers' welfare at heart. In his public speeches, Patton carefully distinguished between the democratic socialist tradition of Sweden, Holland, and Britain on the one hand, and Marxism-Leninism on the other. Patton linked American liberalism to parliamentary democratic socialism, but placed Marxism-Leninism well outside the American consensus. Yet in the process of fighting communism, the NFU pointed out that one does not commit suicide while hampering extremism of the Left. The analogy to Adlai Stevenson's admonition was clear: to get rid of rats you don't burn down the barn.[55] For the NFU in the sixties, "liberalism" meant constructive change. "More liberal laws, housing, agriculture, education, health and all things basic to all people" was the Union's hopeful prognosis for the future.[56] John Kennedy's presidency and, more importantly for the Union, Lyndon Johnson's presidency, gave more hope for farmers and for social programs involving federal intervention.[57]

Although the NFU saw embroilment in Vietnam as a tragic mistake, Johnson's sympathy for agriculture and his War on Poverty gave the NFU hope that what began in the New Deal might continue with the Great Society. Despite the diminishing number of family farmers and the belief of Americans that large-scale agriculture was more efficient than family farms, the NFU rode an ebullient wave of optimism because of Johnson's victory. Thus, a New Deal coalition of "labor, blacks, the elderly, and family farmers would seek full employment, parity and disarmament." None of these materialized, but the NFU maintained its vision for a tempered idealism. As early as 1961, the NFU formed a special committee to eliminate pockets of rural poverty in the United States. It lobbied to rehabilitate and gainfully employ older rural Americans. From its long-standing belief in state intervention, the NFU in 1965 lobbied on the wave of Johnson's victory to push for the Older Americans Community Service Employment Act. Writing to Project Green Thumb, the rural action program for older Americans administered through the NFU, the Office of Economic Opportunity argued that public support, once garnered by the project, would spread "to every area in the United States." The rationale behind extending opportunities for older Americans held that of the eight million elderly in rural America, over 50 percent were below the poverty line and many were retired farmers or farm widows. They were truly "forgotten poor Americans, out of sight, out of mind." Since neither social service agencies nor anti-poverty programs paid attention to this segment of the invisible poor, the federal government, through the NFU, must exploit the talents of the rural poor. As farmers they had "green thumbs," produced an overabundance of food in this country, and ironically were victims of overproduction. Thus the NFU proposed to "take the green thumbs of the poor, older and retired farmers and put them to work to beautify our highways." Through this, reasoned the Union, a ripple effect would be created. By employing older citizens in small town conservation and beautification, both rural areas and people would profit as elderly Americans gained dignity.[58]

Arguing for a role in Green Thumb, the NFU fell back on its heritage of helping rural Americans to combat poverty by "organizing cooperatives which are now doing over a billion dollars worth of business a year." In sponsoring highway beautification, the NFU offered "bread and roses, too" for rural America. Additionally, it would involve workers in job retraining--painting, police dispatch work, street maintenance, historical site preservation and other useful tasks. With high praise from Lady Bird Johnson and with tax-exempt status from the Internal Revenue Service, the program gained headway. As Lady Bird Johnson noted, older farmers suffered hardships through no fault of their own and deserved assistance. Decent intentions, fair play, and a sense of dignity and justice for the elderly also gained favorable publicity for the NFU. But Green Thumb hardly made a dent in the war against rural poverty. The program never received sufficient funding to adequately reach the rural elderly poor.[59]

Green Thumb represented the social arm of NFU political action at a time when the federal government was sympathetic to the organization's aims. Yet even with a sympathetic political administration, Jim Patton, a veteran of farmer protest, noted discernible shifts in social forces. There were fewer family farmers, as each year people left the farms for other occupations. Patton noted that many of those who stayed held down two jobs: "As long as the farmer can drive fifty miles to a job and drive back home to a moonlight farm in order to hang on we are not going to get concerted action among the farmers." Patton recognized that many family farmers simply could not make a decent living from farming alone. But by subsidizing farming by working away from the farm, social consciousness--and militancy-- were dissipated. By 1976 Patton, now president emeritus, admitted that on the national scene the Union and a few intellectuals were never strong enough to gain from the federal government a policy committed to family farms, governmentally supported income, and land use. The fault was neither in the Union nor in farmers. With a vision for economic and political programs, the Union nonetheless lacked sufficient political strength to mobilize massive social change. Writing to Ralph Nader of the Center for the Study of Responsive Law, Tony Dechant, who followed Patton as president of the Union, touched the heart of the issue: "Farmers represent the most widely dispersed power segment in the economy. We in the Farmers Union are trying desperately and sometimes with discouraging results to maintain this pluralistic system. We are the victims of concentrated corporate power as consumers and as primary producers." Dechant's criticism hit the central issue upon which Patton elaborated six years later. President Gerald Ford is "still living in the dark ages of the last century and does not really know what to do with the present situation except to play with the monopolies and multinational corporations which are about to take over the country." What evolved was not the laissez-faire state but a Hamiltonian leviathan which subsidized big business. For Patton, the injustice was obvious. While corporations such as Lockheed received federal aid, "most farmers in the United States are barely getting by." In a populistic vein, Patton noted that farmers are squeezed by both Russia and representatives of corporate agribusiness in the United States who "are manipulating the world and the domestic market."[60]

The NFU never attained its goal of control of agricultural prices by farmers. That view was not isolated to Patton whose roots went back to the Populist movement. A younger generation of Union spokesmen represented by Charlie Nash, executive director of the Ohio Farmers Union, echoed the discontent of small farmers: "Giant multi-national grain corporations and speculators prevent the United States from taking the lead in establishing new international grain agreements with a built-in price regulated for farmers."[61] For the heirs of Populism and Jefferson it appeared to be a never-ending fight.

To transform the Jeffersonian and Populist spirit into a modern setting was the NFU's task. To this end, the NFU sought governmental benevolence through the welfare state, responsive to the signs of change. The National Farmers Union of the late twentieth century became more organizational and managerial--that is, a "business union" in the agricultural sector--but it never lost sight of its original goals. Populistic rhetoric from the late nineteenth century still survived in the NFU side by side with its activities as a legislative pressure and interest group. But the Union remained loyal to its broader goals--an equitable society for the farmer and social justice for all. The NFU served its members' economic aspirations and idealistic vision. It began as an economic interest group and as a moral force. To this day, it emphasizes both themes. After eighty years, the Farmers Union survives because its adherence to non-doctrinaire liberalism implies an ability to change while maintaining a belief in such moral absolutes as individual liberty, democracy, and human justice attained through the welfare state. Like the political movements with which it allied itself in the past, the National Farmers Union today appears quixotic and in eclipse. In the United States, at least, the marketplace and large, well-capitalized enterprises seem more dominant than ever. Still, the NFU's vision of a world of free, autonomous and unexploited producers remains as attractive now as it did for Jefferson and Patton.

Notes

*Grateful acknowledgement is made to Tony Dechant, Victor Ray, Henri Holland, and Vera Shennefels who assisted me in obtaining NFU sources in Denver. Charlie Nash and the staff of the Ohio Farmers Union in Ottawa, Ohio extended numerous courtesies and also aided in the search for source material. Thanks are due to Jack Brennan and the staff of the Western Historical Collection of the University of Colorado. The late James Patton rendered numerous suggestions and ideas. I have benefitted from the criticism of Ronald Lora of the University of Toledo and Patrick Reagan of Tennessee Technological University who read earlier drafts of this paper. William Pratt of the University of Nebraska--Omaha offered additional criticisms. Errors in this essay are mine and mine alone. I gratefully acknowledge research support from the Faculuty Affairs Committee, Kenyon College.

1. T.M. Davis, an NFU organizer, had this poem printed on the back of his business cards. National Farmers Union Historical Archives, "Farmers Union, 1902-1914" File, Box 38, Western Historical Collection, University of Colorado, Boulder, Colorado; hereafter cited as WHC; National Union Farmer, January 24, 1939.

2. Interview with Joseph Ficter, July, 1979. For additional information on Fichter's attitudes, see Roy Wortman, ed., "Remembrances of a Farmers Union Pioneer," Ohio Union Farmer, April, May, June, 1981.

3. Lawrence Goodwyn, Democratic Promise: The Populist

Moment in America (New York: Oxford University Press, 1976) is the most perceptive and sympathetic treatment of the topic.

4. John L. Shover, First Majority--Last Minority: The Transforming of Rural Life in America (DeKalb: Northern Illinois University Press, 1976), pp. 3-50.

5. National Union Farmer, March, 1952, this fiftieth anniversary issue is a valuable source for information on the NFU's origins; James Patton, "Farmers Union First Half Century," in NFU, Minutes, 1952, WHC; see also Theodore Saloutos and John D. Hicks, Agricultural Discontent in the Middle West, 1900-1939 (Madison: University of Wisconsin Press, 1951) and Theodore Saloutos, Farmer Movements in the South, 1865-1933 (Berkeley: University of California Press, 1960).

6. A good account of the Rochdale principles from the NFU perspective is Gladys Talbot Edwards, The Farmers Union Triangle (Jamestown, N. D.: Farmers Union Educational Services, 1941), pp. 19, 59, 110. A brief but thorough examination of the Rochdale Pioneers is Encyclopaedia of the Social Sciences, vol. 4, s.v. "Cooperation in Great Britain and Ireland," by Fred Hall. See also Mancur Olson, The Logic of Collective Action: Public Goods and the Theory of Groups (Cambridge, Ma.: Harvard University Press, 1965), pp. 157-158.

7. National Ritual of the Farmers Educational and Cooperative Union of North America: The Official Ritual (Charlotte, N.C.: The Union, 1910), pp. 14-16.

8. Patton, "Farmers Union First Half Century."

9. Robert L. Tontz, "Membership of General Farmers' Organi-

zations in the United States, 1874-1960," Agricultural History 38 (July 1964): 155.

10. For the current figure, I thank Victor Ray, Vice-President for Field Services, NFU. The NFU's rival organization, the American Farm Bureau Federation, has approximately 3.2 million members according to its Public Relations Office.

11. V. O. Key, Politics, Parties, and Interest Groups (New York: Thomas Y. Crowell, 1964), pp. 156-157.

12. For a discussion of the history of the AFBF, see Grant McConnell, The Decline of Agrarian Democracy (1953; New York: Atheneum, 1969), pp. 44-65 and Richard S. Kirkendall, Social Scientists and Farm Politics in the Age of Roosevelt (Columbia: University of Missouri Press, 1966), pp. 195-261.

13. Quoted in Robert Lee Hunt, A History of the Farmer Movements in the Southwest, 1873-1925 (College Station: Texas A & M Press, 1935), p. 139.

14. Patton, "Farmers Union First Half Century" and Patton, address to American Farm Project participants, Southwest State University, Marshall, Minnesota, June, 1978, author's notes. Patton (b. 1902) was NFU president from 1940 to 1966. For a perceptive biography, see Charles Livermore, "James G. Patton, Nineteenth Century Populist, Twentieth Century Organizer, Twenty First Century Visionary," (Ph.D. dissertation, University of Denver, 1976).

15. Charles Simon Barrett, The Mission, History, and Times of the Farmers Union (Nashville: Marshall and Bruce, 1909), p.44.

16. C. E. Huff to Victor Heyman, 27 February 1957, Historical File, National Farmers Union Headquarters, Denver,

Colorado, hereafter cited as NFU, HQ. Huff, an NFU official, was a strong influence on Patton.

17. Patton, "Farmers Union First Half Century."

18. Patton, personal letter, 30 October 1979. Gilbert Fite, "John A. Simpson: The Southwest's Militant Farm Leader," Mississippi Valley Historical Review 35 (March 1949): 536-584 is critical yet sympathetic; Wesley McCune, The Farm Bloc (New York: Doubleday, Dorran, 1943), p. 193; Chester A. Graham, The Eighty-Year Experience of a Grass Roots Citizen (Grand Rapids: Ammon Hennesy House, n.d.), pp. 204-208.

19. Patton, personal letter, 30 October 1979.

20. NFU, Minutes, 1933, WHC.

21. Ibid.

22. Tony Dechant to Charles Brannan and P. H. Lamphere, 28 May 1954, Box 38, WHC; interview with Dechant, August, 1979. Dechant (b. 1915), a Kansan, was elected national president after Patton's retirement in 1966. Dechant retired in 1980 and was succeeded by George Stone (b. 1919) of Oklahoma.

23. NFU, Minutes, 1934, WHC.

24. Ibid.

25. Ibid.

26. Ibid.

27. Richard Hofstadter's The Paranoid Style in American Politics and Other Essays (New York: Alfred A. Knopf, 1965), pp. 8-9, 238-315 offers the example of Populism as a retrogressive, anachronistic force in American society.

28. Phoebe F. Hayes to Lowell K. Dyson, 21 February 1958;

Edwards, Farmers Union Triangle, pp. 42-43.

29. E. E. Kennedy to S. B. David, 24 October 1935, Kennedy Folder, Box 38, WHC.

30. Resolution of Washington-Idaho Farmers Union to E. E. Kennedy, July 8, 1936, Farmers Union File, 1935-1939, Box 38, WHC; Edwards, Farmers Union Triangle, pp. 42-49. For a detailed description of the Coughlin-Lemke party, see David R. Bennett, Demagogues in the Depression: American Radicals and the Union Party, 1932-1936 (New Brunswick: Rutgers University Press, 1969).

31. NFU, Board of Directors, Minutes, 1938, WHC.

32. F. R. Lennox, "Friends of the Farm and Home Hour, NBC Radio," in National Union Farmer, June 25, 1938.

33. Edwards, Farmers Union Triangle, p. 54.

34. Phoebe Hayes to Tony Dechant, 22 March 1951, in Farmers Union History, General File, Box 38, WHC.

35. NFU, Minutes, 1938, WHC.

36. NFU, Board of Directors, Minutes, 1940, NFU, HQ.

37. F. R. Lennox, Ohio Division, Bulletin, 5 April 1939, Ohio File, NFU, HQ.

38. National Union Farmer, September 10, 1940.

39. Report of James Patton to the National Board, 30-31 January 1943, NFU, HQ.

40. Ibid.

41. Ibid.

42. Ibid.

43. Resolution on Postwar Planning, NFU, Minutes, 1944, NFU, HQ. The NRPB asserted the idea of full employment through economic growth stimulated by private and public sectors.

Southern Democrats and conservative Republicans feared the NRPB as "fascistic" or "communistic" because of its advocacy of long-range planning. Those opposing the NRPB argued that if it were maintained, it would have too much power. In 1943, Congress abolished the Board.

44. Patton to Franklin D. Roosevelt, 1 March 1944, Farmers Educational and Cooperative Union File, OF 899, Franklin D. Roosevelt Library, Hyde Park, New York.

45. NFU, Minutes, 1947, NFU, HQ.

46. Ohio Farmers Union, Articles of Incorporation, Charter and Bylaws, Article V, in Proceedings of the Fifteenth Annual State Convention, 1948, Ohio File, NFU, HQ.

47. Youth educational materials of Mrs. John Stein, Ohio Farmers Union Headquarters, Ottowa, Ohio.

48. NFU, Minutes, 1949, NFU, HQ.

49. Joseph Starobin, American Communism in Crisis, 1943-1957 (Berkeley: University of California Press, 1975), p. 181.

50. NFU, Biennial Report, 1954 and NFU Minutes, 1954, NFU, HQ.

51. NFU, Minutes, 1954, NFU, HQ; interview with Tony Dechant, August, 1979.

52. NFU, Executive Committee, Minutes, 11 October 1950, NFU, HQ; National Union Farmer, May, 1951.

53. National Union Farmer, March, 1951 and February, 1952.

54. NFU, Biennial Report, 1964, NFU, HQ; National Union Farmer, March, June, September, November, 1965.

55. NFU, Board of Directors, Minutes, 13 September 1963,

NFU, HQ.

56. NFU, Biennial Report, 1964, NFU, HQ.

57. Ibid.; Patton to Glen J. Talbot, 26 October 1965, NFU, HQ.

58. NFU, Biennial Report, 1964, NFU, HQ; Theodore M. Berry to Blue Carstenson, 18 August 1965, Box 39, WHC; Blue Carstenson to Tony Dechant, 17 November 1965, Box 39, WHC.

59. Lady Bird Johnson to Blue Carstenson, 18 August 1965, Box 39, WHC; Charles H. Brannon, Memorandum on IRS status, 27 December 1965, Box 39, WHC.

60. NFU, Board of Directors, Minutes, 1976; Patton to Dechant, 7 June 1976; Dechant to Ralph Nader, January 13, 1970; Patton to Alex O'Shea, n.d. [1976?], all in NFU, HQ.

61. Ohio Union Farmer, December, 1977.

James Thurber's Columbus

                by J. Mark Stewart

     In her slim, elegant autobiographical work, <u>One Writer's Beginnings</u>, Eudora Welty examines her sense of place as well as her debt to family and roots. Welty describes the sights, sounds, and smells of her youth in a southern city:

> In our house on North Congress Street in Jackson, Mississippi, where I was born, the oldest of three children, in 1909, we grew up to the striking of clocks. There was a misson-style oak grandfather clock standing in the hall, which sent its gong-like stroke through the livingroom, diningroom, kitchen, and pantry, and up the sounding board of the stairwell. Through the night it could find its way into our ears; sometimes, even on the sleeping porch, midnight could wake us up. My parents's bedroom had a smaller striking clock that answered it. Though the kitchen clock did nothing but show the time, the diningroom clock was a cuckoo clock with weights on long chains, on one of which my baby brother, after climbing on a chair to the top of the china closet, once succeeded in suspending the cat for a moment.[1]

In just half a paragraph, Welty not only puts the reader at ease, she also produces a snapshot that begins to reveal nuances of life in Jackson in the early years of this century. The place of her childhood was a significant influence on the development of Welty, the writer.

     James Thurber was a Columbus, Ohio high school student when Eudora Welty drew her first breath. But like Welty, place was an inextricable part of Thurber's adult view of life. Even after he was long gone from Columbus, Thurber's writing drew on the people and the city of his youth. Thurber put Columbus on the literary map. Perhaps more than any other recent American author, it is difficult to think of the writer without the setting. In a sense, Thurber and Columbus made each other. "I have always waved banners and blown horns for Good Old Columbus Town," said Thurber just two years before his death. His readers, he noted "are all aware of where I was born and brought up, and they know that half of my books could not have been written if it had not been for the city of my birth."[2]

In 1910 James Thurber was a gangling, awkward sophomore at Columbus East High School, reputedly the best in the city. At the time, Columbus was a city of over 181,000 people, twenty-ninth largest in the nation, and third largest in Ohio behind Cleveland and Cincinnati. In the decade between 1900 and 1910, the years of Thurber's youth, Columbus grew over 44 percent. The population was 84 percent native-born white, 9 percent foreign-born white, and 7 percent black. The largest immigrant community was German. It was centered in south Columbus' German Village, an area that now consists of restored Victorian-era homes.[3] To the north was the Ohio State University, a land grant institution with the largest enrollment in the state.

In 1909 the F. & R. Lazarus Company, the city's largest retail store, opened its newly expanded store at Town and High Streets. An advertisement that accompanied the opening listed twenty new departments featuring men's and women's ready-to-wear apparel.[4] Twenty-five dollar princess silhouette suits with long puffed-sleeve coats, shirtwaist dresses, and broad-brimmed, heavily plumed hats were among the most popular items. Lazarus even installed a tea room for tired and thirsty shoppers.[5]

Ten years into the new century, more and more Columbus residents went on their shopping excursions in automobiles. The Columbus Buggy Company even produced an electric car in the city. Whatever the mode of transportation, the citizens of Columbus turned out in force to hear concert bands and take in the amusements at Olentangy Park, or they took in the latest vaudeville acts at B. F. Keith's theatre at the corner of Gay and Pearl. By 1911 Columbus had nine theatres including Memorial Hall, the Great Southern, the Hartman, and Keith's Exhibit. Admission was a dime, and public support was strong.

During the early years of the twentieth century, Columbus grew in all directions along the axes of the cross formed by Broad and High Streets. Older upper and middle class areas such as the University district, Goodale Park, and Thurber's eastside neighborhood between Parsons Avenue and Franklin Park were eclipsed by new, more fashionable suburbs. Blacks clustered on the near northside around Long and High Streets, but were beginning to shift toward the east. The Germans were in the south, and Naghten Street, in a section of the near northside close to the Ohio Penitentiary, was referred to as "Irish Broadway."[6]

Columbus during Thurber's youth was conservative and sedate, the state's capital and center of a rich agricultural region. The college of agriculture at Ohio State was, in fact, for many years the most powerful department at the university. In many respects, Helen Hooven Santmyer's reminiscence of Xenia in Ohio Town could apply as easily to the east side environs of the

Thurbers.[7] Columbus was staunchly Republican as was Charles Thurber, James' father, whose life's work consisted of several minor and intermittent Republican appointments. In 1910 all four representatives from Franklin County to the Ohio General Assembly were Republican; so, too, were all Franklin County elected officials.[8]

"I was brought up in Ohio," wrote Thurber, "a region steeped in the tradition of Coxey's Army, the Anti-Saloon League, and William Howard Taft." He was a boy, he continued, like many others in Columbus "who, as a youngster, bought his twelve-dollar suits at the F. & R. Lazarus Co., had his hair washed with Ivory soap, owned a bull terrier with only one tail, and played (nicely and a bit diffidently) with little girls named Irma and Betty and Ruby."[9]

Thurber's Columbus was a comfortable, midwestern collection of friends, relatives, schoolmates, and eccentrics who later crowded his memory. "There was," he remembered,

> a lot of picnicking and canoeing and cycling, and going for hikes in the woods on Sundays in spring, the men in boaters and bright blazers, the women in shirtwaists and skirts. The men got up baseball games, and the women looked for white violets and maidenhair ferns to take home and tran splant. People liked to sit on the wide verandas on the hotter Sundays, the men with their feet up on the balustrade, reading in the sports pages about Corbett and Jeffries, Maud S and Star Pointer, Cy Young and John McGraw. The women sat more decorously, reading the Lady of Lyons or Lucille, and the children, sprawled on the floor, eagerly followed the comic adventures of the Katzenjammer Kids, Lulu and Leander, Happy Hooligan, Foxy Grandpa, Buster Brown, and Alphonse and Gaston. A couple of young men named Orville and Wilbur were thinking about the laws governing the sustained flight of heavier-than-air contraptions, but people were more interested in the cakewalk than the gas engine. Columbus and the world can never recapture the serene spirit of those years. This is known as Progress.[10]

Thurber's boyhood years coincided with the Progressive movement. But if Thurber and his Columbus cronies were suffering through what Robert H. Wiebe labeled a "crisis of community," they were unaware or unconcerned.[11] Neither Tom Johnson, Sam "Golden Rule" Jones, nor Washington Gladden, who for many years served a church in Columbus, became models for archetypical Thurber characters. Rather, it was the ordinary and colorful characters of his youth who, under various guises, later peopled his stories and sketches.

That is not to say Thurber's youth was dull or uneventful. In Columbus, Thurber found characters enough to fill hundreds of pages with unforgettable stories and vignettes. Nor were his boyhood days free from trouble and tragedy. When James was six years old, his father accepted a political position which required a move to Washington, D.C. While at a summer home in Falls Church, Virginia, James and his brothers, William and Robert, were playing with bows and arrows. In one of those all too frequent childhood accidents, William accidentally shot James in the eye. The village doctor in Falls Church underdiagnosed and undertreated the injury, the result of which was serious damage to Thurber's eyesight. According to William Thurber, if James had been treated promptly by the Washington specialist to whom he was taken three weeks later, his eyesight might well have been saved.[12] Fortunately, Thurber's vision stabilized and enabled him to function partially sighted for the next forty years, until, in 1940, the good eye finally failed. Thurber's last twenty years were spent as a blind writer.

Due to his father's unsteady and less than lucrative employment, Thurber's family was seldom financially secure. The Thurbers moved frequently and more than once had to rely on the largesse of the maternal grandparents. William M. Fisher, Thurber's grandfather, operated a successful wholesale produce business that enabled him to build a large home in a fashionable area just past where Town Street jogged around a big tree and became Bryden Road. Charles and Mary Thurber found it necessary on occasion to call upon the grudging hospitality of eccentric Grandpa Fisher, a vain man who daily clamped a fresh red rose cigarlike between his gold capped teeth and loudly announced himself in public places by saying, "I am William M. Fisher of Columbus, Ohio."[13]

In fact, Jamie, as he was called by his family, came into this life on December 8, 1894 in a house provided by the Fisher money. Grandpa Fisher was so pleased with the birth of William, the eldest, that he bought the Thurbers a house which stood at 251 Parsons Avenue on the east side of the city.[14] That address is now the northbound lane on Interstate 71 just north of its intersection with Interstate 70. Just across the street was the Ohio School for the Blind, a massive, rambling structure, made famous in "The Tree in the Diamond."[15] Currently, it houses the headquarters of the Ohio State Highway Patrol.

In "My Fifty Years with James Thurber," the author, usually a painstaking researcher and stickler for detail, used the wrong address in announcing his birth:

> James Thurber was born on a night of wild portent and high wind in the year 1894, at 147 Parsons Avenue, Columbus, Ohio. The house... bears no tablet or plaque

of any description and is never pointed out to visitors. Once Thurber's mother, walking past the place with an old lady from Fostoria, Ohio, said to her, "My son James was born in that house," to which the old lady, who was extremely deaf, replied, "Why, on the Tuesday morning train, unless my sister is worse." Mrs. Thurber let it go at that.[16]

Thurber lived in that house until he was about five years of age, but it did not play an important role in his stories, as did four other boyhood residences.

Thurber's favorite boyhood home was the one at 921 South Champion Avenue, where he lived for two years prior to moving to Washington, D.C. Today, it is a vacant lot in a deteriorated urban neighborhood. When Thurber lived there, it was the last house on the street.

> Just south of us the avenue dwindled to a wood road that led into a thick grove of oak and walnut trees, long since destroyed by the southward march of asphalt. Our nearest neighbor on the north was fifty yards away, and across from us was a country meadow that ticked with crickets in the summertime and turned yellow with goldenrod in the fall. Living on the edge of town, we rarely heard footsteps at night, or carriage wheels, but the darkness, in every season was deepened by the lonely sound of locomotive whistles. I no longer wonder, as I did when I was six, that Aunt Mary York, arriving at dusk for her first visit to us, looked about her disconsolately, and said to my mother, "Why in the world do you live in this godforsaken place, Mary?"[17]

The Champion Avenue house was also the setting of the story that best illuminates Mame Thurber's eccentric personality. It was there, for instance, that James and his mother went about the neighborhood and gathered up all the dogs that they could find. These they brought to the house, all sixteen of them, and penned them in the basement. These elaborate preparations were in anticipation of a visit from Aunt Mary, a confirmed dog hater, who had cut short her previous visit out of distaste for the

Thurber dogs, Judge and Sampson. Upon Aunt Mary's arrival, Mame somehow cajoled her into lending a helping hand by feeding the two family dogs. When Aunt Mary opened the basement door to call the beasts, all sixteen dogs bounded up the stairs howling and yelping and backing Aunt Mary into a corner where she exclaimed, "Great God Almighty! It's a dog factory!"[18]

Thurber's mother was an inveterate practical joker with a taste for the theatrical. Thurber's love of the absurd predicament, as well as much of his comic sense, came from her. While living at the Champion Avenue home, for example, Mame "bought" a neighbor's house. Her victims in this adventure were the Simonses, members of the Frioleras, a club of young married couples to which the Thurbers also belonged. The Simonses had been trying for some time to sell their "cold, blocky" house near the Thurbers on Champion Avenue and despaired of their chances of unloading the place. One evening Mame whitened her hair and eyebrows with flour, shadowed her cheeks with charcoal, and covered her front teeth with the serrated edge of a soda cracker. Thus disguised, she rang the Simons' doorbell and posed as an interested buyer.

In "Lavender With a Difference," Thurber captures in a sentence much of the substance of his memories of Columbus near the turn of the century. "Harry Simons, opening his front door on that dark evening in the age of innocence, when trust flowered as readily as suspicion does today, was completely taken in by the sudden apparition of an eccentric elderly woman who babbled of her recently inherited fortune and said she had passed his house the day before and had fallen in love with it."[19] Fond remembrances of innocence and hilarity characterize much that Thurber wrote about his boyhood homes.

Another place that looms large in Thurber's sketches was the Fisher home at 695 Bryden Road. Although the four large porches are gone, the building still stands, housing professional offices. While Thurber was not close to his maternal grandfather, the man and his house were imposing figures in his youth.[20] Behind this house stood the grounds of the Ohio State School for the Blind, site of legendary athletic feats of such greats as Billy Alloway, Hank Gowdy, and Chic Harley. Players had to display acute concentration and sure handedness to play for the teams managed and coached by Frank James. This was particularly true in light of the fact that a huge tree sat squarely between first and second bases.[21] Baseball's first "green monster" was located at the Ohio State School for the Blind on Parsons Avenue in Columbus, Ohio, not in Boston's Fenway Park.

The north side of a small, battered frame double at 185 South Fifth Street was also an important place in Thurber's youth. It was the home of Margery Albright, a woman who played an important role in the lives of all the Thurbers, but especially Jamie's. Aunt Margery, as she was referred to by the three brothers, was a folk medicine expert who used the herbs from her garden to concoct solutions for nearly any complaint. In 1905, for example, the Thurbers called for Aunt Margery to come and nurse Charles Thurber back to health. He was suffering from some kind of persistent fever, and the family was concerned for his life. The entire family moved in with the Fishers in the large Bryden Road home and employed a trained nurse, but the patient did not respond. Aunt Margery arrived, ignored the newfangled techniques of Miss Wilson, the nurse, and set about her business. Within a few days, Charles Thurber was on the mend. As soon as he could dress and walk, Aunt Margery returned to her home and garden.[22]

Aunt Margery brought James Thurber into the world. When the doctor was late arriving at the Parsons Avenue home, she took over and delivered the baby. Upon seeing the infant, however, Aunt Margery said to the exhausted mother, "I'm worried. He's got too much hair. I'm afraid he won't be too bright."[23]

Throughout his youth, James spent many happy days with Aunt Margery. His mother, although devoted to her sons, needed occasional respites from the demands of raising three energetic boys. As William put it, two of them were "farmed out." William went to live with the grandparents, James to Aunt Margery's, and Robert, the youngest, stayed at home. Thurber's devotion to the elderly nurse and midwife are obvious in "Daguerreotype of a Lady," and one of his very earliest youthful pieces was a poem entitled "My Aunt Mrs. John T. Savage's Garden at 185 South Fifth Street, Columbus, Ohio." Why he used the name Savage is not entirely clear, and the poem is apparently lost. But Robert Thurber attested to its existence in a Thurber notebook held for many years by the family.[24]

The fourth home that figures prominently in Thurber's writing was the one in which he lived while attending Ohio State

University. Still on the east side of town, just north of Broad Street, 77 Jefferson Avenue is now restored much as it was when Thurber lived there. The Thurber House currently contains memorabilia and serves as a book center for Midwestern writers and presses. It is also a local writers' center that features a prominent writer-in-residence who lives in an apartment constructed in the very same attic where the "bed fell" on grandfather.

The Jefferson Avenue home appears in some of the most memorable Thurber stories--"The Night the Ghost Got In," "More Alarms at Night," and "The Night the Bed Fell,"--as 77 Lexington Avenue. Thurber changed the name of the street to protect the innocent. In a letter to Columbus journalist and artist Bill Arter in 1957, Thurber explained the switch. "I deliberately changed Jefferson to Lexington," he wrote, "for the simple reason that there was a ghost in the Jefferson Avenue house....I didn't want to alarm whoever might be living there when I wrote the story. I think it was a music school for girls then."[25]

The home was in a modest middle class neighborhood, about a forty-five minute streetcar ride from the Ohio State University campus. Like all the Thurber homes, it was the scene of more than its share of improbable events, some of which eventually wound up as jewels of American humor. In the same letter to Arter, Thurber incorrectly predicted, "I doubt if Columbus would ever be interested in placing a marker of any kind on the Parsons Avenue house, or acquiring it."[26] He was right about the location, but not about the devotion and commitment of his admirers.

As it is with all children, schools and schoolmates were

also an important influence during Thurber's Columbus boyhood. He attended Ohio Avenue School for the first grade before moving to Washington, D.C. The injury to his eye resulted in the loss of a year in his education, so that beginning in the second grade, Thurber was a year older than some of his classmates. That was not, however, a problem at Sullivant School where the Thurber boys enrolled when they returned to Columbus. Many of their classmates were well below grade level. James attended Sullivant from the second through the sixth grades.

The site on which Sullivant School used to stand is now the location of the administration offices of the Columbus Public School district. In 1900-1908, it was in a rough, working-class neighborhood. "In seeking an adjective to describe the Sullivant School of my years," Thurber wrote, "I can only think of 'tough.' Sullivant School was tough. The boys of Sullivant came mostly from the region around Central Market, a poorish district with many colored families and many white families of the laboring class."[27] It was not an easy transition for a child who had just lost an eye and had to wear glasses.

Fortunately for Thurber, he soon acquired a guardian of sorts. Floyd, a twenty-year-old fourth grader and the toughest student at Sullivant, was so impressed one day by the fact that Thurber pronounced the word "Duquesne" correctly that he appointed himself the young scholar's protector. "I don't suppose," remarked Thurber, "that I would ever have got through Sullivant alive if it hadn't been for Floyd."[28]

Floyd was a member of what was known at Sullivant as the

"Terrible Fourth." According to the course of study at that time, students were to be taught long division and fractions for the first time in the fourth grade. Moreover, social promotion was not a widespread educational policy at the time. Consequently, several Sullivant students hit the fourth grade and remained there for as long as seven or eight years. Some of the fourth graders were seventeen or eighteen years old. While the existence of the Terrible Fourth may not have done much for Sullivant's standing in Columbus' academic community, it provided the school with a legendary baseball team:

> The Sullivant School baseball team of 1905 defeated several high school teams in the city and claimed the high school championship of the state, to which title it had, of course, no technical right. I believe the boys could have proved their moral right to the championship, however, if they had been allowed to go out of town and play all the teams they challenged, such as the powerful Dayton and Toledo nines, but their road season was called off after a terrific fight that occurred during a game in Mt. Sterling, or Piqua, or Zenia-I can't remember which.... All of us boys were sure our team could have beaten Ohio State University that year, but they wouldn't play us; they were scared.[29]

After his years at Sullivant, Thurber attended Douglas School, more orderly but clearly less exciting. A classmate, Ruth White, remembered him as "quiet and studious and serious." His sixth grade teacher, Miss McElvaine, once told Thurber's mother, "He's so nervous. When I call on him to recite and he stands to his feet, his Adam's apple rolls around so wildly that he can hardly speak."[30] In a letter to Elliot Nugent, Thurber confirmed some of these observations. "When I was a bit of a lad in grammar grades and short pants," he wrote, "I was a wreck-- teacher's pet-- grind..."[31]

Thurber's youthful writing showed little promise of the craftsmanship to come. Nevertheless, while at Douglas he often carried a notebook about with him in which he doodled and wrote poems and stories about interesting experiences. Thurber also liked to perform for the family in the living room. "One time," recalled cousin Earl Fisher, "he wrote a play which he acted out as the family sat around the living room. I guess it really consisted of little more than Jamie's reading a list of jokes that he had clipped from newspapers and magazines." Unfortunately, he exhausted his repertoire of stories prematurely. Thurber resolved the dilemma by running to his grandmother's house and clipping more jokes before the audience lost interest.[32]

Douglas School provided Thurber with an early outlet for his writing. His fellow eighth graders elected him Class Prophet, whose duty it was to produce a written prophecy in which all the class members were mentioned. Catherine C. Hislop, one of the two girls elected to assist Thurber, recalled that "he did all the writing and we did all the laughing." The prophecy was a fantasy about a trip aboard an invention called the "Seairoplane," a vehicle "that travels in the water as well as thru the air and on land." The main character was Harold Young, a popular eighth grader who, ironically, later became an aviation pioneer and World War I fighter pilot. While the piece is juvenile and hackneyed, glimpses of Walter Mitty sneak through:

> One day as we were sailing easily along, Harold came rushing out of the engine room with dishevelled hair and bulging eyes. We asked him what on earth was the matter. For answer he pointed to a piece of rope that had caught in a part of the machinery that was situated on the farthest end of a long beam which extended far over the side of the Seairoplane.

Then he said, "Unless that rope is gotten out of the curobater we will all be killed."

These awful words astounded us and we all became frightened. Suddenly amid all our lamentations a cry from Harold was heard and we all looked up. What was our surprise to see James Thurber walking out on the beam.

He reached the end safely and extricated the rope, but when he turned to come back his foot caught and he pitched head foremost toward the deck. His unusual length saved him, for he landed safely on the Seairoplane. We were all very happy that the terrible crisis had been safely passed and afterwards learned that James was a tight rope walker with the Barnsell and Ringbailey's circus.[33]

In 1909 Thurber matriculated from Douglas to East High School where he continued to carry a notebook in which he scribbled and wrote. He remained quiet and shy, but gradually gained the reputation of being bright. While athletic heroes like Chic Harley and his brother Robert garnered most of the attention, Thurber participated sparingly by writing for the school paper, the X-Rays, and assisting with dramatic productions. A boyhood friend, Thomas Meek, recalled Thurber in high school as a "studious and sometimes withdrawn type, a kind of loner. But he wrote much better than the rest of us, and that made the teachers love him." He bloomed slowly, but perceptively. By the time he attended East, noted younger brother Robert, "Jamie stayed with Aunt Margery much less. Even so, he wasn't around home as much as William and I were. He was quiet about where he went. We knew he was always thinking, but we never knew what he was thinking."[34]

One reason Thurber was home less than the other brothers was that he held various jobs while a student at East High. The variety of jobs added to his store of information and anecdotes about the city. At various times, he worked as a delivery boy for an optical store, in a steel factory, a cigar store, and for the State-City Free Employment Agency.[35]

In the fall of 1912, Thurber wrote a theme for English class which is the best example of his early work. Entitled simply, "Election Night," it captured the excitement of the Taft-Wilson-Roosevelt-Bull Moose presidential contest. The prose is still strained and stilted, but the eye for detail and the sense of place is unmistakable:

> Excitement was at a fever heat in Columbus as elsewhere last Tuesday night when the fate of the candidates hung in the balance. From early evening until late at night and even into the 'wee sma' hours of Wednesday the city, and High Street especially, was the scene of great action and irrepressed excitement. A mighty crowd thronged the sidewalks brilliant with the myriads of electric lights strung along the thorofare in blinding array.
> Everybody jostled everybody else, but all in a spirit of hilarity and good feeling; at least before the election returns counted out all but the winning man.
> As ten o'clock rolled around and it was established without a doubt who was to be our next president pandemonium reigned in the street. Millions of horns kept up an incessant and strident song of victory. One could scarcely force his way thru the struggling pushing throng and at best emerged with a mouthful of confetti and a pair of ringing eardrums.

The teacher remarked in the margin, "Very good James. You sometimes use quotation marks where they are not needed."[36]

It goes without saying that Thurber's Columbus experience went far beyond the people, houses, and schools noted above. Thurber's Columbus was also his beloved dogs, Rex and Scottie, the summertime trips to Olentangy and Minerva Parks, and the daredevils lifting up in their hot air balloons from Driving Park. It was Mr. Ziegfeld and elections, drives around Franklin Park, and sneaking into State games at the old Ohio Field.

Columbus was also his later relationships at the university with professors like Joseph Russell Taylor, Billy Graves, and Dean Joseph Villiers Denney. And, it was his fateful friendship with Elliot Nugent along with the work on the university's newspaper and humor magazine. Thurber's Columbus was all this and much more.

Thomas Meek, a boyhood friend born just two blocks from Thurber, noted that in many ways, Thurber never really left his hometown. "The reason I say he didn't leave Columbus," explained Meek, "is because whenever you were with Jim he'd always come back to incidents that had happened in their early years there and to his friends there."[37]

Just as Eudora Welty associated clocks with her childhood memories of Mississippi, so too did Thurber. Upon his return to Columbus in 1953 to accept the Ohioana Sesquicentennial Medal, Thurber underscored his indebtedness to his boyhood home. His books, he said, "prove that I am never very far away from Ohio in my thoughts, and that the clocks that strike in my dreams are often the clocks of Columbus."[38]

Notes

1. Eudora Welty, One Writer's Beginnings (New York: Warner Books, Inc., 1984), p. 3.

2. Ohio State Journal, 14 February 1959.

3. U.S. Department of Commerce, Bureau of the Census, Thirteenth Census of the United States, 1910: Population, 1: 68, 81, 82, 86, 178, 836-837.

4. Chronology of F. & R. Lazarus Company Growth, Vol. 1, Box 9, Lazarus Family Papers, The Ohio Historical Society, Columbus, Ohio.

5. Betty Garrett, Columbus: America's Crosswoods (Tulsa: Continental Heritage Press, Inc., 1980), p. 105.

6. Ibid.

7. Helen Hooven Santmyer, Ohio Town (New York: Harper & Row, 1962).

8. Ohio, Secretary of State, Annual Report to the Governor, 1910, pp. 36, 292-293.

9. James Thurber, "The Secret Life of James Thurber," The Thurber Carnival (New York: Harper & Row, 1945), p. 32.

10. James Thurber, "Return of the Native," Credos and Curios (New York: Harper & Row, 1932), pp. 57-58.

11. Robert H. Wiebe, The Search for Order (New York: Hill and Wang, 1967).

12. William F. Thurber, "Early Years," 1971, Thurber Collection, The Ohio State University Library, Columbus, Ohio.

13. James Thurber, "Man with a Rose," The Thurber Album (New York: Simon and Schuster, 1952) and Burton Bernstein,

Thurber, A Biography (New York: Dodd, Mead & Company, 1975), p. 21.

14. Bernstein, Thurber, pp. 13-14.

15. James Thurber, "The Tree in the Diamond," The Thurber Album.

16. James Thurber, "My Fifty Years with James Thurber," The Thurber Carnival, p. xi.

17. James Thurber, "Lavender with a Difference," The Thurber Album, p. 130 and William A. Arter, "Thurbertown, Ohio," Columbus Vignettes (Columbus: by the author, 1967), p. 93.

18. James Thurber, "Lavender with a Difference," The Thurber Album, pp. 132-133; Samuel B. Baker, "James Thurber: The Columbus Years" (M.A. thesis, The Ohio State University, 1962), pp. 4-6; Martha Brian, "Thurber's Columbus, Then and Now," Columbus Monthly, March 1976, pp. 37-40.

19. James Thurber, "Lavender with a Difference," The Thurber Album, pp. 134-136 and Ruth White, "James Thurber, His Life in Columbus," The Columbus Dispatch, 10 March 1940.

20. Rosemary O. Joyce, et. al., eds., Of Thurber & Columbustown (Columbus: The Thurber House, 1984), p. 94.

21. Arter, "Thurbertown, Ohio," Vignettes, p. 94; James Thurber, "The Tree in the Diamond," The Thurber Album, pp. 75-76.

22. James Thurber, "Daguerrotype of a Lady," The Thurber Album, pp. 100-101.

23. Arter, "Thurbertown, Ohio," Vignettes, pp. 92-93 and White, "Thurber," The Columbus Dispatch, 10 March 1940.

24. William Thurber, "Early Years," 1971, Thurber

Collection and Baker, "Thurber: Columbus Years," pp. 6-9.

25. James Thurber to Bill Arter, 6 May 1957, William A. Arter Papers, The Ohio Historical Society, Columbus, Ohio.

26. Ibid.

27. James Thurber, "I Went to Sullivant," from <u>The Middle-Aged Man on the Flying Trapeze</u> in <u>Ninety-Two Stories</u> (New York: Avenel Books, 1985).

28. Ibid.

29. Ibid.

30. White, "Thurber," <u>The Columbus Dispatch</u>, 10 March 1940.

31. James Thurber to Elliot Nugent, 25 August 1918, Thurber Collection.

32. Baker, "Thurber: Columbus Years," pp. 17-18.

33. Baker, "Thurber: Columbus Years," pp. 20-21 and Charles S. Holmes, <u>The Clocks of Columbus: The Literary Career of James Thurber</u> (New York: Atheneum, 1972), pp. 17-18.

34. Bernstein, <u>Thurber</u>, p. 29 and Baker, "Thurber: Columbus Years," p. 22.

35. Bernstein, <u>Thurber</u>, p. 32.

36. James Thurber, "Election Night," 1912, Thurber Collection.

37. Lewis Branscomb interview with Thomas Meek, 2 August 1972, Thurber Collection.

38. James Thurber, "The Response to His Award of the Ohioana Sesquicentennial Medal," 24 October 1953 (Columbus: Ohioana Library Association, 1953), p. 9.

Peace-Church Conscientious Objectors and the War Department in World War I
by Albert N. Keim

For the small communities of Quakers, Mennonites and Church of the Brethren scattered across the United States in 1917, the war in Europe was a distant but troubling rumble just over the horizon. For them war was always worrisome, for their religiously grounded conscientious objection to war placed them in opposition to their societies in time of war. Their memories of the Civil War, a half century earlier, still persisted.

The Civil War was the first mass conscription war these centuries-long pacifists had ever encountered. In March 1863, Congress assumed for the states the administration of conscription. The original draft act provided an exemption for anyone who furnished a satisfactory substitute or paid a $300 commutation fee. Less than a year later in February 1864, the act was amended to recognize only conscientious objectors who were members of religious denominations whose "rules and articles of faith and practice" prohibited military service. The Secretary of War could assign them to duty in military hospitals, the care of freedmen, or payment of the $300 for the benefit of sick and wounded soliders. The payment of the $300 fee was the only provision ever carried out.[1]

In the Confederacy, the draft law of 1862 exempted Quakers, Brethren, Nazarenes, and Mennonites with the understanding that they would hire a substitute or pay a tax of $500 to the Confederate Treasury. The Peace Churches found these conditions severe and often violated by the authorities. A number of Mennonites and Brethren were imprisoned and a Church of the Brethren leader in the Shenandoah Valley was shot to death by a band of masked men.[2]

The Civil War provisions for conscientious objectors were not very satisfactory. Thus when the crisis of 1917 erupted into war, few desirable precedents existed. The Peace Churches not only lacked coordinated organizations, but had not given much thought to the problem of the CO in wartime.

American entry into the European war came as a surprise; within eighteen months it was over. That pervasive element of total war, the military draft, took on its characteristically draconian feature of total equality enforced with all the unremitting power of the warfare state. In a few short months, the military enlistment machinery catalogued and mobilized an entire generation of young Americans for military purposes. A few months later, their elders felt the bite of the war bond, an ingenious device to finance the war effort. The twin resources of modern warfare, manpower and money, were mobilized with swift thoroughness. For those conscientiously unable to cooperate in the war effort, it was a fearful time.

World War I was total war, fought not only with guns, but with factory lathes and farmers' plows. Powerful propaganda aroused enthusiasm for a "war to end war" and "to make the world safe for democracy." That there were dissenters whose consciences forbade joining the war effort came as a surprise to governments and people on all sides of the conflict. Reliance on war as a means to settle differences among nations seemed to most people a necessary and inevitable, if undesirable, course of action. Objection to war to the point of refusal to participate was not only considered unrealistic, but treasonous; a breach of faith with one's nation and people.

With the breaking of diplomatic relations with Germany in early 1917, American Friends began to reflect on an appropriate response to the mounting emergency. During a faculty meeting at Quaker Haverford College in early March, a committee of five was appointed "to consider the formation of a training unit of some sort, possibly an ambulance corps." The purpose of the Haverford Emergency Unit was "To provide a reasonable opportunity for Haverford men to prepare in unison for a national emergency without necessitating withdrawal from college work or the sacrifice of individual conscience." On April 6, the day war was declared by Congress, the Haverford College Student Association voted 158 to 6 in favor of a training plan. A joint faculty-student meeting later in the day formally adopted a comprehensive training program in motor touring, shop work, Red Cross work, camping, hiking, and drill. Within a few weeks $10,000 was raised and a strenuous training schedule was launched.[3]

But the Emergency Unit faded as quickly as it had been formed. With commencement in May its members scattered. Its significance lies in the idea. It served as a prelude to the Haverford Reconstruction Unit which formed in the summer, after conscription began in earnest and alternative forms of service became a high priority for absolute conscientious objectors.

The declaration of war and the introduction of a conscription bill in April precipitated a historic meeting of thirteen Friends on April 30, 1917. They met at the Friends meetinghouse at 15th and Race Streets in Philadelphia "to consider what might be appropriate Quaker action in the war emergency." The group represented a variety of American Friends. Henry J. Cadbury, a professor at Haverford College, served as Clerk of the Meeting and recorded the following minute: "We are united in expressing our love for our country and our desire to serve her loyally. We offer our services to the government of the United States in any constructive work in which we can conscientiously serve humanity."[4] Thus was born the American Friends Service Committee. Rufus Jones was elected chairman; Alfred G. Scattergood, vice-chairman; Charles F. Jenkins, treasurer; and Vincent D. Nicholson, executive secretary to handle day-to-day details of the new organization. Headquarters were established in the historic Friends Meetinghouse at 20 South 12th Street in Philadelphia.[5]

The founding of the American Friends Service Committee (AFSC) gave the Society of Friends, and subsequently the other Peace Churches, an organization to implement two basic concerns which devolved on conscientious objectors in World War I: (1) securing exemption from military service, both combatant and noncombatant, and (2) forging a program for alternative service satisfactory to a government at war and to consciences that could not support war.

In regard to means for alternative service, several hopeful possibilities appeared. One was the appointment by President Wilson of Grayson Murphy as Chief of the American Red Cross in France. Murphy, a graduate of the William Penn Charter School in Philadelphia, had been a student at Haverford College where he was on close terms with Rufus Jones, Professor of Philosophy. Jones now approached Murphy about a prospective Friends Unit for relief work in France. The idea appealed to Murphy. After a conference with the AFSC, he suggested a delegation of Friends visit France, confer with English Quakers there and survey the needs. After receiving the blessing of Henry P. Davison, President Wilson's new director of foreign relief work, J. Henry Scattergood and Morris Leeds left New York on June 2, and reached France before the first contingent of American troops. The investigation and reports of Scattergood and Leeds became the basis for the plans already underway for a reconstruction unit of American Friends in France.[6]

The training program for what came to be known as the Friends Reconstruction Unit began in early June. A committee screened candidates for service as applications streamed in. An intensive six-week course of study, work and worship was designed including physical conditioning, French language, study, public sanitation, social service, first aid, carpentry, auto repair, and a time for silent gathered worship each evening. The reports of Scattergood and Leeds indicated that a desperate need for housing existed. Hence a model house was constructed, based on plans from France, to give trainees experience in construction. The last days at Haverford were spent in packing tools and medical and surgical equipment. Hopes ran high--the AFSC slogan, "A Service of Love in Wartime," seemed to be coming to fruition. During the hectic summer of 1917, it appeared that an alternative peace program was being constructed.[7] "As Friends we cannot bear arms against fellow men," wrote Walter C. Woodward in an editorial in the April 19 American Friend. "Neither are many of us clear to do service of any kind under the direct command of the military arm of the government. In our right, however, we can repair the waste places, relieve the suffering, bind up the wounds, and help bridge the chasm of hate which is the fruit of war."

But dedication and skills were not enough. America was in the tightening vise of total war. Factory, farm, railroad, post office and store--all were being pressed into one gigantic war machine. Exceptions and exemptions were hard to come by. By late summer of 1917, Rufus Jones ruefully admitted, "we assumed, no doubt too hastily, that the President and exemption boards would gladly recognize that our reconstruction work abroad was a voluntary and unforced type of noncombatant service, entirely satisfactory for the fulfillment of the provisions."[8]

When the war began in August 1914, Americans were secure in the conviction that it was not their concern. President Wilson declared that America "neither sits in judgment upon others nor is disturbed in her own counsels." America would remain "neutral in fact as well as in name... impartial in thought as well as in action."

Americans saw the war as a case of European militarism run

amok whose ultimate denouement would not affect the United States. The Lusitania incident in May 1915 marked a turning point in American attitudes about the war. For the first time, it became apparent that the U.S. could find itself drawn into the maelstrom. During the great debate over neutral rights in the summer of 1915, President Wilson came out for preparedness and the cabinet began drafting plans for rearmament. Preparedness, Wilson argued, was no longer a partisan cause, but a national necessity.

In January 1916, Wilson toured the East and Midwest explaining and defending his preparedness program. But on his return to Washington on February 4, it was clear Congress would reject the Continental Army plan proposed by Secretary of War Garrison. Garrison resigned. His replacement was Newton D. Baker, mayor of Cleveland, popular with Democrats in Congress, and an early supporter of preparedness. Wilson's preparedness program in Congress began to make steady progress.

The passage of the National Defense Act on June 2, 1916, enlarged the Military Academy, doubled the authorized peacetime strength of the Regular Army, integrated the National Guard into the national defense system, and established a program of volunteer summer military training camps. It also introduced a selective draft option, known as the "Haydon Joker," buried in an obscure paragraph of the bill. Since any mention of a draft bill would have been anathema to a majority in Congress, the congressional managers of the bill played down its presence. Only a few members of Congress knew of its existence. Wilson and Baker knew of the clause, but Wilson, with wonderful verisimilitude, argued that it applied only in time of war and was not really conscription, but a "draft in a more limited sense of the term."[9]

Wilson was reelected in November 1916 by a narrow margin after a campaign built around the slogan, "He kept us out of war." But events began to shorten the President's neutrality options. On January 31, 1917, Germany announced an unrestricted submarine warfare zone around the British Isles and the coast of Europe. In response Wilson severed diplomatic relations with Germany on February 3, 1917.

The next day, Wilson suddenly appeared, unattended and unannounced, at Secretary of War Newton D. Baker's office for a conference. Upon his departure, the Secretary sent for General Crowder, his Judge Advocate General. The President, Baker informed Crowder, had decided upon a draft to recruit manpower for the Regular Army. He wanted a legislative draft proposal drawn up by 10:00 a.m. the next morning. Crowder, taken aback, inquired whether the President had expressed any opinion regarding the components of such a proposal. No, replied Baker, the War Department would need to rely on its own resources.

At that moment, Crowder realized that his extracurricular interest in military manpower recruitment issues had not been in vain. Years earlier, as a young cavalry officer stationed at a frontier army post, Crowder, trained at West Point and the Law School of the University of Missouri, had made an exhaustive study of the Civil War draft act and its administration. The essential features of an improved draft law were already present in Crowder's well-organized mind. Justice required all male citizens of a designated age cohort to be enrolled. The law would ask for personal registration at a designated place rather than a house-to-house census. Draftees would be credited to their district of permanent residence. Quotas would be based on states rather than congressional districts. The use of bounties or the employment of substitutes definitely would be prohibited. Finally, the term of service would be for duration of the war.

Crowder sketched out his ideas in general form, identified the major elements of the proposal, and then asked each of his four assistants to work on a draft of a designated section. During the night refinements were made and early on February 4, Crowder wrote out in almost final form the language subsequently submitted to Congress. A few minutes before 10:00 a.m., Crowder handed the prepared typescript to Secretary Baker. During the following weeks the document was further refined. On April 7, the day after formal entrance by the United States into the war, the bill entitled "An Act to Authorize the President to Increase Temporarily the Military Establishment of the United States," was laid before the Congress by Secretary Baker.[10]

Conscription had many opponents in Congress. Hearings and debate consumed more than a month. It was not until May 18 that the Selective Training Act was finally signed into law by President Wilson. He hailed it as "in no sense a conscription of the unwilling; rather it is a selection from a nation which has volunteered en masse."[11]

The Act had a conscientious objector provision:
Nothing in this act contained shall be construed or compel any person to serve in any of the forces herein provided for, who is found to be a member of any well

recognized religious sect or organization at present
organized and existing and whose existing creed or
principles forbid its members to participate in war in
any form and whose religious convictions are against
war or participation therein in accordance with the
creed or principles of said religious organizations;
but no person so exempted shall be exempted from
service in any capacity that the President shall
declare to be noncombatant.[12]

The conscientious objector clause presented a serious problem for the Peace Churches. It provided no remedy for conscientious objectors who could not engage in noncombatant activity. This limited its utility for Peace Church conscientious objectors, although the phrase giving the President authority to define noncombatancy was interpreted by the Peace Churches as a means to meet their expectations and needs. President Wilson's delay in defining noncombatancy for a year and then defining it only in military terms, left Peace Church conscientious objectors at the mercy of the powerful, sometimes evasive officials of the War Department. Even before the Selective Training bill became law, several groups attempted to effect changes. On April 12, a week after Congress began its deliberations on the bill, three Mennonites, P.H. Richert, Maxwell H. Kratz and Peter Jansen visited Washington to lobby for explicit exemption of the conscientious objector from military service.[13] That same day Lillian Wald, Jane Addams and Norman Thomas made an eloquent plea to Secretary of War Baker to base conscientious objector exemption on an individual basis and to make clear provision for those conscientious objectors who could not accept noncombatant service.[14] The three spoke for the American Union Against Militarism (AUAM), a prestigious anti-war group which was soon to create the American Civil Liberties Union. Secretary Baker had once been a member of the AUAM. And the presence of Jane Addams, respected and admired by Wilson and Baker, on the executive committee of the AUAM, led the group to believe its representation might have some effect. However, Baker's noncommittal response gave faint hope. As debate continued on the bill in Congress, Norman Thomas wrote a letter to General Crowder and to Senator Chamberlain, Chairman of the Senate Military Affairs Committee, urging that "an alternative service of recognized value to the state" be created for those unable to do noncombatant service.[15] Jane Addams followed Thomas' letter with a strongly worded telegram to Baker demanding that the AUAM concerns presented on April 12 be taken seriously.[16] Baker replied:

> Your telegram of the 27th reached me. I think it is unlikely that we can secure a legislative exemption for conscientious objectors. I will, however, see that your view is presented to the Conference Committee. In the meantime I hope that the Administration of whatever law is passed will make it possible for us to avoid the unhappy difficulties which occurred in England and which you mention.[17]

Roger Baldwin of the new American Civil Liberties Union wrote to the Senate and House committees urging especially the recognition of the CO's who were not members of a "well recognized sect opposed to war."[18] Baker and Crowder gave three days testimony before the House and Senate Military Committees and at one point were closely questioned by congressmen who objected to any exemptions, religious or otherwise. Baker stoutly responded: "It is a part of the policy of the government to allow liberty of conscience, and where men are actually members of religious bodies which have entertained that view, they have never been required in this country to fight." But, a question persisted, are members of religious groups totally exempted? Replied General Crowder: "That is right. Here the exemption is complete for religious people." Then, in an exchange fateful as a foretaste of things to come, a congressman observed: "It occurs to me that the class of men you propose to draft under this bill are to be from 19 to 24, and all active men, their religious beliefs must be rather immature, and would it not really be better to give them service in the noncombatant corps?" "I have no objection to that," replied Baker.[19]

From the outset, both Wilson and Baker had taken a firm stand against individual conscientious exemption. Wilson insisted it would be "impossible... because it would open the door to do so much that was unconscientious on the part of persons who wished to escape service."[20] Baker was aware of the abuses of exemptions in the Civil War. Thus he observed to Wilson that, "So many kinds of people have asked for class exemptions that our only safety seems to be in making none."[21] Congress agreed, for when Senator Robert M. La Follette and Representative Edward Keating offered an amendment recognizing political conscientious objectors, it was supported by only a few of their colleagues. Congress and the War Department were afraid of anything which would encourage "slackers and draft dodgers."[22]

June 5, 1917 was registration day. Wilson hailed it as a "great day of patriotic devotion and obligation."[23] For the Peace Churches, it was another step closer to the drafting of their young men without knowing the true implications of that process. Furthermore, the pressure of the war spirit began to make itself felt. Wilson led the charge with a Flag Day speech in which he called the peace movement one of traitors and schemers. The next day, Congress passed the Espionage Act.[24] Summer 1917 was a time of anxiety for the Peace Churches, as they sought to bring their concerns to the attention of the War Department.

A number of Peace Church leaders felt a strong need to organize a common effort to deal with the War Department. A few days after the passage of the draft act, six representatives of the Peace Churches met in Washington, D.C. to explore common action. Their call for a "Committee which, in a united and concerted way, may have watch over the situation, devise plans, present our position and claims to the various departments of our government, and labor together in the interests of our time-honored and Scriptural teachings of peace" appears in retrospect as a timely and important initiative, but was never carried out in the course of the war.[25] The absence of such a unified effort contributed to the difficulties encountered by Peace Church conscientious objectors in World War I.

The lack of a strong concerted Peace Church lobby did not mean an absence of effort. On the contrary, a constant stream of delegations visited Washington from all the Peace groups, and they found surprisingly quick and easy access to Secretary Baker, General Crowder, and others at the War Department. In fact, it is difficult to believe that more activity could have been useful. The problem was not representation and presence. Secretary Baker was bombarded by Peace Church concerns. Rather, the unorganized and episodic character of the initiatives gave

Baker freedom to maneuver. He very skillfully used the situation, cajoling and shifting ground as he met delegation after delegation.

Baker sought to be reassuring. When three members of a newly created Mennonite War Problems Committee visited him in late summer, he concluded the interview by affably putting his hand on D. D. Miller's knee with the words, "Don't worry. We'll take care of your boys."[26] Baker insisted that the deficiencies in the legislation would be remedied by administrative process, but refused to define how that process would occur. General Crowder, brusque and genuinely unsympathetic to conscientious objectors, played a tough role. The churchmen were continually thrown off balance by his hard line interpretations of policy, although he probably represented the true line of policy more accurately than his superior, Secretary Baker.

The failure of the Peace Churches to unite their efforts was largely due to the decentralized character of the church organizations and a genuine confusion among the groups about what constituted appropriate noncombatant behavior. The immobilization resulting from an inability to get consensus on the issue of how far to cooperate was graphically portrayed by C. E. Boyers, who represented the Church of the Brethren at Camp Meade. Reported Boyers:

> Only last week the captain said he needed men in the Medical Corps badly and asked whether our church would oppose work there. Finally, I ventured to say I thought they would not. He asked if I would put that in writing. I replied that I had no authority to speak for the church. You see? Would appreciate a word on this point.[27]

From Camp Funston came the plaintive, "We don't know how far to go because our church hasn't defined our privilege."[28]

For Peace Church leaders, the ability to answer such queries was linked to what could be hoped for by way of War Department policy. The Peace Churches sought total exemption as an ideal. Only the more conservative Mennonites were prepared to insist on that stance for all of their young men. The Brethren and Friends were less directive, giving their young men freedom of choice.

The uncertainties felt by Peace Church leaders during the summer of 1917 were heightened by two policy statements in August from the War Department. A ruling on August 8 for the first time stated in unmistakable language that all draftees are "in the military service of the United States from the time specified for reporting to the Local Board for military service."[29] The Peace Churches had hoped to avoid becoming part of the military apparatus. The second ruling, on August 11, was equally disconcerting. All designated conscientious objector draftees would be "forwarded to a mobilization camp" and treated as part of the draft quota of a state and district.[30] Conscientious objectors were to be physically placed in Army camps, a development viewed with alarm by all the Peace Churches.

During the discussions following these rulings, a forceful advocate for the Peace Churches emerged in the person of W. W. Griest, congressman from Lancaster, Pennsylvania, whose district included large populations of Friends, Mennonites and Brethren. Griest was a Quaker, minority leader of the Agriculture Committee in the House of Representatives, and genuinely interested in the rights of his Peace Church constituents. He not only opened doors for Peace Church representatives in Washington, but actively worked on their behalf. Thus, in July even before the War Department rulings, he had written to Wilson and Crowder requesting agricultural deferments for Mennonites, acting on a request from the Lancaster Mennonite Conference Bishop Board.[31] After the August War Department rulings, Griest wrote an eloquent and strongly worded letter to President Wilson:

> Living in the midst of the nonresistant religious sects of Southeastern Pennsylvania--the Dunkards, the Amish, the Quakers, and the Mennonites--I wish to direct your attention to the unrest and alarm recently aroused among them by your regulations which they think will deprive them of the considerations accorded their religions by the Selective Draft Act.[32]

Why were they so alarmed?:

> To be posted as selected for military service on Form 164, to be assembled and sent to mobilization camp as one selected for military service; probably to be dealt with there either as a menial or arrayed in uniform which is a dress contrary to his religious beliefs and principles and the Creed of his church, and to be treated in all respects as one selected for military service except for the certificate he holds and which the government will have no record of, is according to these plain, but loyal folk a lack of consideration which would appear to be unnecessary and in contravention of the spirit of the Selective Draft Law, and contrary to all draft measures ever enacted in this country from colonial days down to the present time, during all the wars of American History.[33]

Griest also urgently encouraged the Peace Churches to send delegations to Baker and the War Department. The most important thing, he told W. J. Swigert of the Brethren Peace Committee, "is to reverse the order by Crowder that conscientious objector registrants be consigned at once to military encampments."[34]

The Peace Church leaders responded with alacrity. On August 17, the American Friends Service Committee commissioned Issac

Sharpless and Henry Bartlett to see Baker about the matter. They did so on August 22. Baker was cordial but tough. Would hospital service be agreeable with Quakers?, he asked. Not generally, was the reply. How will Friends be treated when they get to camp?, the Friends inquired. They will be given the hospital option. If they refuse that they will be locked in the Guard House and court martialed, replied Baker. Why not exempt conscientious objectors for service with the Friends Reconstruction Unit and avoid such troubles?, the Friends asked. That can't be considered because it would generate too many conscientious objector exemption cases, Baker replied. Would it help to see Wilson? No, replied Baker, but he would see that Wilson received their letter of concern.

As usual, Baker's anteroom was crowded with persons waiting to see him, so he quickly ushered the Friends into the next office to see Crowder. The latter was taciturn and dour. I wrote the act, he said. It is a military measure. Where the word "service" is used it means military service. What, the Friends asked, would happen if Friends refused all service? "I'm sorry you asked that for it would not be pleasant for you to know or for me to contemplate." Sharpless and Bartlett assumed he meant the men would be shot.[35]

Two days later on August 25, four Hutterites from South Dakota visited Baker and were assured that "the best will be done" for them. Their young men, Baker said, would "not be compelled to do that which is contrary to the dictates of their conscience." The editor of the Mennonite Gospel Herald was relieved: "this is indeed good news to us whose positions on the question of military service is the same as theirs."[36] On August 28, a delegation of Friends led by Rufus Jones presented an eloquent proposal to Baker. The War Department rulings created, as they put it, "a very grave situation." You have a problem: Many of our young men will not be able to cooperate with your definitions of noncombatancy. We can help you solve the problem by having the American Friends Committee find "service of national importance" for all Friends who are conscientious objectors. Under the provisions of the draft regulations, the Committee argued, the President may discharge conscientious objectors, and "this Committee pledges itself to find forms of service to be approved by the President, for all such men." They pointed to the success of such a plan in Britain and New Zealand and the precedents established during the American Civil War.[37]

On September 1, two delegations visited Baker. An eight-man Mennonite group reported on the Mennonite position, just defined at a conference at Goshen, Indiana, a few days earlier. One member of the group, A. G. Clemmer, had the foresight to summarize the main lines of the discussion with Baker and cited ten provisions the Secretary promised to follow.[38] Later that same day, W. J. Swigert, I. W. Taylor and W. M. Lyon of the Church of the Brethren carried Clemmer's summary into an interview with Baker. Baker was surprised by the document, but after a careful perusal agreed to its essential accuracy, taking exception only with item eight, the key issue at hand. "It would not possible," he said, "to say finally: 'Those who accept noncombatant service will be assigned to some other service not under the military arm of the government.' It may possibly be so, but that would have to be worked out." To the dismay of the churchmen, he went on to say "and on the absolute refusal to obey orders and accept assignments from officers in charge, some might be imprisoned for a time. But provisions will be made for adjustment. Go as far as you can, and all claims for conscience will be heard."[39]

Thus, after a series of five visits by Peace Church delegations within a period of one week, Baker at the very last was still unwilling to concede the most important point: that Peace Church conscientious objectors be freed from military control. Nor did he respond to Peace Church proposals for alternative service. In the midst of this intense lobbying, Baker revealed his real intentions in a letter to President Wilson:

> It does not seem to me that it would be wise now to designate this work of reconstruction as the sort of noncombatant service contemplated for religious objectors, chiefly for the reasons that any definition of that sort of work at this time may have the effect of encouraging further "conscientious objecting." On this whole subject my belief is that we ought to proceed with the draft, and after the conscientious objectors have gotten into camps and have made known their inability to proceed with military work, their number will be ascertained and a suitable work evolved for them.[40]

The first wave of draftees, aged 21-31, began to arrive at the training camps on September 5. The inability of the Peace Churches to gain War Department action on the conscientious objector issue now meant that the burden of what constituted appropriate behavior--where to draw the line in terms of cooperation in the training camps--fell swiftly and forcefully on the shoulders of young conscientious objector draftees, a situation the War Department immediately began to take advantage of.

In late September 1917, Secretary Baker visited Camp Meade in Maryland to inspect an "interesting group of conscientious objectors."[41] Out of that visit evolved a strategy he hoped would persuade conscientious objectors to cooperate with the government. His policy, he informed President Wilson, was to segregate the conscientious objectors from their fellow soldiers. The feeling of rejection, he was sure, would soon bring them around to cooperation and only a hard core of Amish, Quakers, and Fundamentalists would be left.[42] In October he issued orders that conscientious objectors should be separated from military personnel, treated with tact and consideration, and unless they refused a lawful order, they should not be court-martialed.[43] But the Army soon made a shambles of Baker's intentions. Courts-martial handing down twenty-five year sentences became common-place. Physical abuse became rampant. Clarifying orders by the War Department on handling conscientious objectors did not improve matters. The problem lay in the absence of a clear policy and the fact that the officers in charge were almost never in sympathy with such policy as existed. The powerful public propaganda machine, designed to mobilize support for the war effort, combined with the formalized military legal machinery, place conscientious objectors in a parlous position; their religious convictions and civil rights counted for little. Baker and the War Department were intent on keeping the nimber of conscientious objectors who persevered as few as possible, even at the price of an abridgment of civil liberties.

As autumn became winter, the plight of young conscientious

objectors caught in the web of a military system geared to wean them from their conscientious objector convictions became ever more difficult. Peace Church leaders struggled to create a network of support to help mitigate some of the worst cases of mishandling and abuse. The War Department became increasingly unresponsive to the plight of conscientious objectors as the weight of the war effort began to strain the available economic, transport, and personnel systems. Until some definitive resolution could be made to remand conscientious objectors to useful civilian pursuits, the dilemma of the conscientious objectors would continue to worsen. The Peace Churches sought to pressure the President to declare what constituted noncombatancy, but given his and Baker's intentions vis-à-vis the conscientious objector problem, it was not surprising that they were not inclined to move on a definition.

The conscientious objector problem would not go away. Finally, on January 8, 1918, Baker addressed a letter to Senator Chamberlain of the Senate Military Affairs Committee:

> I enclose herewith for the consideration and appropriate action of the Senate Military Committee, a joint resolution authorizing the Secretary of War to grant furloughs to enlisted men of the army without pay and allowances, to permit said enlisted men to engage in civil occupations and pursuits. The main purpose for which it is intended to use this authority is to furlough soldiers in the National Army during harvest and planting time to enable them to assist the agricultural production of the country. Under the law as it now stands the furloughed men would be entitled to pay and allowances during the period of their absence. It is necessary, therefore, to have authority to grant such furloughs without raising a claim against the Government for pay.[44]

Clearly the Wilson Administration was reaching for a resolution of the conscientious objector problem. On February 12, President Wilson confirmed this in a letter to H. C. Early, moderator of the Church of the Brethren:

> The Secretary of War has presented to the Congress for approval, a bill which will authorize the War Department to furlough, without pay, men in the military service. Should the Congress enact this legislaion, it will then be possible under its provision, to assign, by conditional furlough, men whose conscientious scruples cannot otherwise be met, to civilian occupations of the general sort of which you indicate.[45]

The Furlough Act was passed on March 16. A few days later Rufus Jones, reporting on yet another trip to the War Department, observed that the new act gave the Secretary of War authority to furlough conscientious objectors for civilian work. Thus, he remarked, the President will not need to rule on what constituted appropriate noncombatant work for conscientious objectors.[46] However, almost as Jones was speaking, the President did rule on appropriate noncombatant work. On March 20, he issued Executive Order 2823, an order, as the American Friends Service Committee Peace Committee noted, which made the conscientious objector position even more tenuous, for now conscientious objectors refusing any of the options became subject to punishment for refusing such service.[47] The administration, however, had adroitly managed to find a way to move conscientious objectors quietly into civilian service while preserving the guise of being tough on conscientious objectors. By not recognizing a civilian alternative in his March 20 order, Wilson preserved himself from criticism for being soft on conscientious objectors--a serious problem, largely generated by the powerful war propaganda campaign underway. For the President in the spring of 1918 to have reflected sympathy for the conscientious objector would have been politically inexpedient.

In any case, the American Friends Service Committee Peace Committee accurately diagnosed the meaning of these events. Rufus Jones, Stanely Yarnall and Vincent Nicholson immediately visited the War Department. Baker was absent in France but Baker's secretary, Dr. Frederick Keppel, agreed that the Furlough Act did provide a loophole for furloughing conscientious objectors to civilian work. Keppel went on to suggest that the Mennonites, Brethren and Friends should form a joint commission to organize and give direction to the young men released by the Furlough Act.[48]

Jones acted swiftly. On April 4, a conference of Peace Church leaders convened in Philadelphia and created a Joint Commission, composed of nine men of "broad and understanding sympathies," three from each of the Peace Churches. The Commission would be responsible for arranging employment for and giving oversight to men furloughed by the War Department. The Commission would place men in civilian employ on a priority basis, first to agriculture, second reconstruction and relief abroad, third forestry, and finally, such other general civilian work agreed upon by the Commission and the War Department. The Commission would be committed to make periodic reports to the War Department regarding the status of each man in its charge.[49]

Frederick Keppel, Third Assistant Secretary of War, formerly Dean of Columbia University, became the key War Department official in the development of the plan to solve the conscientious objector problem. However, resolution of the issue continued to founder on the desire of the War Department to appear tough on the conscientious objector. The Department no longer feared large-scale conscientious objector defections. As reported by the <u>New York Times</u>, the War Department was at pains to note that as of June 1, 1918, only 600 bona fide conscientious objectors had emerged out of a total of 1,300,000 men drafted. As the article noted, the War Department hoped the newly created Board of Inquiry would reduce the numbers even more.[50] At issue now was simply the need to avoid all appearance of special privilege for conscientious objectors, given the temper of public opinion. Having found a device to furlough conscientious objectors, the problem now was to design a means, a test, to determine sincerity. Keppel found the answer in a Board of Inquiry.

On May 31, Rufus Jones reported to Professor Swigert of the Church of the Brethren that he had just met with Keppel, who assured him that the plan for furloughing conscientious objectors was "practically perfected, with a few alterations." Keppel was sure the Secretary of War would agree with the plan and announce it in a very short time. Jones acknowledged that "this proposed plan is by no means what we want. It is, however, almost certainly the best we can get through the War Department." Jones went on to observe that

> it is the settled judgment in Washington that the so-called exemption clause in the draft law never looked toward the exemption of our conscientious objectors from noncombatant service. It apparently did not occur to the Washington people that our objection was anything more than an objection to the direct killing of people. They do not seem to understand that we are opposed to the military system and all forms of service

under such a system. I find it difficult to make anybody in Washington realize that attitude."[51]

The War Department announced the new plan for handling absolute conscientious objectors on May 30. All conscientious objectors were to be moved to Fort Leavenworth, Kansas. A Board of Inquiry, chaired by Major Richard C. Stoddert of the Judge Advocate's office (later Walter C. Kellogg replaced Stoddert) was created. The other members were Judge Julian W. Mack of the Federal Court and Dean Harlan F. Stone of Columbia University Law School. Absolute conscientious objectors were to be furloughed without pay for agricultural service. If the farmer provided compensation, it was to be at the compensation level of private. In exceptional cases, the Board of Inquiry could furlough men for service in France with the Friends Reconstruction Unit. All concientious objectors recommended for furlough had to accept it. Finally, to the dismay of Peace Church leaders, the directive decreed that in no case could the furloughed men escape their military status. All military regulations remained in effect.[52]

Rufus Jones was again dispatched to Washington by the Executive Committee of the American Friends Service Committee. Once the sincerity of the conscientious objector was validated, who would the men be remanded to?, he inquired of Keppel. Keppel identified three possibilities--the Department of Agriculture, local draft boards of the respective men, or the Peace Church Joint Commission. Jones urged the latter. The War Department was uneasy about that idea, however, and proposed a military commissioner. As Jones later acknowledged, the Peace Church Commission was "sure to be open to criticism on the part of those who wanted severe measures used toward these men, and persons of such attitude could hardly approve of turning the conscientious objectors over to the tender mercies of their own friends and people." Jones, trading on his good relations with Keppel, was able to have the appointment be a civilian commissioner who, as he put it, "understands the conscientious objector point of view." Jones acknowledged that the Joint Commission will "not have any large amount of work to do," but would serve as counsel to the Commissioner.[53]

Unfortunately, Keppel's optimistic hopes of finding a civilian commissioner "in a few days" lapsed into a few months. It was not until August 3, 1918, that he informed the Peace Churches of the appointment of Dr. Roswell N. McCrea of the Columbia University School of Business as the new commissioner. McCrea was a graduate of Haverford College and understood the Historic Peace Church perspective on war. But by then the war was almost over and the work of the Commissioner never really got under way.[54]

During World War I, no solution was found which dealt adequately with the problem of the absolute conscientious objector. The War Department plan placing young conscientious objectors in military camps to test their sincerity and, if possible, convince them to accept some form of military or noncombatant service was clearly unsatisfactory. But the logic of the warfare state with its all-consuming need to bring everything and everyone into the orbit of the war effort, created nearly insurmountable obstacles to non-military alternatives for those who could not participate. The solution for conscientious objectors lay in the design of a civilian alternative to military service. Passed by an unsuspecting Congress and administered with gingerly reticence by the War Department, the Farm Furlough Act did not resolve the issue. It failed to free the absolute conscientious objector from the tentacles of the military machine. The only resolution with promise was sending conscientious objectors to the Friends Reconstruction Unit in France, a process which became possible only late in the war and which absorbed only a limited percentage of conscientious objectors.

The failure to achieve a satisfactory resolution for the absolute objector was not a result of an absence of effort by the Historic Peace Churches. A better-coordinated effort might have helped, but given the obdurate posture of the War Department, it is doubtful that even a united front would have accomplished much more. Not having waged a conscript war for more than fifty years, the War Department was unprepared for the tenacious convictions of conscripted conscientious objectors. By the time War Department officials realized their mistake, the war was over.

World War I was a searing experience for the Peace Churches. The memory of that experience would bulk large in the search for an early resolution of the problem at the onset of World War II. The general shape and form taken by the Civilian Public Service for conscientious objectors in World War II was a product of the failure of the War Department and the Peace Churches to develop a viable policy and program in World War I.

Notes

1. Guy Hershberger. War, Peace and Nonresistance (Scottdale, Pa.: Herald Press, 1944), pp. 98-106.

2. Samuel L. Horst, Mennonites in the Confederacy: A Study of Civil War Pacifism (Scottdale, Pa.: Herald Press, 1967), p. 80.

3. "A Documentary Record of the Formation and Operations of the Haverford Emergency Unit, 1917," Book H., Haverford College Library.

4. Elizabeth Gray Vining, Friend of Life: The Biography of Rufus M. Jones (Philadelphia: J.B. Lippincott, 1958), p. 158.

5. Ibid.

6. Rufus M. Jones, A Service of Love In Wartime: American Friends Relief Work in Europe, 1917-1919 (New York: Macmillan, 1920), pp. 10-11.

7. Ibid., pp. 17-20.

8. Ibid., p. 50.

9. Blanche Cooke, "Wilson and the Anti-Militarists" (Ph.D. dissertation, Johns Hopkins University Press, 1970), pp. 78-78.

10. David A. Lockmiller, Enoch H. Crowder: Soldier, Lawyer and Statesman (Columbia: University of Missouri Studies, 1955), p. 152.

11. Daniel R. Beaver, Newton D. Baker and the American War Effort, 1917-1919 (Lincoln: University of Nebraska Press, 1966), p. 33.

12. U.S., Congress, An Act to Authorize the President to Increase Temporarily the Military Establishment of the United

States, Pub. L. 65-12, 65th Cong., 1st sess., 1917.

13. Hershberger, p. 116.

14. Cooke, p. 203.

15. Ibid., p. 310.

16. Ibid., p. 204.

17. Beaver, p. 231.

18. Cooke, p. 210.

19. U.S. Selective Service System, Conscientious Objection, Special Monograph No. 11, Volume I, ed. Mapheus Smith and Kenneth H. McGill (Washington, D.C.: Government Printing Office, 1950), p. 55.

20. Charles Chatfield, For Peace and Justice: Pacifism in America, 1914-1941 (Knoxville: University of Tennessee Press, 1971), p. 70.

21. Baker to Wilson, May 26, 1917, Newton D. Baker Papers, Library of Congress, Washington, D.C.

22. Donald Johnson, The Challenge To American Freedoms: World War I and the Rise of the American Civil Liberties Union (Lexington: University of Kentucky Press for Mississippi Valley Historical Society, 1963), p. 17.

23. Beaver, pp. 33-34.

24. Cooke, p. 214.

25. The Friend, 21 June 21 1917, pp. 616-617.

26. Oral Interview, Orie O. Miller, 4 March 1972, Stoltzfus notes, file 237, Eastern Mennonite College, Harrisonburg, Virginia.

27. C. E. Boyer to W. J. Swigert, 5 November 1917,

Sappington notes, Eastern Mennonite College.

28. D. A. Crist to W. J. Swigert, 25 October 1917, Sappington notes.

29. American Friend, 6 September 1917, p. 712.

30. Ibid.

31. Griest to Crowder, 2 July 1917, W.W. Griest Papers, Swarthmore College, Swarthmore, Pennsylvania.

32. Griest to Wilson, 27 August 1917, Griest Papers.

33. Ibid.

34. Griest to W. J. Swigert, 28 August 1917, Griest Papers.

35. Executive Committee, Report, 22 August 1917, American Friends Service Committee Archives, Philadelphia, Pennsylvania.

36. Gospel Herald, 3 September 1917, p. 409.

37. Friends Intelligencer, 1 September 1917, p. 553.

38. Conscientious Objection, Special Monograph No.11, Vol. I, p. 58.

39. Ibid., pp. 58-59.

40. Cited in Frederick Palmer, Newton D. Baker: America At War (New York: Dodd, Mead & Company, 1931), Vol. I, p. 341.

41. Beaver, p. 232.

42. Ibid.

43. Ibid.

44. U.S. Congress, Senate, Senate Report, No. 202, 65th Cong., 2nd sess., 1917.

45. Wilson to H.C. Early, 12 February 1918, quoted in Gospel Messenger, 2 March 1918, p. 136.

46. Peace Committee Minutes, 22 March 1918, American Friends Service Committee Archives.

47. Ibid., 23 March 1918.

48. Executive Committee Minutes, 1 April 1918, American Friends Service Committee Archives.

49. Ibid., 4 April 1918.

50. New York Times, 2 June 1918.

51. Jones to Swigert, 31 May 1918, File 29, Stoltzfus File.

52. Statement Authorized by the War Department and Text for the Order of the Secretary in Reference to Conscientious Objectors, 30 May 1918 (Washington, D. C.: War Department, 1918).

53. Jones to Swigert, 31 May 1918, American Friends Service Committee Archives.

54. Jones, A Service of Love in Wartime, p. 113.

The Black Legion: A Paramilitary Fascist Organization of the 1930s
by David J. Maurer

On the night of May 12, 1936, Charles A. Poole, a Works Progress Administration worker, was murdered on a rural road in Wayne County, Michigan. Ten days later, Duncan C. McCrea, Wayne County Prosecutor, prepared warrants for the arrest of seven men on a charge of murder.[1] The next day, Detroit newspapers told their readers that the alleged murderers were members of a secret paramilitary organization similar to the Ku Klux Klan. In the months that followed, grand juries and newspapers investigated the activities of the Black Legion.

The organization, according to fairly reliable evidence, was organized in Lima, Ohio sometime in 1931.[2] Virgil F. Effinger, an electrical contractor, wanted to save America "from communism, fascism, and any other kind of ism."[3] He appropriated some of the trappings of the Ku Klux Klan (ritual, organizational format, and prejudices) in creating his new organization. A veteran of the Spanish-American war, he decided on a paramilitary framework and styled himself as the "Major General" of the Black Legion.

The organization was basically military. It was composed of regiments made up of battalions which were made up of companies. Members of the organization were ranked into various degrees: Foot Legion, Night Riders, Black Knights, and a kind of praetorian guard, the Iron Guard. Recruiting efforts were undertaken primarily in Ohio, Michigan, and Indiana. Duncan McCrea's charge that the Black Legion was operating in fifteen or eighteen states is not supported by evidence in the Department of Justice files or other sources. Charges of Black Legion activity outside of the three north central states appeared in newspapers around the nation and in letters to the U.S. Department of Justice, but none of the accounts of lynchings, arson, and floggings offer any credible link to the Black Legion. Malcolm X's charge that the Black Legion was responsible for the burning of his family's home in 1929 and the murder of his father in 1931 is not supported by any evidence.[4] Probably a number of Klan-like organizations were promptly labeled the "Black Legion," once that organization's activities were exposed.

In 1936 Effinger claimed six million members nationwide. Sheriff George Gillis of Allen County, Indiana (Ft. Wayne), reported rumors of three to ten thousand members. Maurice Sugar, a Detroit labor attorney, estimated membership at between twenty and thirty thousand in Michigan "with perhaps one-third [of the members] being centered within the city of Detroit."[5] Membership probably numbered under fifty thousand in the three states, although one investigator believed that a figure close to one hundred thousand was possible.[6]

A Black Legion auxiliary was created by some of the "Regiments." According to one source, the women exchanged "recipes for lemon pie and talked about impending visits of the stork."[7] In addition to the regular organization, various front organizations were established. In Michigan, the Black Legion established or controlled the Wolverine Republican League, the

Wayne County Rifle and Pistol Club and the Twenty and Eight Club. In Ohio, some regiments called themselves the United Brotherhood of America. In Indiana, some of the membership styled themselves the Mystic Order of the Black Snakes.[8] Many members were or had been members of the Ku Klux Klan in Ohio, Michigan and Indiana. However, Ohio Grand Dragon James A. Colescott and the national Klan Imperial Wizard Hiram W. Evans denied any connection with the Klan.[9] As former Klan members, Legion recruits had no difficulty in accepting racist views or the outlandish Klan-like ritual. Arthur F. Lupp, Sr., identified as the leader of the Michigan Legion, noted that the attraction of the organization was its willingness to fight communism and attack any "un-American" organization whether "alien," "radical" labor, civil rights, or church.[10]

Organization literature claimed the Legion was anti-communist, anti-Catholic, anti-Jewish, and anti-Negro. One Legion tract asserted, in an evident desire to establish patriotic credibility, that the Legion was responsible for the Boston Tea Party and that the Minute Men were early members.[11] But the most important reason for a growing membership was economic. Legion recruiters acquired jobs or promised them to potential recruits. The lure of employment undoubtedly interested men suffering from the effects of the Depression. In Ohio, Legionnaires were enrolled on WPA projects in Allen County (Lima was Effinger's home town). Some evidence suggests that labor leaders or company officials were able on occasion to influence the employment of Legion members in the automobile plants. Others in Michigan found employment at the Pontiac State Hospital and with the municipal governments of Pontiac, Ecorse, Detroit, Highland Park, and Royal Oak.[12]

Walter White, NAACP Executive Secretary, speculated after reading a 1937 study of the Legion prepared by Professor Elmer Akers of the University of Michigan's Department of Sociology that

> one of the chief means of recruiting members in the Black Legion was their practice of getting jobs for newcomers from the South. I read several stories, for example, of how southern whites were given jobs almost upon arrival in Detroit while native-born whites who had lived in Detroit for some time were unable to find work. Was not this one of the reasons for the rapid growth of the Black Legion?[13]

Undoubtedly another recruiting device was the mystic fraternalism of the Legion. Effinger borrowed the regalia of the Klan and added a few embellishments. Members wore black robes and hoods with a pirate hat emblazoned with the skull and crossbones. A prospective member was initiated with a pistol pointed at his heart while swearing that he was a

> native-born, white, Protestant, gentile, American citizen...[and would] tear down, lay waste, despoil, and kill our enemies...[to] exert every possible means [to exterminate] the anarchist, Communist, the Roman hierarchy and their abettors... before violating a single clause or implied pledge [to] pray to an avenging God and an unmerciful devil to tear [his] heart out and roast it over the flames of sulphur...[14]

The initiate was then given a bullet and informed that his fellow Legionnaires kept a matching one which would be used in his execution if he violated his oath.[15] Perhaps a few of the initiates smiled inwardly at the ludicrousness of the ritual, but the majority seemed to accept the fanaticism inherent in the oath. Mrs. Margaret Dean, wife of the confessed killer of

Charles Poole, Dayton Dean, told the <u>Detroit Times</u> that the membership was prepared to murder, bonb, steal, and flog without remorse anyone judged by the members to be in violation of the code of the Black Legion.[16]

By 1934, enough members existed in Allen County, Ohio and Oakland County, Michigan for the leadership to try to influence local political activity. Although the Legion did not realize the kind of political power that it wanted to exercise and did not gain the political power of Ku Klux Klan in the early 1920's, the Legion did gain a little political influence even as it was frustrated at the ballot box.

Virgil Effinger was unable to win the sheriff's office in Allen county and a number of Legion-supported candidates in Oakland County were defeated in their bids for county and municipal offices.[17] Elmer Akers' study noted that the organization made little headway in its efforts to wield substantial political influence.[18] The Legion's political success was generally limited to some previously elected officials in Ohio and Michigan. Grand jury and newspaper reports indicated that relatively few elected officials were members. The Oakland grand jury report speculated that these individuals "would gladly forego the stigma of membership in the Black Legion" once the organization's activities were exposed.[19] However, the Legion did have some success in attracting membership in some of the public agencies--state hospitals, relief organizations, police and sheriff departments. Leadership ranks were filled by men in the lower echelons of local and state government (city inspectors, firemen, policemen, state hospital and relief organization employees, etc.), small businessmen, factory foremen, and would-be political figures. These individuals may have had some success in securing jobs for other Legion members, but a number of investigations failed to turn up any evidence of criminal conspiracy or violation of state or federal laws.

In 1935 the Federal Bureau of Investigation conducted an inquiry into the organization's activities in Lima, Ohio at the request of William Stanley, Assistant to the Unites States Attorney General. Its report indicated that the organization had many members in the local Federal Emergency Relief Admisistration and that the police department refused to take action against the Legion for its terrorist activities because the Chief of Police was a member of the Black Legion. The report concluded with the belief that there was no evidence of a violation of federal law.[20] On May 28, 1936, Carl Watson, Works Progress Administrator in Ohio, reported to Washington that an investigation into Black Legion activities revealed a high number of Legion members in the relief apparatus of Allen County, but "no present or former Black Legion member occupies any position under WPA that would permit him to influence labor policies or exercise discrimination."[21] The Oakland County investigation uncovered evidence of Legion membership in several of the police departments in the county but was unable to document criminal activity.[22]

Unable to develop any substantial political clout, the Black Legion seemed to turn increasingly to terrorist activities. The Legion's terrorist activities began shortly after its creation but reached full-flower between 1934 and the Poole murder in

1936. Members of the Black Legion confessed to setting fires at the homes of alleged communists, engaging in a plot ot kill William Voisine, the Village President of Ecorse, Michigan, and the murders of Charles A. Poole and Silas Coleman.[23]

Poole's murder by the Legion occurred because he had boasted of knowing Legion members and secrets and had allegedly beat his pregnant wife. Coleman was killed as a "thrill" because Legion members wanted to kill a black man. Bombs and arson were used to destroy the meeting places of communists and socialists in all three states and the Legion was accused of bombing Father Charles Coughlin's Shrine of the Little Flower in Royal Oak, Michigan. Other murders, attempted murders, arson, and bombings were alleged to have been committed by the Legion.[24] The successful prosecution of the murderers of Poole and Coleman and those involved in the attempted murder of Arthur L. Kingsley, editor of the Highland Park, Michigan newspaper, undoubtedly caused county prosecutors to forego further charges, since the alleged guilty parties had been sentenced to long prison terms.

By mid-1937, the Black Legion had ceased to exist and attempts to resurrect it failed. Indictments, imprisonment, grand jury reports, and newspaper accounts destroyed the organization. Members and potential members could not brave the general disgust and horror that most of the community had for the Legion. The best example of the popular revulsion from the Legion was the movie, Black Legion, directed by Archie Mayo, written by Robert Lord and made by Warner Brothers in late 1936 starring Humphrey Bogart. The picture made it clear that in spite of the patriotic purposes of some of the Legion members, the organization spawned terror, disrespect for the law, and subversion of the American way of life.[25]

The meteoric life of the Black Legion needs additional attention beyond the recital of the activities that the organization engaged in between 1931 and 1936. The first question a researcher with the advantage of a nearly fifty-year perspective that Professor Akers' 1937 study did not have would be, why was the Legion limited geographically? The answer seems to include several reasons. The leadership was limited to those with earlier Klan relationships and these men were limited to their acquaintanceship in the three-state area of Indiana, Michigan, and Ohio.[26] All three states had experienced migration from southern states where the Klan had been strong in the 1920s. The influx of unskilled laborers that supported the prejudices of the Klan was primed for Legion propaganda that attributed the nation's economic problems in the 1920s to those groups that were the traditional targets of the Klan. In Ohio, Indiana, and particularly in Michigan, jobs and promises of jobs could be made by Legion leaders because of their positions in local or state government, relief organizations, and certain industrial establishments in these states.[27] The same situation might have developed in other states if Klansmen or former Klansmen in hiring positions had been acquainted with the Ohio and Michigan leadership.

Another question regarding the Legion's success in Michigan was raised by labor leaders in 1936.[28] Homer Martin, president of the United Automobile Workers, testified before a congressional committee on his beliefs regarding the purpose of the Legion. "The anti-labor character of the Black Legion is definitely revealed by the murders of George Marchuk and Jacob Bielak, the latter a member of the AFL local of the Hudson Motor Car Company. Bielak was killed on the day following a stoppage of work in his plant department, of which he was the leader."[29] Marchuk was allegedly slain because of his union activity at Ford Motor Company.[30] Charges were made that Harry Bennett, Chief of Security at Ford, was supporting the Legion. Bud Simons, a labor activist in the 1930s, stated in an oral history interview that the "Black Legion played quite an important role in fighting the organization in the union."[31] Although Legionnaires were sometimes used as strikebreakers, the evidence of active participation and funding of anti-union activities by the auto companies in Detroit is slim. But what credible evidence exists suggests that shop superintendents and foremen were willing to be sympathetic to any movement that attempted to thwart unionization of their workers. John C. Leggett in his study of class consciousness in Detroit observed that these people felt labor organizations were a threat to capitalism and they were prepared to support fascist and crypto-fascist movements if necessary to protect "their system."[32]

Elmer Aker's sociological study of the Legion suggests that a primary reason for the success of the Legion was its ability to fill a social vacuum.[33] A great many of the Legion members were without the money to pay dues in various fraternal organizations and were without religious affiliation. The Legion provided legitimate social activities for women in the auxiliary and the men could join rifle club offshoots of the Legion. Illegitimate activities often provided an excitement to the otherwise drab existence of many trapped by the poverty of the Depression--especially if the violence was cloaked with the belief that the perpetrators were acting in the defense of white, Anglo-Saxon, Protestant America. The burning of the Worker's Book Store and Worker's Camp in Michigan was justified by the Legion as an attack on communism.

Many of the Legion members took pride in being part of what they believed was a growing nation-wide army. The leadership used the classic device of exaggerating the membership.[34] The device was so successful that after the Legion was exposed, newspapers, grand juries, and district attorneys reported, on the basis of testimony offered by Legion members, that the organization had millions of members and was active in most states. Only subsequently was it apparent that the average Legion member had been misled by the leadership.

Legion members believed that when the code word "lixto" was given, all Legionnaires would assemble with their arms and be prepared to either thwart a communist uprising or initiate their own coup d'état.[35] Typically, the leadership boasted that the Legion had friends in high places who were anxious to support the Legion in its fight against alien influences and would protect them in their capacity as dispensers of justice and "true" Americanism. Virgil Effinger allegedly stated that highly placed members of the U. S. Department of Justice were members of the Legion and they were helping the Legion. FBI investigation of the assertion failed to disclose any proof of this.[36]

The nativism and terrorism of the Legion, cloaked with patriotism and fraternalism, provided an outlet for frustration and boredom for those disaffected by the economic, political, and social turmoil of the mid-Depression years. The violence and attempts to acquire political influence could have been nation-wide if the original leadership had had acquaintanceships outside of Michigan, Indiana, and Ohio and had the exposure of the Legion's terrorist activities not come to light in 1936. Even so, the question whether the Legion could have become a truly significant organization is debatable. The violence of the Ku Klux Klan in the 1920s and the terrorism of the White Citizen's Councils in the 1950s caused revulsion in the majority of the American population. The popular reaction to the revelations of murder, arson, and violence of the Legion in 1936 demonstrated that the American public was generally opposed to such vigilantism. An attempt to reestablish the Legion in 1938 failed completely.

Notes

1. Urban Lipps, Harvey Davis, Dayton Dean, Irvin Lee, George C. Johnson, Paul R. Edwards, and Edgar Baldwin.

2. Report of Black Legion Activities in Oakland County, State of Michigan, In the Circuit Court for the County of Oakland, George B. Hartrick, Circuit Judge, Clinton McGee, Special Prosecuting Attorney, Filed with Clerk of the Court 31 August 1936; Morris Janowitz, "Black Legions on the March," America in Crisis: Fourteen Crucial Episodes in American History (New York: Alfred A. Knopf, 1952) ed. Daniel Aaron, p. 305.

3. J.M. Carlisle, "A Black Legion General," Detroit News, 29 May 1936.

4. Classified File 202600-2866, Department of Justice, Record Group 60, National Archives, Washington D. C.; Malcolm X [Little] with the assistance of Alex Haley, The Autobiography of Malcolm X (New York: Grove Press, 1965), pp. 3, 9-10.

5. Effinger statement in Lima News, 26 May 1936; Allen County Sheriff in Akron Beacon Journal, 28 May 1936; Maurice Sugar File, Box 7, Henry Kraus Collection, Archives of Labor History and Urban Affairs, Wayne State University, Detroit, Michigan.

6. J.M. Carlisle, "How Many Men in the Black Legion," Detroit News, 31 May 1936; Time, June 1, 1936, pp. 12-13; Nation, June 10, 1936, pp. 728-729.

7. Cleveland Plain Dealer, 29 May 1936.

8. Michael Clinansmith, "The Black Legion: Hooded Americanism in Michigan," Michigan History 55 (Fall 1971): 354 and Akron

Beacon Journal, 23 and 28 May 1936.

9. Akron Beacon Journal, 27 May 1936 and Lima News, 24 May 1936.

10. Detroit Free Press, 26 May 1936.

11. Akron Beacon Journal, 23 May 1936 and Cleveland Plain Dealer, 25 May 1936.

12. Carl Watson to Col. L. Westbrook, WPA Assistant Administrator, 28 May 1936, Box 610, Ohio, "State" Series, WPA Records, National Archives, Washington D. C.; Tracy Doll, U. A. W. official at Hudson, Oral History Transcript 24, pp. 7-8 and Wyndham Mortimer, V. P. of U. A. W., to Executive Offices [27 Sept. 1936], Box 1, Correspondence, Homer Martin Collection, Archives of Labor History and Urban Affairs, Wayne State University; Janowitz, "Black Legions on the March," p. 307; Detroit Free Press, 29 May 1936; Clinansmith, "Black Legion," p. 251; Report of Black Legion Activities in Oakland County, pp. 23-24.

13. Walter White to Elmer Akers, 28 February 1938, Akers Manuscript, Robert F. Wagner Papers, Georgetown University, Washington, D. C.

14. Report of Black Legion Activities in Oakland County, pp. 7-13; Dayton Dean, "Secrets of the Black Legion," Official Detective Stories, October 1, 1936, pp. 3-7, 35-37; George Morris, The Black Legion Rides (New York: Workers Library Publishers, 1936), p. 5.

15. Clinansmith, "Black Legion," p. 254.

16. Detroit Times, 2-7 June 1936.

17. Detroit News, 31 May 1936 and Report of Black Legion Activities in Oakland County, pp. 18-19.

18. Akers Manuscript, p. 16, Wagner Papers.

19. Report of Black Legion Activities in Oakland County, pp. 19-24.

20. Memorandum, 2 June 1936, 202600-2866, Section 1, Department of Justice, Record Group 60, National Archives.

21. Carl Watson to Col. Lawrence Westbrook, WPA Assistant Administrator, 28 May 1936.

22. Report of Black Legion Activities in Oakland County, pp. 18-23.

23. Akron Beacon Journal, 10 June 1936 and Detroit News, 22 May 1937.

24. Report of Black Legion Activities in Oakland County, pp. 25-28; Anna Damon for the International Labor Defense to Homer Cummings, 8 July 1936, 202600-2866, Section 2, Department of Justice, Record Group 60, National Archives; "The Necessity and Basis of an Investigation by the Senate Committee on Violations of Civil Rights and Collective Bargaining Into the Activities of the Black Legion," 1936, File PR, Box 12, Series 2, Civil Rights Congress of Michigan Collection, Archives of Labor History and Urban Affairs, Wayne State University, Detroit, Michigan.

25. Review of "Black Legion," Detroit News, 29 January 1937.

26. Lima [Ohio] News, 25 and 31 May 1936; Chicago Tribune, 24 May 1936; Akron Beacon Journal, 27 May 1936.

27. John L. Spivak, "Who Backs the Black Legion," New Masses, 23 June 1936, pp. 13-14; Report of Black Legion Activi-

ties in Oakland County, pp. 23-24.

28. Spivak, "Who Backs the Black Legion," pp. 9-10; Detroit News, 13 June 1936; Detroit Labor News, 3 July 1936; Memorandum on the Black Legion, Maurice Sugar File, Box 7, Henry Kraus Collection; United Automobile Worker [Detroit], 7 July 1936.

29. United Automobile Worker [Detroit], 7 July 1936.

30. "The Necessity and Basis of an Investigation... into the Activities of the Black Legion" and Black Legion--KKK, 1936, File PR, Box 12, Series 2, Civil Rights Congress of Michigan Collection.

31. Bud Simons, Oral History Interview, University of Michigan-Wayne State University Institute of Labor and Industrial Relations, September 6, 1960, Detroit, Michigan.

32. John C. Leggett, Class, Race, and Labor: Working-Class Consciousness in Detroit (New York: Oxford University Press, 1968), pp. 51-52.

33. Akers' Manuscript, pp. 6-8, Wagner Papers.

34. Lima News, 26 May 1936 and Cleveland Plain Dealer, 27 May 1936.

35. Report of Black Legion Activities in Oakland County, p. 31.

36. Memorandum, 2 June 1936, 202600-2866, Section 1, Department of Justice, Record Group 60, National Archives.

Governmental Planning in the Late New Deal

by Patrick D. Reagan

Wednesday, March 28, 1938 proved a trying day for Charles E. Merriam. Since July 1933, Merriam, a political scientist at the University of Chicago, had served on the New Deal's planning board. While his fellow planners Beardsley Ruml, Henry S. Dennison, and Frederic A. Delano took part in the economic recovery debate of 1937-1938, Merriam worried about the continued existence of the planning board. Merriam had just learned that the U.S. Senate was considering dropping a provision of the revised executive reorganization bill which would place the planning agency as a staff advisory group within a new Executive Office of the President. On that March day in 1938, Merriam began work on a memorandum for use by Senate Majority leader Alben Barkley to allay the fear of senators concerned that the reorganization bill was another attempt by President Roosevelt to extend executive authority at the expense of congressional prerogative.[1]

Merriam acted as a kind of philosopher of American national planning. He argued that the planning board should serve both the President and the Congress as an advisory staff agency availing itself of social scientific expertise while taking into account the interest group politicking that dominated the American political economy. Merriam viewed national planning from a broadened perspective as "governmental planning" which went beyond physical planning, conservation of natural resources, planning of public works projects, or support for moderate New Deal economic reforms. He defined national planning as process rather than as blueprint. The planning board which the reorganization bill proposed would carry on work accomplished since July 1933:

> The [proposed] National Resources Planning Board would be wholly advisory in its functions, without any executive power whatever. This board would collect the facts, analyze and interpret them, and from time to time make various suggestions to the President and Congress. The Board proposed is not an executive planning board, or a legislative planning board, but strictly and solely an advisory planning Board.[2]

Since his days as an independent Republican alderman in Progressive-era Chicago, Merriam had come to see planning, personnel, and budget making as interrelated parts of the process of governmental administration. In his dual roles as vice chairman of the planning agency and member of the President's Committee on Administrative Management, Merriam was instrumental in attempting to bring order to the national planning process. He hoped to make federal governmental administration as efficient as that of private corporations.[3]

From 1937 to 1939, Roosevelt's planners took part in two of the most significant reform efforts of the late New Deal. The recession of 1937-1938 revived the policy debate over retaining orthodox economic policies inherited from the 1920s or drastically shifting toward deficit spending measures. A number of scholars continue to refer to the debate as a turning point in New Deal economic policymaking which inaugurated "the Keynesian revolution" in fiscal policy. Herbert Stein dramatically refers to the debate as "The Struggle for the Soul of FDR," while more recently Albert Romasco terms the debate, "The Crisis of the New Deal Program." Traditional accounts of the 1937-1938 debate begin with the orientation of intellectual history in assuming the influence of British economist John Maynard Keynes via his The General Theory of Employment, Interest and Money (1936). Actually, the course of the debate had little to do with Keynes or Keynesian economics in light of the role of the New Deal planners. More central to the economic policy recommendations of Ruml, Dennison, and Delano was the idea of compensatory spending policy while balancing the federal budget over the course of the business cycle as a way to promote economic stabilization and to avoid social upheaval.[4]

For Merriam the idea of applying corporate efficiency concerns to the running of the federal government hardly sounded new. As Barry Karl has noted, executive reorganization and reform had roots as far back as the late nineteenth century.[5] Leadership of the reorganization movement in the 1930s came naturally to Merriam who saw it as part of the process of advisory national planning. While his fellow planners joined the debate over economic recovery, Merriam simultaneously took up the cudgels for reorganization. In the process, the planners acted just as they argued advisory national planning should act in the American context.

The New Deal planning board began as an outgrowth of ideas originally broached in one of the subcommittees of the Unemployment Conference of 1921 directed by Secretary of Commerce Herbert

Hoover. In 1931 Congress passed the Economic Stabilization Act sponsored by Senator Robert F. Wagner (D-N.Y.). The act created an agency to plan a shelf of public works projects which could then serve as an economic balancing wheel promoting stabilization in recessionary times. Title II of the National Industrial Recovery Act of 1933 established the National Planning Board as an adjunct to the Public Works Administration. President Roosevelt appointed Charles E. Merriam, Frederic A. Delano, and Columbia University institutional economist Wesley Clair Mitchell as members of the operative Advisory Committee of the NPB. In late 1935, Mitchell resigned from the board to continue his work as research director of the National Bureau of Economic Research. In consultation with Roosevelt, Secretary of Commerce Daniel C. Roper, and PWA Administrator Harold Ickes, Merriam and Delano decided to replace Mitchell with a two-member Advisory Committee comprised of representatives of the business community. They chose liberal businessman Henry S. Dennison, head of a paper manufacturing firm in Framingham, Massachusetts and Beardsley Ruml, treasurer of the New York City-based R.H. Macy's Department Stores. Merriam had worked closely with Ruml throughout the 1920s in founding the Social Science Research Council. He had met Dennison while serving on President Hoover's Research Committee on Social Trends (1929-1933).[6]

Initially the planning board restricted itself to developing plans for the shelf of public works projects, but with the release of the June 1934 *Final Report*, the definition of planning had expanded considerably. From 1934 to 1937 the planning agency broadened its research focus beyond public works planning to include pioneering studies in conservation of natural resources, the social impact of technology, declining population, and the structure of the economy. The planners supported creation of two regional planning groups in New England and the Pacific Northwest, state planning boards in a majority of the states, and consideration of more extensive public works measures.[7]

With the explicit recognition of business interests by the addition of Ruml and Dennison, the planning agency moved into the more controversial arena of economic policy advising. None of the planners had more than a passing acquaintance with changing ideas in the economics profession that later scholars would capture in the term "the Keynesian revolution." Rather, their ideas stemmed from their own practical experiences in the 1920s and participation in a variety of economic discussion groups amidst the recession of 1937-1938. Each of the planners played a somewhat different role in the recovery debate: Dennison as educator of his fellow businessmen, Ruml as informal policy adviser within government circles, and Delano as mediator between the orthodox budget-balancing group around Secretary of the Treasury Henry Morgenthau, Jr. and the "spenders" centered around Chairman Marriner Eccles of the Federal Reserve Board of Governors.[8]

Dennison's whole career pointed toward his acceptance of advisory national planning during the New Deal. From 1900 to 1936 the common threads tying together Dennison's work included the extension of managerial rationalization from the firm-specific to the trade industry to the national level, the necessity and usefulness of socioeconomic research, careful study of the business cycle, and promotion of economic stabilization efforts. After reorganizing the family firm, the Dennison Manufacturing Company, between 1911 and 1916, he broadened his horizons to establish a reputation as a liberal businessman.[9]

During World War I, Dennison followed his friend Edwin F. Gay, first Dean of the Harvard Business School, into war mobilization work. As Gay's assistant in the Planning and Statistics divisions of the Shipping Board and the War Industries Board, Dennison helped collect economic statistics, promote stabilization efforts, and plan for war production. Gay and Dennison went on to found the federal Central Bureau of Planning and Statistics. Dennison rapidly came to believe in the necessity of cooperation between business and government and the importance of research as noted in his founding of the Twentieth Century Fund with fellow Boston businessman Edward A. Filene in 1919 and work as business representative to President Wilson's First Industrial Conference in October 1919.[10]

Dennison's work with industrial trade associations, the Taylor Society, private individuals, and government committees during the New Era of the 1920s helped form his idea of planning. His own firm began corporate planning in 1919, when its Research Department predicted a downturn in the business cycle for late 1920. Dennison argued that firms should cut back on investment, purchasing, and production before the peak in the cycle. Firms should increase expenditures for advertising, sales, credit, and new product lines during slow periods. Dennison probably began developing these ideas after 1914 in discussions with Dean

Wallace B. Donham of the Harvard Business School and business cycle economist Wesley Clair Mitchell of Columbia University. He kept up the discussions with these people throughout the 1920s.[11]

By 1929 Dennison seemed the perfect choice to write the "Management" chapter for a landmark study in economic research sponsored by a continuing subcommittee of the Hoover-inspired Unemployment Conference of 1921. Recent Economic Changes in the United States (1929) received partial financial support from the Laura Spelman Rockefeller Memorial directed by Beardsley Ruml. In his essay, Dennison emphasized the long-range impact of the managerial revolution led by corporate businessmen since the late nineteenth century. He argued for the necessity of cooperation among businessmen in trade associations, the usefulness of social scientific research, and the emergence of corporate-oriented industrial planning. Help might come from the federal government. Between 1929 and 1933, Dennison tried to implement these recommendations through formation of a Business Reseach Council modeled after the Merriam-Ruml initiated Social Science Research Council founded in 1923. The onset of the Depression, lack of concerted interest from corporate businessmen, and failure to garner funds from the Rockefeller Foundation put a premature end to that effort.[12]

From 1933 to 1936, Dennison honed his corporate liberal views in work with the U.S. Chamber of Commerce's Committee on the Continuity of Business Employment and the Department of Commerce's Business Advisory and Planning Council (BAPC). During discussions in a Harvard study group at the same time, Dennison developed the idea of a "plan for planning." His interest in business cycle research led in the direction of a moderate compensatory spending policy. When his own faith in corporate leadership faltered as the Depression deepened, Dennison turned toward the idea of governmental planning as a way to enact industrial self-government--the older notion of the business commonwealth revived. While on the BAPC, Dennison met Ralph Flanders of the Jones and Lamson Company of Springfield, Massachusetts and Morris Leeds of the Leeds and Norththrup Company of Philadelphia. Dennison, Flanders, and Leeds joined in 1935 with Dennison's old Boston business friend, Lincoln Filene, to search for a way out of the economic morass. They eventually moved toward consideration of a full employment economy based on high production and high consumption--a transmogrification of New Era capitalism from the 1920s.[13]

To guide him through the thicket of economic theory, Dennison hired a young economist, John Kenneth Galbraith. Dennison and Galbraith influenced one another before publishing their work as Modern Competition and Business Policy (1938). They argued for a middle way between an outmoded policy of antitrust prosecution and total government control of the economy. Later that same year--during and immediately after the policy debate of 1937-1938--Dennison, Filene, Flanders, and Leeds published Toward Full Employment. The authors recommended a combination of policies including adoption of compensatory spending over the course of the business cycle, creation of a flexible federal budget, careful use of more traditional monetary policy, and federal income tax reform to increase federal revenue during recessions. The recommendations included both old and new ideas without endorsing permanent deficit spending policy. They hoped to educate fellow businessmen about the need for pragmatic, flexible policies that would promote recovery and aid in stabilizing the economy. Dennison did discuss economic matters with some members of the Harvard economics seminar directed by Alvin Hansen and John Williams, but no record exists as to its significance. Dennison and his fellow businessmen never sought to so outpace orthodox monetary and fiscal policy that federal government expenditures would displace private investment as the predominant force for economic growth. The bottom line came in the area of predominant control. For these liberal businessmen, corporate control--industrial self-government--remained the ideal toward which economic policy should converge.[14]

While Dennison hoped to move businessmen toward an accommodation with government in a corporate liberal sense, Beardsley Ruml quietly moved within governmental circles as an informal "man of ideas" and sometime policy adviser. Ruml started his career in the emerging field of psychological testing with a doctorate from the University of Chicago. He moved on to work with the pioneering applied psychologist Walter Van Dyke Bingham at the Carnegie Institute of Technology before joining the Committee on Classification of Personnel in the Army in the Adjutant General's Office during mobilization for World War I. After a short-lived effort in industrial consulting work, Ruml rejoined his old University of Chicago mentor, James R. Angell, at the Carnegie Corporation. In 1921 President Angell and assistant Ruml of the Corporation developed the use of "income warrants" which committed present funds for future projects of the philanthropy. They ultimately committed $30 million of the Carnegie Corporation's funds in their brief one-year tenure. One Corporation official later intriguingly suggested that the policy was akin to Keynesian spending policy. Angell and Ruml did not stay around long enough to reveal whether the policy possibly could have remained permanent.[15]

When Angell left the Corporation in 1921 for the presidency of Yale University, he recommended Ruml for work with Rockefeller family surveys. Family adviser Raymond B. Fosdick and John D. Rockefeller, Jr. liked Ruml's work so well, they appointed him director of the Laura Spelman Rockefeller Memorial in 1922. Ruml now headed a philanthropy with a principal of over $74 million and an annual working capital of $4 million. Ruml went to work reorienting the focus of the Memorial's grants away from female and child welfare toward a consciously planned program. He hoped to support the creation of a national social science research network centered on large research universities, private research bodies, and cooperative governmental bureaus. Twenty-six per cent of the total funds granted within the United States by the Memorial from 1923 through 1927 went toward supporting the Merriam-inspired Social Science Research Council and research projects in the social sciences at Merriam's own school, the University of Chicago. The Memorial also granted funds for research done by Wesley Clair Mitchell's National Bureau of Economic Research for the committee which produced <u>Recent Economic Changes</u> (1929) and for financing of President Hoover's

Research Committee on Social Trends (1929-1933). Chairman Wesley Clair Mitchell and vice chairman Charles Merriam of the latter committee wrote the summary chapter of the final report in <u>Recent Social Trends in the United States</u>, published in the spring of 1933, which recommended establishing an advisory national planning agency. Several months after public release of the report, President Franklin D. Roosevelt appointed Mitchell and Merriam as two of the three members of the New Deal's National Planning Board. Advisory national planning moved from the Hooverian New Era to the Rooseveltian New Deal. Philanthropic manager Ruml eased the way.[16]

While not directly tied to economic policy concerns, Ruml's work as director of the Memorial should be seen in the broader light of the long-range effort at planning and financing research in the social sciences at the national level, promoting business-government cooperation, and using a kind of compensatory spending policy in philanthropic grants over the course of the early business cycle of such new organizations as the Social Science Research Council. In 1929 Rockefeller trustees decided to merge the Memorial with the larger Rockefeller Foundation. Ruml sided with the more modern corporate-oriented trustees to argue for administrative reorganization of the Foundation with functionally divided divisions operating through an overall staff and line structure. The new Social Science Division took over most of the Memorial's work but not all. Research in public administration would be supported by the new Spelman Fund of New York initially headed by Ruml and then by Merriam. The Spelman

Fund provided funds for the establishment of New Deal state planning boards that were sponsored by the governmental planning agency.[17]

After a brief tenure as dean of the new Social Science Division at the University of Chicago, Ruml in 1934 took the position as treasurer of R.H. Macy's Department Stores in New York City. By late 1937, Ruml became a quiet, but influential policy adviser with access to officials within the Roosevelt administration. He played some role in the development of the domestic allotment plan, part of the New Deal's agricultural policy, and in committee discussions which led to drafting of the Social Security Act of 1935. The particulars are unknown. In late 1937 Ruml wrote Leon Henderson suggesting the idea of partial forgiveness of federal income tax debts as a way of temporarily and indirectly creating increased purchasing power. Nothing came of the idea in 1937. On April 1, 1938 while on his way to visit the Macy's store in Atlanta, Ruml received a call from Harry Hopkins, Leon Henderson, and Aubrey Williams to attend an informal meeting at Pine Mountain Valley near Roosevelt's Warm Springs, Georgia retreat. The memorandum--written by Ruml--that emerged from the meeting served as Hopkins' backup for a meeting with Roosevelt regarding the appropriate policy response to the recession. The end result involved Roosevelt's famous turn toward a resumption of spending policy called for in his April 14, 1938 address to Congress. Roosevelt used whole sections of the memorandum in almost verbatim form. Ruml did not refer to Keynesian theory or permanent deficit spending policy. He argued that the federal government had historically stimulated purchasing power through alienation of the public lands, land grants to railroad corporations, and tariff protection for emerging industries. Rather than promote expanded production through governmental fiat--the path taken by Soviet Russia, Fascist Italy, and Nazi Germany--Ruml called for government spending to take up the slack left by lagging private investment. Government spending could then stimulate consumption which would in turn leave open "competition" which he thought "indispensable." To promote an increase in national income, Ruml said "that hand in hand with government spending must go the risking of private capital." Though not clearly stated, Ruml implied that compensatory spending could only be a temporary policy course which would be abandoned after an increase in private investment, employment, and production.[18]

Roosevelt received even more authorization for spending than he asked for in April 1938, but the larger issue remained unresolved--would this economic policy become permanent? Dennison clearly thought not. Ruml's advocacy of a flexible budget and the tax cut alternative to direct deficit spending from 1943 on would indicate he thought not as well. We do know that both Dennison and Ruml discussed matters with the "spenders" in the informal groups centered around the employees of Marriner Eccles' Federal Reserve Board of Governors. Yet as Dean Lowe May has noted in his recently published history of the response to the recession of 1937-1938, Eccles came to fiscal policy via the unusual circumstances of the Mormon economy in Utah where he worked as a banker. At best then, the policy process of 1937-

1938 did not resolve the long-range issue, but settled on the compromise solution that some form of spending by the federal government was necessary both to promote economic recovery and to preserve the political economic equilibrium through economic stabilization. Only the massive deficit spending to prosecute World War II would confirm a distinct trend toward Keynesian fiscal policy as advocated by a small group of younger professional economists.[19]

Frederic A. Delano moved into the economic policy debate as a kind of mediator between the Morgenthau-Treasury-budget balancing / Eccles-Federal Reserve Board-spending factions. Prior to 1933, Delano had been a more prominent individual than his nephew, Franklin Delano Roosevelt. From 1886 to 1914, Delano moved up the managerial ladder of the Chicago, Burlington and Quincy Railroad. As a member of the Commercial Club of Chicago, Delano helped architect Daniel Burnham gain business support for the famous 1907 Chicago City Plan. After brief service on the first Federal Reserve Board, Delano worked as Director of Transportation for the American Expeditionary Force in France during World War I. He then shifted toward city and regional planning. In 1921, Delano joined his old Chicago friend Charles D. Norton on the Regional Plan of New York and Its Environs. Through the American Civic Association's Committee of One Hundred, Delano helped bring regional planning to Washington, D.C. with the creation of the National Capital Park and Planning Commission in 1926. Delano served as the Commission's head from 1929 through 1943.[20]

Like Dennison, Ruml, and Merriam, Delano sought a middle way out of the economic problems of modern American industrial capitalism. Since his days as a railroad manager, Delano had advocated creating "a community of interest" among business, labor, and government. For most of the 1920s and into the early 1930s, this meant advocating a transformation of the older ideal of voluntary association in the private sector with a new role for the federal government. After election of his nephew to the presidency, Delano wholeheartedly supported New Deal programs. Between July 1933 when he became acting head of the planning board and August 1943 when the agency was abolished, Delano served as the go-between man within the board, among other government officials, and between Roosevelt and private businessmen. After Roosevelt's call for resumption of spending on April 14, 1938, Delano acted on a Ruml memorandum which proposed creation of a new advisory group, the Fiscal and Monetary Advisory Board. The agency would include Secretary of the Treasury Morgenthau, Chairman Eccles of the Federal Reserve Board of Governors, Budget Director Daniel Bell, and a representative of the National Resources Committee, the new name of the planning agency. When Morgenthau proved reluctant about institutionalizing the economic policy dialogue, Delano turned to President Roosevelt who approved the idea. The Board met from late 1938 until swallowed up and forgotten in the defense production effort after June 1940.[21]

While Dennison, Ruml, and Delano played key roles in the debate over economic recovery in 1937-1938, they never advocated permanent deficit spending policy. Delano's private correspondence reveals contradictory ideas mixing older economic orthodoxy and guarded support for short-run compensatory spending policy. Dennison and Ruml argued in a non-theoretical way that lacked the sophistication of later professional Keynesian economists that in severe economic times, the government could compensate for a falling off of private investment as a temporary policy over the course of the business cycle to restore economic stability. Robert M. Collins has noted that Keynesian fiscal and monetary policy advocates were ranged in several variant factions--"pump primers," "compensatory spenders," and the more well-known "interventionists" or "stagnationists." Yet he mistakenly identifies both Dennison and Ruml as "proto-Keynesians" in the compensatory spending group. The planners sought to give general advice which would both promote economic stabilization and avoid the dangers of social upheaval. Their ideas stemmed from personal experience and institutional connections between 1900 and 1938 as well as discussions with businessmen, people at Harvard University and the Harvard Business School, and members of the Eccles' faction in Washington, D.C.[22]

In May 1939, Henry Dennison, probably the most theoretically sophisticated of the planners, testified before the Temporary National Economic Committee regarding the role of government spending for public works. When pressed to comment on the impact of government spending, he replied, "Under the present situation I don't see how [government spending] could amount to more than a fraction of the contribution [toward the restoration of prosperity]." Dennison went on to say that "I think the principal thing is to look for private expenditure." Just over three years later, Beardsley Ruml proposed his famous Pay-As-You-Go tax plan which foreshadowed his postwar advocacy of the tax cut alternative to permanent direct deficit spending that would be taken up by the Committee for Economic Development which he helped establish in 1942. Robert M. Collins has detailed the growth of this "commercial Keynesianism"--though his terminology retains the traditional scholarly fascination with the intellectual history of those professional economists calling themselves Keynesians rather than focusing on the actual policy advisers on the postwar Council of Economic Advisers.[23]

While the national economic policy of federal compensatory spending aimed at promoting cooperation between business and government, the issue of executive reorganization sought to bring corporate administrative efficiency to the presidency. As leader of the reorganization forces, Charles E. Merriam hoped to integrate planning, personnel, and budget making in an advisory staff structure. Part of his concern lay in resolving the ambiguous status of the planning board. Established by Title II of the National Industrial Recovery Act in July 1933, the planning agency lost legislative status with the Supreme Court's May 1935 decision invalidating the Recovery Act. Between 1936 and 1939, Roosevelt continued the board through the use of executive orders and line appropriations under the public works and emergency relief acts of 1936-1938. Efforts to create a permanent planning organization through congressional action from 1936 through 1939 came under political attack from conservative Democrats, Republicans, old progressives, and even a few New Deal Democrats. These politicians argued that reorganization represented Roosevelt's latest effort to abuse executive power following in the wake of the Supreme Court "packing" plan and the attempted purge of conservative Democrats in the election of 1938. Merriam worked for reorganization in the midst of this hostile political climate.[24]

The immediate origins of the reorganization movement lay in a complex organizational network built up during the 1920s. After completion of the Hoover-sponsored Recent Social Trends volumes (1933), Merriam took a proposal to continue some of the work to the Problems and Policy Committee, the policy planning body of the Social Science Research Council (SSRC) created with Laura Spelman Rockefeller Memorial funds in 1923. The policy committee appointed a subcommittee consisting of Merriam, Ruml, and popular economist Stuart Chase which in turn recommended creation of a Special Committee of Inquiry on Public Service Personnel. New Deal planning board members Merriam and Delano convinced Executive Director Robert T. Crane of the SSRC and their superior, Public Works Administrator Harold Ickes, to seek presidential sponsorship of the effort to implement recommendations of President Hoover's Research Committee on Social Trends. In November 1933, Roosevelt approved the idea, but refused to give official sanction or money. The group then asked for and received $57,500 to conduct the study from the Spelman Fund of New York. Luther Gulick of the Institute for Public Administration at Columbia University served as research director. Upon completion of its work in the area of civil service, the Special Committee hoped to spark a broader study of executive reorganization.[25]

While Merriam took the idea to his colleagues on the planning board, Louis Brownlow, head of both the Public Administration Committee of the SSRC and the Public Administration Clearing House on the University of Chicago campus, sent the idea to President Roosevelt through Harold Ickes. Cooperation which extended from President Hoover's Research Committee on Social Trends through the SSRC and the Spelman Fund through the planning board led to Roosevelt's appointment of the President's Committee on Administrative Management on March 20, 1936. On the Committee sat Luther Gulick, Louis Brownlow, and Charles E. Merriam. Commonly referred to as the Brownlow Committee, the group worked through 1936 and into early 1937 on a huge study of the executive branch searching for ways to rationalize agencies created in the wake of the New Deal.[26]

Yet rising congressional opposition to the growth of executive power, bureaucratic infighting among government agencies, protection of pork barrel turf by politicians, and fear of the only new idea--creation of a permanent national planning board--led to defeat of the administration bills of 1937 and 1938 that came out of the study. By April 3, 1939 a compromise reorganization bill emerged from Congress which established the modern presidency. The bill set technical specifications for civil service work, created the Executive Office, brought the old Bureau of the Budget into the executive branch, and provided for six administrative assistants for the President.[27]

But no provision for a permanent planning agency existed in

the revised bill of 1939. Roosevelt again had to temporize in creating the National Resources Planning Board (NRPB) within the new Executive Office of the President through Reorganization Plan No. 1 and Executive Order 8248. Opposition to the possibility of permanent federal deficit spending surfaced in the economic policy debate of 1937-1938. Similar political opposition to a permanent planning board created by legislative authority arose in the reorganization controversy of 1937-1939. Neither Roosevelt nor the planners squarely faced the rising tide of political resistance in Congress. In the 1943 appropriations hearings for the NRPB, these same two issues cropped up. This time political resistance aimed at curbing Roosevelt's wartime extension of executive power led to abolition of the planning board amidst charges by critics that the planners were advocating adoption of permanent spending policies for the postwar period.[28]

The planners' participation in the economic recovery debate and the executive reorganization controversy in the late New Deal revealed their conception of an advisory national planning process. Dennison, Ruml, and Delano moved toward acceptance of a moderate compensatory spending policy based on balancing the federal budget over the course of the business cycle and hinted at the tax cut alternative to direct deficit spending. Their ideas came from their own experiences between 1900 and 1938 rather than from any self-consciously emerging school of professional economics later termed "Keynesian." Their program intended to promote business-government cooperation as a way to both stabilize the economy and preserve the social peace that had disappeared in other parts of the world. Merriam sought executive reorganization as a way to make federal governmental administration more efficient, i.e. more businesslike.

The planners' advocacy and practice of governmental planning in the late New Deal indicates that Barry Karl's recent suggestion of a "Third New Deal" may not be so off the mark as a first reading might imply. Construed more broadly, the planners can be viewed as one part of the wider evolution of the corporate liberal world in twentieth-century America discussed in the works of such scholars as Ellis W. Hawley, Kim McQuaid, and Robert M. Collins.[29] Like other modern liberals, Roosevelt's planners sought to preserve the best of nineteenth-century American voluntary values and institutions while wrestling with the implications of the new organizational society that was urban-industrial America in the twentieth century. We know that the corporate liberals never won total victory, but at times they played key policy-making roles. Governmental planners in the late New Deal acted as part of this larger historical process in their attempt to deal with the issues of national economic policy responses to the recession of 1937-1938 and perceived needs to make executive branch organization and administration both more modern and more efficient in the wake of the New Deal response to the Great Depression.

Notes

1. Richard Polenberg, Reorganizing Roosevelt's Government, 1936-1939: The Controversy Over Executive Reorganization (Cambridge, Ma.: Harvard University Press, 1966), especially pp. 134-135; Barry D. Karl, Charles E. Merriam and the Study of Politics (Chicago: University of Chicago Press, 1974), pp. 226-283; Charles E. Merriam, "Planning Agencies in America," American Political Science Review 29 (1935): 197-211 and "The National Resources Planning Board: A Chapter in American Planning Experience," Ibid. 38 (1944): 1075-1088.

2. [Charles E. Merriam], "Memorandum on a National Resources Planning Board," 23 March 1938, File F-VIII, Papers of the President's Committee on Administrative Management, Franklin D. Roosevelt Library, Hyde Park, New York, hereafter cited as FDRL.

3. Charles E. Merriam, "Investigation as a Means of Securing Administrative Efficiency," Annals 41 (May 1912): 281-303 and "Budget Making in Chicago," Annals 62 (November 1915): 270-276; Steven J. Diner, A City and Its Universities: Public Policy in Chicago, 1892-1919 (Chapel Hill: University of North Carolina Press, 1980); Karl, Charles E. Merriam, pp. 61-83.

4. On the economic recovery debate, see Theodore Rosenhof, Dogma, Depression and the New Deal: The Debate of Political Leaders Over Economic Recovery (Port Washington, N.Y.: Kennikat Press, 1975) and "New Deal Pragmatism and Economic Systems: Concepts and Meanings," The Historian 49 (1987): 368-382; Melvin D. Brockie, "Theories of the 1937-38 Crisis and Depression," The

Economic Journal 60 (1950): 292-310; Kenneth Roose, The Economics of Recession and Revival: An Interpretation of 1937-38 (New Haven: Yale University Press, 1954). Quotations are from chapter titles in Herbert Stein, The Fiscal Revolution in America (Chicago: University of Chicago Press, 1969) and Albert U. Romasco, The Politics of Recovery: Roosevelt's New Deal (New York: Oxford University Press, 1983). For standard accounts of the Keynesian revolution, see The New Economics: Keynes' Influence on Theory and Public Policy, ed. Seymour E. Harris (New York: Alfred A. Knopf, 1947); Robert Lekachman, The Age of Keynes (New York: Random House, 1966); Alan Sweezy, "The Keynesians and Government Policy, 1933-1939," American Economic Review 62 (May 1972): 116-124; John Kenneth Galbraith, "How Keynes Came to America," originally published in New York Times Book Review, May 16, 1965, and reprinted in Galbraith's A Contemporary Guide to Economics, Peace, and Laughter (1971: New York: New American Library, 1972); Robert M. Collins, The Business Response to Keynes, 1929-1964 (New York: Columbia University Press, 1981), pp. 1-20.

5. Barry D. Karl, Executive Reorganization and Reform in the New Deal: The Genesis of Administrative Management, 1900-1939 (Cambridge, Ma.: Harvard University Press, 1966), pp. 37-81 and Peri E. Arnold, Making the Managerial Presidency: Comprehensive Reorganization Planning, 1905-1980 (Princeton: Princeton University Press, 1986), pp. 81-117.

6. Patrick D. Reagan, "From Depression to Depression: Hooverian National Planning, 1921-1933," Mid-America, forth-

coming; Delano to Ickes, 21 September 1935, Merriam to Delano, 16 October 1935, Delano to Ickes, 2 December 1935, Roper to Ickes, 3 December 1935, Ickes to FDR, 3 December 1935, all in 153.3, Central Office Correspondence, 1931-43, Record Group 187, Records of the National Resources Planning Board, National Archives, Washington, D.C. Merriam's work with Ruml in the 1920s is discussed briefly in Karl, Charles E. Merriam, pp. 118-139, while Merriam's friendship with Dennison is noted in correspondence in Box 28, Merriam Papers.

7. Byrd L. Jones, "A Plan for Planning in the New Deal," Social Science Quarterly 50 (1969): 525-534; Charles E. Merriam and Leon Henderson, "Emerging Industrio-Governmental Problems," November 9, 1939, Box 184, Charles E. Merriam Papers, Univesity of Chicago Library; Albert Lepawsky, "Style and Substance in Contemporary Planning: The American New Deal's National Resources Planning Board as a Model," Plan Canada 18 (September-December 1978): 153-187; Philip W. Warken, A History of the National Resources Planning Board, 1933-1943 (New York: Garland Publishing, 1979).

8. The best work on the Morgenthau/Eccles factional debate is Dean Lowe May, "New Deal to New Economics: The Response of Henry Morgenthau, Jr. and Marriner S. Eccles to the Recession of 1937," Ph.D. dissertation, Brown University, 1974 published as From New Deal to New Economics: The Liberal Response to the Recession of 1937 (New York: Garland Publishing, 1980). Lowe briefly discusses the role of the planners on pp. 99-102, 202-204, 212-215, 229-232 of the dissertation.

9. Patrick D. Reagan, "The Architects of Modern American

National Planning," Ph.D. dissertation, Ohio State University, 1982, pp. 146-195.

10. Herbert Heaton, A Scholar in Action: Edwin F. Gay (Cambridge, Ma.: Harvard University Press, 1952), pp. 98-138; articles in Quarterly Publications of the American Statistical Association 16 (March 1919); Adolf A. Berle, Jr. Leaning Against the Dawn: An Appreciation of the Twentieth Century Fund (New York: Twentieth Century Fund, 1969), pp. 3-24; Henry S. Dennison and Ida Tarbell, "The President's Industrial Conference of October, 1919," Bulletin of the Taylor Society 5 (April 1920): 79-92.

11. Dennison-Donham correspondence in 1921, General Correspondence, 1919-1923, Dean's Office Records, Archives of the Harvard Graduate School of Business Administration, Cambridge, Massachusetts; Dennison, "Management and the Business Cycle," Journal of the American Statistical Association 18 (March 1922): 20-31; Johnson Heywood, "How the Dennison Manufacturing Company Meets the Slumps," Advertising and Selling Fortnightly, March 11, 1925, pp. 15-16, 72-75; Dennison-Mitchell correspondence in Business Cycles file, Henry S. Dennison Papers, Archives of the Harvard Graduate School of Business Administration.

12. Henry S. Dennison, "Management," President's Conference on Unemployment, Committee on Recent Economic Changes, Recent Economic Changes in the United States (New York: McGraw-Hill, 1929), II, pp. 495-546 and Business Research Council file, Dennison Papers.

13. America Faces the Future, ed. Charles A. Beard (New

York: Vanguard, 1932), pp. 196-264; Kim McQuaid, "The Business Advisory Council of the Department of Commerce, 1933-1961: A Study in Corporate/Government Relations," Research in Economic History 1 (1976): 171-197; Dennison, "Planning," memorandum for BAPC meeting of March 5, 1932, 153.3B, Record Group 187; Dennison, "A Five Year Plan for Planning," August 1932, Dennison Papers; Dennison, "Suggestions for a Popular Presentation of Planning" and correspondence among Dennison, Flanders, Leeds, and Filene, Ralph Flanders Papers, Syracuse University, Syracuse, New York.

14. John Kenneth Galbraith, A Life in Our Times: Memoirs (Boston: Houghton Mifflin, 1981), pp. 61-67; Dennison and Galbraith, Modern Competition and Business Policy (New York: Oxford University Press, 1938); Dennison et al. , Toward Full Employment (New York: Whittlesey House, 1938) and correspondence regarding the book in Flanders Papers; Office Diary entries for August 7 and 10 and November 18, 1937 and May 12, 1938, Dennison Papers. Dennison, Ruml, and Delano all worked with the Federal Reserve system at some point. Dennison was Deputy Director and Chairman and Director of the Federal Reserve Bank of Boston from January 1938 through 1945. Ruml was appointed by Eccles to replace the resigning Owen D. Young for the New York Federal Reserve Bank in the summer of 1937 and served until December 1946. Delano had worked as an agent for the Richmond Federal Reserve Bank from 1921 through 1936.

15. Alva Johnston, "The National Idea Man--I, II, and III," The New Yorker, February 10, 17, 24, 1945, respectively 28-32 ff., 26-30 ff., 30-34 ff.; C. Hartley Grattan, "Beardsley Ruml

and His Ideas," Harper's Magazine, May 1952, pp. 78-86; Daniel Kevles, "Testing the Army's Intelligence: Psychologists and the Military in World War I," Journal of American History 55 (December 1968): 565-581; "The Reminiscences of Samuel S. Hall, Jr. (1968)," pp. 27-34 and "The Reminiscences of Francis Keppel (1967)," p. 5, Columbia Oral History Collection.

16. Leonard Outhwaite, "The Life and Times of the Laura Spelman Rockefeller Memorial," typescript, Outhwaite Papers, Rockefeller Archive Center, Tarrytown, New York; Raymond B. Fosdick, The Story of the Rockefeller Foundation (New York: Harper & Brothers, 1952), pp. 134-148, 192-209; LSRM, Annual Reports (New York: LSRM, 1922-1933); per centage figures from "Appropriations for Social Science and Social Technology Made by the LSRM up to December 1, 1927," Box 63, Subseries 6, Series I, LSRM Collection, Rockefeller Archive Center; Barry D. Karl, "Presidential Planning and Social Science Research: Mr. Hoover's Experts," Perspectives in American History 3 (1969): 347-409; President's Research Committee on Social Trends, Recent Social Trends in the United States (New York: McGraw-Hill 1933), Vol. I, p. lxxiii.

17. SSRC, Decennial Report: 1923-1933 (New York: SSRC, 1934); Fosdick, Story of the Rockefeller Foundation, pp. 134-144, 202-209; Abraham Flexner, Funds and Foundations: Their Policies Past and Present (New York: Harper & Brothers, 1952), pp. 77-83; Robert E. Kohler, "A Policy for the Advancement of Science: The Rockefeller Foundation, 1924-29," Minerva 16 (1978): 480-514; Spelman Fund of New York: Final Report (New York: Spelman Fund,

1949).

18. Henderson to Ruml, 1 November 1946, Ruml, "Remarks by way of Introduction to the CED Tax Fiscal Policy Proposals of 1947," Ruml, Warm Springs Memorandum, 1 April 1938, Memorandum of E[meline] N[ollen] Conversation with Leon Henderson for Ruml Memoirs, all in Beardsley Ruml Papers, University of Chicago Library; Aubrey Williams to Ruml, 14 September 1938, Aubrey Williams Papers, FDRL; Hopkins to David Lynch, 10 November 1942, FDR--Monopoly Message, 1938 File, Harry L. Hopkins Papers, FDRL; "Leon Henderson in the Lion's Den" clipping in L-H Speeches-Etc.-Postwar File, War Production Board Papers, Leon Henderson Papers, FDRL; The Public Papers and Addresses of Franklin D. Roosevelt (New York: Macmillan, 1940), Vol. 1938, pp. 221-248.

19. May, "New Deal to New Economics," pp. 66-102, 130-137, 192-206, 209-215, 230-237, 251-259; Rosenhof, Dogma, Depression and the New Deal, pp. 50-58, 113-132; Romasco, Politics of Recovery, pp. 226-240; Stein, Fiscal Revolution, pp. 165-196. For evaluations of the impact of the spending policy see E. Cary Brown, "Fiscal Policy in the Thirties: A Reappraisal," American Economic Review 46 (1956): 857-879; Larry Peppers, "Full-Employment Surplus Analysis and Structural Change: The 1930's," Explorations in Economic History 10 (Winter 1973): 197-210; Byrd L. Jones, "The Role of Keynesians in Wartime Policy and Postwar Planning, 1940-1946," American Economic Review 62 (May 1972): 125-133.

20. David Cushman Coyle, "Frederic A. Delano: Catalyst," Survey Graphic, July 1946, pp. 252-254; Delano, "The Chicago Plan with Particular Reference to the Railway Terminal Problem,"

Journal of Political Economy 21 (1913): 819-831; Michael P. McCarthy, "Chicago Businessmen and the Burnham Plan," Journal of the Illinois State Historical Society 63 (Autumn 1970): 228-256; World War I Papers, Series I, Frederic A. Delano Papers, FDRL; Harvey A. Kantor, "Charles Dyer Norton and the Origins of the Regional Plan of New York," Journal of the American Institute of Planners 39 (1973): 35-42; American Planning and Civic Association folder, Series I, Delano Papers; Frederic Gutheim for the Commission, Worthy of the Nation: The History of Planning for the National Capital (Washington, D.C.: Smithsonian Institution Press, 1977), pp. 139-233.

21. Delano, "Our Recent Crisis and the Future," Review of Reviews, December 1932, pp. 27-29 and "Shifting Bureaus at Washington," Review of Reviews, May 1933, p. 33; materials in PPF 72, FDRL; Delano-FDR correspondence,, OF 72, FDRL. On the Fiscal and Monetary Advisory Board see Delano-Morgenthau correspondence on 12, 27, 28 April 1938, Morgenthau Diaries, FDRL; Charles W. Eliot, II, "Confidential Memorandum of Conference with the President, June 6, 1938," Box 174, Merriam Papers; Albert Lepawsky, "The New Deal at Midpassage," University of Chicago Magazine 67 (Summer 1975): 29-35.

22. Collins, Business Response to Keynes, pp. 8-10, 63-71. Cf. Kim McQuaid, Big Business and Presidential Power: From FDR to Reagan (New York: William Morrow, 1982), pp. 186-187.

23. U.S. Congress, Temporary National Economic Committee, Hearings (Part Nine: Savings and Investment), testimony of Henry S. Dennison on May 22, 1939 (Washington, D.C.: Government

Printing Office, 1940), pp. 3786-3787; materials on Tax Plan of 1942-43 in Box II, Ruml Papers; Collins, Business Response to Keynes, pp. 77-209 and "American Corporatism: The Committee for Economic Development, 1942-1964," The Historian 44 (1982): 151-173.

24. Warken, History of the NRPB, pp. 38-104; Richard Kalish, "National Resource Planning: 1933-1939," Ph.D. dissertation, University of Colorado, 1963; Marion Clawson, New Deal Planning: The National Resources Planning Board (Baltimore: John Hopkins University Press for Resources for the Future, 1981), pp. 52-63, 210-218; Polenberg, Reorganizing Roosevelt's Government.

25. Minutes of the Problems and Policy Committee of the SSRC, 25 February 1933, Box 146, Crane-Merriam correspondence, Box 47, and Merriam-Soule-Ruml correspondence of June-July 1933, Box 56, Merriam Papers; correspondence in OF 868, FDRL; SSRC Commissions 1934 file, Box 26, William F. Ogburn Papers, University of Chicago Library; Notes on Development of Spelman Fund Policy and Program, Box 157, Merriam Papers; Harold F. Gosnell, "Commissions of Inquiry Appointed by the SSRC in 1933," Box 131, Merriam Papers; File A-II-5, Papers of the President's Committee on Administrative Management, FDRL, hereafter PCAM Papers.

26. Merriam to Bruce Bliven, 15 April 1938 and Merriam to Delano, 4 October 1935, Merriam Papers; Ickes to FDR, 20 December 1935, OF 285, FDRL; Ickes to FDR, 8 February 1936 and Merriam to Brownlow, 20 February 1936, Merriam Papers; Memorandum on Conference with the President, 4 March 1936, File A-II-7, PCAM Papers; Louis Brownlow, "Management Study," 16 March 1936,

Merriam Papers.

27. Polenberg, Reorganizing Roosevelt's Government.

28. Kalish, "National Resource Planning," passim and Philip L. White, "The Termination of the National Resources Planning Board," M.A. thesis, Columbia University, 1949.

29. Barry D. Karl, "In Search of National Planning: The Case for a Third New Deal," paper delivered at the Organization of American Historians' convention, Cincinnati, Ohio, April 1983 and The Uneasy State: The United States From 1915 to 1945 (Chicago: University of Chicago Press, 1983), pp. 160-181. On the debate over the nature of corporate liberalism, see David W. Eakins, "The Development of Corporate Liberal Policy Research in the United States, 1885-1965," Ph.D. dissertation, University of Wisconsin, 1966; James Weinstein, The Corporate Ideal in the Liberal State: 1900-1918 (Boston: Beacon Press, 1968); R. Jeffrey Lustig, Corporate Liberalism: The Origins of Modern American Political Theory, 1890-1920 (Berkeley: University of California Press, 1982); Ellis W. Hawley, The Great War and the Search for a Modern Order (New York: St. Martin's Press, 1979); Guy Alchon, The Invisible Hand of Planning: Capitalism, Social Science and the State in the 1920s (Princeton: Princeton University Press, 1985); special issue on corporate liberalism of the Business History Review 52 (Autumn 1978); Ellis W. Hawley, "The Corporate Ideal as Liberal Philosophy in the New Deal," The Roosevelt New Deal: A Program Assessment Fifty Years After, ed. Wilbur J. Cohen (Austin: Lyndon B. Johnson School of Public Affairs, 1986), pp. 85-103; McQuaid, Big Business and Presidential Power; Robert M.

Collins, "The Persistence of Neo-Corporatism in Postwar Business-Government Relations," paper delivered at the Organization of American Historians' convention, Detroit, Michigan, April 1981; Robert Griffith, "Dwight D. Eisenhower and the Corporate Commonwealth," American Historical Review 87 (1982): 87-122; Thomas J. McCormick, "Drift or Mastery? A Corporatist Synthesis for American Diplomatic History," Reviews in American History 10 (1982): 318-330; John Lewis Gaddis, "The Corporatist Synthesis: A Skeptical View," and Michael J. Hogan, "Corporatism: A Positive Appraisal," in Diplomatic History 10 (1986): respectively, 357-362 and 363-372.

Ambassador Claude G. Bowers and the Chilean Decision to Break
Relations with the Axis Powers, September 1939-January 1943
by Jack Ray Thomas

In the early years of World War II, Chile and the United States became embroiled in a diplomatic skirmish that threatened the long-term friendly relationship between the two nations. The problem centered around Chile's reluctance to sever diplomatic relations with Germany, Japan and Italy and ultimately to declare war on them. Chile's stance conflicted with Washington's desire to bring all of Latin America into line on the Allied side in the struggle. After the outbreak of World War II in Europe, the neighbors clashed over this issue until finally in January 1943, Chile broke diplomatic relations with the Axis. But the disagreement was a serious one for both nations and taxed the diplomatic skill and patience of both governments before it was finally resolved.

Through the decade of the 1930s, the United States had tried to create a policy of unity in Latin America.[1] President Franklin Roosevelt's Good Neighbor Policy was an effort to dispel the old Latin American hostility toward the United States, and, at the same time, to create a union of nations that would act in concert relative to events that transpired outside the hemisphere. Therefore, with the coming of war in Europe the United States wanted the Latin Americans to remain aloof from the struggle. But when Japan attacked Pearl Harbor, Washington changed immediately and now, as a participant in the war, hoped to gain solid support from its neighbors. Most of the Latin American countries immediately broke diplomatic relations with the Axis and some declared war. However, the long sought unanimity of action was blocked by the refusal of Argentina and Chile to agree to an anti-Axis policy. Argentina was particularly adamant in its refusal to oppose the Axis. Therefore, Secretary of State Cordell Hull aggressively applied pressure to force a diplomatic rupture, but without immediate success. His Argentine policy created a great deal of enmity toward the United States, even among Argentinians who were not sympathetic to the Axis, but who resented Yankee meddling in what they regarded as their internal affairs.[2]

The Roosevelt administration did not pursue the same strategy against Chile, even though the Chilean government's refusal to break diplomatic relations with the Axis caused almost as much anguish in the State Department as Argentina's independent course of action. But Chile had some advantages over Argentina in its dealings with the United States. Chile was a democracy with a government that had come to power in a free election in 1938, while Argentina was dominated by the military. United States Ambassador to Chile, Claude G. Bowers, related that Chile's Foreign Minister, Juan B. Rossetti, told him that Argentina was in a difficult position relative to the United States because pro-Nazis were in the Argentine army and government. Rossetti went on to tell Bowers that Chile was more fortunate. Bowers wrote, "He said the army here is democratic and that the higher officers are all friends of [President] Aguirre Cerda."[3] Consequently, Chile, regarded as one of the most stable, democratic regimes in Latin America at the time, was valuable to Washington as an example of the virtue of democracy over dictatorship. High ranking officials in Santiago made it clear, although usually off the record, that their sympathies were with England and the United States, and that they were not averse to breaking diplomatic relations with Germany and Japan.[4] Yet they refused to make the break quickly, because they believed a sufficiently large proportion of their population opposed such action strongly enough to unleash a disastrous internecine clash that could damage the democratic tradition of Chile and plunge the nation into a bitter civil war. Arguments such as these satisfied the State Department for a time, but later only increased Washington's exasperation with Chile's recalcitrance.

To understand Chile's reluctance to sever diplomatic relations with the Axis and to declare war on those nations, Chilean history during World War I and between the wars must be taken into account. At the time of the First World War, Chile was in the midst of political turmoil and the Santiago government refused to break relations with the Kaiser's Germany. The result was an economic bonanza for Chile, as she furnished critical primary materials for Europe. Chile's copper and nitrates were in great demand throughout the war, increasing the nation's foreign trade and thereby strengthening the economy. This fact was in the minds of government leaders when World War II broke out in 1939.[5]

More pressing reasons for remaining neutral in World War II

were Chile's domestic economic problems and continuing political chaos. From 1920 to 1940, the country was in a severe financial crisis. When Arturo Alessandri entered the presidential office in 1920, he learned of the monetary plight of the nation. When he set out to work up a budget for 1921, he found the national coffers empty. The 1921 budget was spent before the end of 1920 and the economic future looked exceedingly bleak.[6] To his credit, Alessandri made some progress during the early years of his administration, but then in 1924 the military became restless and Alessandri was overthrown and exiled. A military government took over under the direction of Major Carlos Ibanez del Campo who ruled as a dictator until 1931. Ibanez was a typical Latin American dictator, but he too managed to make some economic progress until 1929, when the world-wide depression struck. Once again the nation floundered, and at that point a military officer with socialist inclinations led an insurrection that overthrew Ibanez and set up the short-lived Socialist Republic of Chile. There followed more confusion and considerable political infighting and intrigue, until Alessandri emerged once again as the legal president in 1933. Now, however, Alessandri was not as liberal as he had been in 1920. Having experienced the overthrow of his government and exile to Europe, Alessandri tended to be more concerned with maintaining control over the nation and less committed to reform than in his first term. Meanwhile, a variety of political parties fought for popular support. A Christian Falange movement emerged, while the Communist Party grew slowly and the more powerful Socialist Party continued to expand. On the right, the old Conservative Parties were joined now by the less liberal, Liberal Party. More importantly, for the immediate period, the Nazi Party under the leadership of Jorge Gonzalez von Marees gained more and more adherents. Between right and left, the Radical Party occupied the middle ground. At the close of the decade of the 1930s, the Radicals comprised the strongest single party in the nation. Still, they were not likely to gain the presidency alone, because the Conservative-Liberal alliance could still outpoll them.

In 1936, the Radicals approached the left-wing parties with the idea of a coalition resembling that which had been arranged in Spain and France; a coalition that could defeat the Liberal-Conservative union. Fortunately for the Radicals, Moscow called for the cooperation of its Communist parties around the world with other reform groups at this time. This was a reversal of earlier policy of remaining apart from such coalitions. The Democrats also agreed to join, realizing that alone they had little strength but allied with other parties, they might become part of a victorious alliance and thereby gain positions in the cabinet. With the three parties in agreement, the only major left-of-center group outside the coalition was the Socialist Party, but its participation was crucial because of its size; in the proposed union only the Radicals had greater numbers. At first, the Socialist leadership refused to join on the grounds that the already existing Block of the Left coalition performed the very same function and that the parties should concentrate on that union and forget about European Popular Front ideas. But the Popular Front was a more binding arrangement and the potential for such an alliance appeared limitless. Finally, the Socialist leadership consented and the Popular Front was created.[7]

In a nominating convention, the Radical Party candidate, Pedro Aguirre Cerda, was chosen as the Popular Front's presidential candidate. He subsequently won the 1938 presidential election.[8] While this election was legitimate and Aguirre Cerda was a competent president, Chile was not able to ease its political and economic distress despite the widespread hope people placed in the Popular Front regime. For this reason then, when the Second World War broke out in Europe, the Chilean government wanted to ignore it if possible and concentrate on solving its own problems.

Still another reason for Chile's refusal to break diplomatic relations was the large immigrant population of Germans, Italians and Spaniards in the nation. Many of these people still had emotional ties to their home countries, and they did not want their adopted land to go to war against their former countrymen.[9] The southern provinces were heavily populated by Germans, many of whom held dual citizenship and did not want to break their ties to Germany. Some lived along the border with Argentina where they maintained contact not only with other German-Chileans, but with German-Argentines as well. In any election, these German-Chileans possessed voting strength, and when aligned with Italian and Spanish fascist immigrants their political influence soared. At the outset of the war, most Chileans were not fearful of the Fascist and Nazi immigrants; some influential Chileans even applauded these foreigners. But the government in Santiago had to concern itself with the immigrants and their voting strength and with all the domestic problems the nation faced, governmental leaders did not want to add to their difficulty by touching off civil strife with the European immigrants.[10]

For these reasons, Chile did not join the other Latin American countries that, with the exception of Argentina, broke diplomatic relations with the Axis. When the United States entered the war, Chileans now had a new concern: the possibility of a Japanese attack on their long, exposed, practically indefensible, 3200 mile coastline on the Pacific Ocean.[11] Chileans were not alone in the Western hemisphere in fearing an eventual invasion from Asia. Every other Latin American country that bordered on the Pacific felt the same way, and the United States also expected an invasion in California or the state of Washington. In this atmosphere, the Chilean government held firm to its position of remaining neutral. For the Chilean people, this decision made a great deal of sense. The old cliche that they had everything to lose and nothing to gain rang true in their ears. It was for them a reasonable stance that Under Secretary of State for Latin American Affairs Sumner Welles, Secretary of State Cordell Hull, and President Rossevelt could not fully grasp and that led to many diplomatic clashes between the two nations before Chile finally broke diplomatic relations and then declared war.

The United States position in the diplomatic maneuvering resulted from its desire to build hemispheric solidarity in the face of Axis aggression. If the Axis tried to gain a foothold on the continent, a Latin American union of nations, joined by the United States, could come to the assistance of any one country assaulted. Consequently, the United States believed this unified position crucial throughout the war. As late as 1945, Secretary of State Edward R. Stettinius emphasized the policy of unification. His predecessors, Cordell Hull and Sumner Welles, made the same point frequently during the early stages of the war. In addition to the fear of Nazi penetration into Latin America, there was constant concern for the safety of the Panama Canal. Latin American nations at war with the Axis, even if their declarations of war would be largely symbolic, could be asked to assist in protecting the canal. Chile would become especially important if the Canal were closed, because shipping between the Atlantic and Pacific coasts of the United States would have to pass through the Straits of Magellan which were controlled by Argentina and Chile.

While in the throes of this diplomatic disagreement, the United States was fortunate in having Claude Bowers as its Ambassador to Chile.[12] Bowers had a measure of influence in the upper echelon of the State Department even before he arrived in Chile, largely because of his long career in national Democratic Party politics. A self-proclaimed Jeffersonian Democrat, he worked hard for local Democrats in Indiana, and eventually he went to Washington to serve as personal secretary to a midwestern senator. He also ran unsuccessfully for Congress on two different occasions. After writing a couple of political histories that were well received, he went to work as a journalist for the New York World where he consistently publicized his party's views in a political column. By 1928 he also had acquired a reputation as a forceful orator delivering the keynote address at the Democratic National Convention held that year. During his lengthy association with the party, Bowers came to know Franklin Roosevelt and Cordell Hull reasonably well. This friendship with the future president and future secretary of state was a distinct advantage for Bowers after he entered the diplomatic corps.

After Roosevelt was elected in 1932, he appointed Bowers ambassador to Spain. In that capacity, Roosevelt told him to write directly to the White House when significant events occurred that Bowers thought should be made known to the president.[13] Later when civil war ravaged Spain, Bowers counseled support for the Loyalist forces, but the State Department called for a hands-off policy and the Spanish fascists, with Axis support, triumphed. With the fascists in power, their archenemy Bowers was no longer welcome in Spain. He was reassigned to Chile in 1939, where he remained for the next fourteen years.

Bowers' experience in Spain gave him a credibility within the State Department that enabled him to calm some of those who wanted to apply heavy pressure on Chile to break diplomatic relations with the Axis. Most State Department officials and Roosevelt himself told Bowers that he had been right about Spain and those who had refused to help the Loyalists had made a mistake.[14] Bowers' relationship with Roosevelt and Hull also gave him an opportunity to openly disagree with policy and provide his own substantial contribution to the decision-making process relative to Chile. Bowers was in a strong position, because his policy of patience with Chile could not be assailed as pro-Nazi. Bowers was one of the very few United States diplomats to understand clearly the threat of Nazi Germany to the United States and to oppose early the Axis power that was developing in Europe.[15]

With a solid diplomatic reputation bolstered by a good working relationship with his superiors, Bowers was able to push the idea of a patient policy toward Chile. This did not mean that some members of the State Department would not seek to apply pressure, or that Bowers himself did not, in a variety of discreet ways, seek to line up the Chilean government behind the United States, but Bowers was able to soften the impact of those who tried to force Chile into a diplomatic break with the Axis early in the war.

Bowers and the State Department did not always fathom the internal Chilean difficulties that influenced the nation's foreign relations decisions. Prior to Pearl Harbor when Popular Front President Aguirre Cerda was in office, he received nominal support from the Chilean Nazi Party even though the Popular Front was a moderate leftist coalition. The Nazis supported Aguirre not because of any ideological affinity, but because they hated and feared his major opponent in the 1938 election, Gustavo Ross Santa Maria. Ross had been a prominent member of the preceding government headed by Arturo Alessandri. Near the end of Alessandri's administration in 1938, a group of Nazi college students launched an insurrection that was quickly suppressed by the national police. Some sixty of the young men were rounded up and held prisoner on an upper floor of the Seguro Obrero (Social Security) Building located just across the street from the presidential offices. While no one has ever been able to prove Alessandri's implication in what transpired, the Nazis believed that he gave the order to slaughter the men on the spot.[16] This carnage convinced the Nazi leaders in Chile that they would be better off even with a slightly left-of-center president, than with one who might more closely approximate their political views, but who had the blood of Nazi youth on his hands.

Because of the electoral support he had received from the Nazi Party, Aguirre was loathe to take action against that party at home or against Germany abroad when the war began. He maintained this attitude throughout his tenure as president.[17] While Aguirre was a man of strong democratic tendencies, he was enough of a politician to understand that political debts had to be honored. Aguirre, like many other Chileans, was anything but certain about the outcome of the war in its early years. As the German army raced through Europe with apparent ease, Chileans suspected that Hitler might emerge victorious. Should this happen, they did not want to be alienated from a Germany that dominated Europe. Chilean historian Ricardo Donoso noted that so long as Germany was winning, Chilean public opinion did not line up against the admired and respected Germans. However, when the Allies invaded North Africa on November 8, 1942, Chileans concluded that the initiative had passed to the Allies, and public opinion began to swing away from support of Germany.[18] Ambassador Bowers also believed that so long as Germany had a chance to win the war, Chile would remain neutral. Ernesto Barros Jarpa, a leading Chilean politician and for a time Foreign Minister, was convinced that Germany would either win the war or it would end in a stalemate. In either case, if Chile remained neutral, she would be in a better position to benefit from postwar trade with the Axis nations.[19]

Still another reason for Chile's reluctance to support the Allies was the nagging suspicion that Argentina, which strongly supported the Axis cause, might attempt to invade Chile, if the Chileans threw in their lot with the Allies. Public statements had been made by Argentine officials to the effect that Argentina needed a port on the Pacific Ocean in order to be a truly great nation. One way such a port could be acquired would be by taking some of Chile's territory.[20] As late as December 1944, Chilean leaders still feared Argentine aggression. Bowers wrote that, "There is no question that the President (now Juan Antonio Rios) and his Foreign Minister (Joaquin Fernandez) are rather seriously worried about the intentions of Argentina vis-a-vis its neighbors."[21]

It has been suggested that an even more compelling reason for Chile's refusal to cut her ties with the Axis was that she hoped to force the United States into providing her with more material aid and a better trading agreement in exchange for a break in relations with the Axis. However, there is little evidence to support this view. In fact, under the Lend Lease program the United States offered Chile fifty million dollars worth of military equipment over a five-year period for which

Chile would have to repay only fifteen million dollars. Yet, the Chileans exasperated Hull and Welles by refusing to take up the offer immediately. Instead, the Chilean Foreign Ministry found countless reasons why the agreement should be rewritten time and time again. Negotiations dragged on for almost a year, until Hull finally set a deadline after which the offer would be withdrawn. This was hardly the action of a government that was trying to extort material from Washington.[22]

Ambassador Bowers, sensitive to all these Chilean concerns, was also aware that there was a group of pro-Axis politicians who, while in the minority, could cause extensive trouble for the Popular Front government. Every action involving the United States had to be carefully scrutinized so as not to give ammunition to the pro-Axis forces for their rather extensive propaganda network.[23]

Meanwhile, prior to Pearl Harbor, Washington wanted to limit the apparent growth of German influence in Chile. At the same time, the British feared that Germany was establishing a network of agents that could sabotage the nitrate and copper industries at any given moment, and they convinced the State Department that Axis subversion was a real possibility throughout the country. In September 1939, the chief of German espionage in South America, Walter Scharpp, arrived in Santiago, lending greater weight to the English argument that Chile was a primary target for the Germans.[24] Rumors also circulated widely that the Nazis were stationing spies around the country to prepare for the overthrow of the Chilean government. By the spring of 1940, many North Americans in Chile and in Washington, and even some

Chileans, were convinced that the Germans planned a coup d'état for the near future.[25]

As the rumors of Nazi subversion circulated widely throughout Chile, the United States Embassy made an effort to check out each one. Ambassador Bowers did not get overly excited about the threat of a German incursion into Chile, but he was concerned about the strides made by German propagandists and about the growth of Nazi influence inside the Chilean government. At one point, the Nazis worked through sympathetic officials in the Chilean Ministry of Interior to censor a film, The Nazi Spy, which depicted the Germans in an unfavorable manner. Bowers believed that the Minister of the Interior might be leaning toward the Germans, and he was certain that the man's brother was a Nazi. He concluded that "I am afraid that the Government itself, including the army, is honey-combed with Nazi spies." To underscore this assessment, the same theater from which the pro-British film was banned showed a pro-Nazi film, The Storm Trooper, over the objections of the British Embassy.[26]

Meanwhile, public opinion in the United States speculated on German infiltration in Chile. In June 1940, the New York Times acknowledged that there had been no definite proof of German fifth column work in Chile according to a Santiago police department report. But the same article pointed out that some Santiago newspapers were unconvinced by the investigation and insisted that Nazi activity pointing toward an eventual takeover of the nation was continuing.[27] There was widespread talk of Nazi plans to destroy power plants, water supplies, and railroads.[28]

In July 1940, the *Times* sent a reporter to Chile to investigate the allegations, and he wrote a lengthy article on the Nazi propaganda and sabotage efforts. He found the group of German-Chileans to be the best financed Axis subversion force in all of Latin America. He concluded that this organization was so extensive that everything was in place for an assault on Santiago whenever the signal should be given from Berlin. That order, he thought, would come when the United States entered the war on the side of the Allies. He worried about Nazi infiltration into government circles but concluded that "The responsible heads of the government are generally regarded as sincere advocates of democracy, and friends of the United States and opposed to any foreign interference in Chilean affairs, but Nazi intrigues are said to have corrupted some minor national and local officials." The reporter went on to comment on Nazi influence in the Chilean army. In the nineteenth century, the army had been trained by German officers who were greatly respected and admired by most Chilean military men. Contact with Germany had continued throughout the twentieth century. The army even dressed like the Germans, right down to the distinctive German-style helmets. Even more dramatic was the Chilean army's adoption of the German "goose step" when marching. Therefore, the reporter was apprehensive about the way the army would go in the event of an attempted German takeover. Like others in Chile, he was not certain of the outcome.[29]

Another fear among North Americans was that Hitler was in a position to dominate the Chilean economy, thereby forcing the nation into dependence on Germany. Loss of markets due to the war made Santiago vulnerable, and a "worsening depression" pushed Chile closer to economic disaster.[30] In this period of economic downturn, Nazis tried to console Chilean businessmen by telling them that when the war ended in Germany's favor, Berlin would buy Chilean products at better prices than the Allies and the United States were then paying. North American companies found that this tactic had some success when they learned that many of their orders had been canceled, especially for products such as heavy machinery, hardware and electrical equipment which the Germans were trying to sell to foreign markets. Before the war, Germany bought 52 percent of Chilean agricultural production. From 1930 to 1935 when Chile had no money, she bartered to get the needed imports. This barter arrangement enabled the Germans to get a three million dollar railway equipment order. In an effort to offset the German advantage, the United States Export-Import Bank loaned Chile twelve million dollars.[31]

One Chilean writer suggested that the separate nations of Latin America were always going to be at a disadvantage in dealing with large countries like the United States and England, unless they joined together economically to form a large, economic unit throughout the region which might at some time in the future lead to political union. But, using Hitler and Mussolini as examples, he wrote that for such a union to work all economic and political freedom would have to be suppressed just as in Germany and Italy. Few Chileans were willing to take such a drastic step.[32]

Assisting the German cause in Chile in the early war years

was the Communist Party which was part of the Popular Front government. Hitler and Stalin had a non-aggression pact, and pro-Allied groups feared that the Communists would create disorders during which the Germans would have a pretext for stepping in to save the nation from Communism and to restore law and order. This concern ended on June 22, 1941, when Hitler marched into Russia, thereby making the Chilean Communist Party an automatic supporter of the Allies.[33]

Even without Communist assistance, violent acts continued to be perpetrated by the Nazis, until the Chilean government finally lost its patience. In August 1941, police raided a number of German strongholds in the South, confiscating official papers and documents. From the information they collected in these raids, Chilean police arrested several Nazis, including three who worked in the German Embassy in Santiago. Two of the three claimed diplomatic immunity, including the commercial attache. He had earlier openly boasted of his association with a subversive organization. United States diplomatic personnel believed he would have been declared persona non grata long before, had the Chilean government not feared reprisals from Germany.[34]

Despite the official position of ignoring German subversion and propaganda activity, some individual Chileans spoke out against the danger inherent in coddling the Axis. One outspoken writer attacked the entire concept of pacifism in World War II. He argued that neutral nations played into Nazi hands and that Hitler used peace and neutrality to benefit himself. But when it was to his interest, he would attack former neutral nations in Latin America just as he had in Europe. The writer concluded,

"We cannot be misled about peace. It is a Nazi strategy but the goal remains world dominance."[35]

Despite periodic raids on suspectd Nazis, the Chilean government continued to publicly insist that no serious Nazi anti-government activity was taking place in the nation. Following Pearl Harbor and United States entry into the war, the Chileans still moved slowly against subversive agents. In April 1942, Raul Morales became Minister of the Interior and Prime Minister. He confided to Bowers that he could find no background information on subversion and fifth column action in the department's files. He asked Bowers for any United States information that might be available. Bowers was pleased to pass it all along to him.[36] Soon thereafter, authorities discovered that a private phone wire between the Ministry of Marine in Santiago and the headquarters of Naval Authorities in Valparaiso had been tapped by some German youth living in a dormitory near the line. The official German explanation was that the young men had attached a wire to the naval line as an antenna for their innocent radio. One report said the line had been used exclusively for secret communications on the movements of foreign and Chilean vessels in Chilean waters. But the Popular Front government was unmoved by all the revelations, and the policy of neutrality continued.[37]

From May through September 1942, Nazi propaganda and sometimes sabotage plagued the Chilean government. One police raid netted eighty-four packages of dynamite in the house of a Nazi party member, while other raids turned up explosives in the homes of other Nazis.[38] The police believed that the dynamite was to be used to disrupt communications and spread terror throughout the country. Nazi Party leader, Gonzalez Von Marees, denied that his party had any such intention. He insisted that the whole issue of bombs and explosives was a police effort to distract attention from the assassination of a retired army officer.[39] This facile explanation was discounted by Washington. The United States press speculated that there was an extensive Nazi sabotage plan for Chile that would so preoccupy the nation that the government would never break diplomatic relations with the Axis nations.[40]

Events ultimately convinced the Chilean government that some significant action had to be taken. When the Chamber of Deputies named a committee to investigate Nazi subversion, the United States diplomatic corps could only sigh that it was about time! Ambassador Bowers wrote, "It is incredible that any Chilean with any desire to maintain his country's dignity and independence should cling to the asinine idea that Chile can stay neutral and escape the fate of all the would-be 'neutral' countries of Europe."[41] When word of Chile's determination to investigate Nazi activity reached the United States, the press hailed the action and reported that various groups, including the Socialist Party, were now committed to the severance of diplomatic relations with the Axis nations as soon as practicable.[42]

The United States continued to express concern over Nazi espionage in Chile throughout the second half of 1942. Radio transmitters were uncovered that were being used to notify German submarines of Allied shipping off the Chilean coast. Bowers constantly provided evidence of subversive action to the Chilean government. But while some raids on Nazi groups were carried out and some Nazis were arrested or expelled from the country, the government steadfastly refused to sever diplomatic ties. In one typical incident, a famous Chilean writer, Benjamin Subercasseaux, published an article in the Santiago newspaper, La Nación, charging that "Nazi espionage has a free hand in Chile." But the Minister of Foreign Affairs, Ernesto Barros Jarpa, denied any knowledge of espionage and announced that Subercasseaux would be prosecuted for unwarranted criticism of his government. Bowers had shown Barros Jarpa intercepted messages to Berlin on ship movements which supported Subercasseaux's charges, but the foreign minister claimed no knowledge of such activity. The ambassador wrote in his diary, "In other words the Minister deliberately lies." The United States embassy was willing to employ a good lawyer to defend Subercasseaux, but when the case came to trial the writer was acquitted without Bowers' assistance. By that time, however, Barros Jarpa had been replaced as foreign minister, and the government was moving toward rupture of relations with the Axis although still at a very deliberate pace.[43]

Upon the death of President Aguirre Cerda, Juan Antonio Rios was elected to the presidency. He sought to improve the relationship of his government with Washington by announcing a good will tour of the United States. Plans were launched in the spring of 1942, but no firm date was agreed upon. From time to time, a general schedule was floated for diplomats on both sides, but when the time approached something always seemed to come up to interfere with the President's departure.[44] On August 13, President Roosevelt sent Rios a personal invitation. It appeared that the visit finally was going to materialize. But in October 1942, Undersecretary of State for Latin American Affairs, Sumner Welles, delivered a speech in Boston that so infuriated the Chileans that relations immediately became strained. Welles said in part that Chile and Argentina were stabbing their neighbors in the back by not breaking diplomatic relations with the Axis nations which were carrying out espionage activity in those countries that could spill across their borders and damage other Latin American nations.

President Rios immediately suspended consideration of his trip to the United States. At the same time, the Chilean ambassador to Washington was ordered to meet with President Roosevelt and read him a statement complaining of Welles' speech as offensive to the dignity of Chile and protesting the accusations. Roosevelt was conciliatory and told the ambassador that he hoped that President Rios would make the trip so that he and the Chilean president could sit down together and discuss the problems that existed between the two nations.[45]

But in Chile public opinion was outraged by the Welles speech. The press was filled with excerpts from the now infamous address. Bowers tried desperately to ease the anger, but for a time words from Yankees could not penetrate the veil of hostility that the Welles speech had created. Before the speech was delivered, Welles had cabled part of it to Bowers whose reaction was that "It seems a shocking mistake just as Rios is about to leave for Washington as our guest and I tremble for the reaction here."[46] Bowers read the temper of Chile correctly. The press continued its denunciation of Welles, Roosevelt, Bowers and the United States in general. Bowers lamented that "Our enemies are jubliant and our supporters depressed." Bowers believed that he had been patiently leading Chile toward a break with the Axis; he even targeted the date for such action as the return of Rios from his United States sojourn. He recalled that arrests of high-ranking Nazis in the country had picked up in August and September 1942, and that Chile had denied Germany the use of its codes. He wrote that "It seems that Welles speech was bad timing."[47]

The Chilean opponents of a diplomatic rupture now came storming to the fore, openly condemning the United States. Ex-president Arturo Alessandri was especially critical, but Foreign Minister Ernesto Barros Jarpa was even more outspoken. He quoted from a June 30, 1942 memorandum compiled by the United States secret service attached to the United States embassy which stated that Chile had relatively less espionage than the United States, Cuba, or Brazil. He further vented his hostility by calling the Welles speech "a gratuitous imputation against our country." The speech took on the "gravity of an insult to the honor of a dignified and independent nation and it was an unjustifiable act." Barros Jarpa, who had opposed breaking diplomatic relations all along, took the opportunity to tell his countrymen that the speech represented a turn to a far more aggressive policy toward Chile than the United States had pursued in the past. Alessandri agreed, and both men sought to turn the event to the favor of those opposed to rupture.[48]

Bowers desperately tried to ease the anger of the Chileans, but a couple of demonstrations in front of the United States embassy indicated clearly that it would require a major effort to overcome the hostility generated by the Welles speech. At one point Bowers, tired and disappointed, wrote in his diary, "I must say I think Rios could have adopted no other course." Bowers speculated that only two steps by the United States could have saved the Rios trip. If Welles had acted on Bowers' suggestion and stated publicly that he was unaware of Chile's recent action against Nazi espionage when he made the speech and if he then expressed gratification at that action, Rios might have gone ahead with his planned trip. The only other action that might have enabled him to make the trip would have been for Roosevelt to make a conciliatory statement for the press. But neither course was followed. Bowers believed that the State Department prevented either statement. He wrote, "But the State Department wise men were very cold to this and the result is that all the ground we have gained by hard work during the last four months has probably been lost and Barros Jarpa has been made a national hero." On top of everything else, Rios asked Bowers to cancel a dinner that Bowers had scheduled for him. The Ambassador sighed, "The end of a perfect day."[49]

Meanwhile, some quarters in Chile concluded that perhaps the Welles speech was not far off the mark. Articles began to appear in the press demanding Barros Jarpa's resignation as foreign minister. Also, critics like Alessandri cooled their attack and wrote of their friendship for the United States. Bowers concluded that Rios might retract the cancellation of his United States trip. He thought that if this occurred, Barros Jarpa would have to resign. While the visit was not made, on October 20 all the Chilean ministers resigned which meant that Barros Jarpa was in fact eliminated. But Bowers lamented that some of the friends of the United States also were driven from the cabinet at that time.[50]

Rios named Joaquin Fernandez as his new foreign minister. There were rumors that he was a Nazi, but some of Bowers' friends in the Chilean government denied this and reported that at one point Fernandez had told Rios, "This simply cannot go on. You have to break relations." Bowers, however, was concerned about the new cabinet which he characterized as politically weak. Nonetheless, with each passing day the furor over Welles' speech steadily declined. Roosevelt responded to Rios' protest, but he did not apologize. He said the facts in the speech were accurate.[51]

Despite the outcries over Welles' speech, U.S. criticism of Chilean policy did not go unnoticed within the Rios government. It became evident that the only course of action that would satisfy the United States was to sever relations with the Axis. With that realization in mind, Rios began planning for the eventual diplomatic rupture with the Axis. Early in December, he sent Minister of the Interior, Raul Morales Beltrami, to the United States to explain the Chilean position. But Morales stopped first in Argentina and Brazil before moving on to Washington. Rios wanted to be certain that his neighbors understood his new policy before it was presented to the North Americans. In all three countries, Morales was well received, and all three governments voiced understanding of the policy change. Roosevelt told Morales that he understood Rios' deliberate action because, like the United States, Chile was a democracy and democratic governments had to gain the support of their people before significant action could be taken. In particular, the act of severing relations with a friendly nation was a difficult step which the Chilean people had to understand the reasons for before they voiced support.

Another more pressing reason for the Morales mission was to get the United States to send military equipment quickly to Chile, so that if the Axis decided to attempt an attack on the long, exposed coastline, Chile would be able to defend itself. When the United States agreed to send the material immediately, Rios concluded that the Morales mission scored a victory, because up to this point Washington had insisted that military equipment would be sent only after diplomatic relations were broken. Washington also assured Morales that the moment the break came, Chile would be regarded as an ally of the United States and, as such, would be eligible for the protection of the military power of the United States.[52]

By the end of 1942, it was clear to all concerned that Chile was going to end diplomatic relations with the Axis. The only question was the exact date for such action. In early November, a Vichy France radio broadcast pointed out that Germany was now reconciled to an imminent diplomatic break with Chile. The forecast was based on the policies and statements of President

Rios and on the fact that Chile stepped up its attacks on Germans accused of subversion. In late October, two illegal radio transmitters were uncovered and destroyed. They had been used to send information to Europe on military activity in Latin America and on shipping in Latin American waters. A number of people were arrested when the transmitters were found.[53]

Despite Chile's apparent drift away from neutrality, some apologists for Chile and Argentina argued that by remaining neutral these countries were serving the cause of the democracies by keeping diplomatic channels to the Axis open that would be otherwise closed. Supporters of rupture, however, did not accept such a view and insisted that a greater asset for the democracies would be a completely united Western Hemisphere.[54]

As the Chilean Senate prepared to vote on the rupture resolution in January 1943, many prominent Chileans came out in support of the President. Even people who earlier were linked to the Nazis now joined the pro-rupture forces, including the former president, Carlos Ibanez del Campo. Only former president Alessandri remained firmly in opposition. He still insisted that Chileans would pay for such a move by suffering an attack from the Axis powers. He and others were convinced that in the postwar world, Chile would lose trading partners by renouncing its neutrality. But Rios was careful and moved slowly, preparing the political and economic segments of the population in Chile for the inevitable. When the break finally came on January 20, 1943, the government was ready to make the move as painless as possible. Decrees of January 20 and February 18 provided for the confiscation of all property held by people from Axis countries worth a total of 688,840,566.36 pesos. Additionally, all businesses of the Axis were closed and their commercial activity was banned. Goods belonging to members of the Axis countries in Chile were frozen. While all of these acts looked exceedingly detrimental to the Axis, Rios saw to it that Germany, Japan and Italy were not unduly harmed. The possessions of these countries in Chile were placed under the Superintendent of Banks and under a Development Corporation that protected them from illegal seizure. While other countries that had earlier broken relations expropriated Axis property, Chile guarded such property. When the war ended and diplomatic relations were reestablished, the property was returned. Consequently, after the war, both Germany and Japan praised Chile for the correctness of its handling of the diplomatic break.[55]

When the Senate passed the resolution ending diplomatic relations with the Axis, President Rios went on the radio and in a thirty-five minute speech explained his government's position to the Chilean people, many of whom continued to favor a policy of neutrality. In the speech, he emphasized that the breaking of relations was strictly diplomatic and was not directed at the people of the Axis nations "to whom Chile owed much of its progress, culture and military training." He also stated that Chile had always favored the Allied cause, but that now it was giving its moral support to the struggle and that the break "followed the principles of continental solidarity." Finally, he pointed out that his government was merely following Chilean public opinion which strongly endorsed the move.[56]

To ease the tension of the moment, Rios arranged a parade of 100,000 people which marched to the Presidential Palace where their president told the participants that they must join together at this moment in history, discipline themselves, and increase production. This was one of the largest celebrations in all of Chilean history. People in the crowd carried pictures of Roosevelt, Churchill, and Stalin along with large pictures of President Rios.[57]

The United States had finally nudged Chile to end its relations with the Axis, but the Chilean government had defied Washington since the outbreak of the war while it worked to build a favorable climate among German-Chileans and Italian-Chileans. It had managed to maintain relations while Japan was strong enough in the Pacific to threaten the Chilean coast. After the Battle of Midway in June 1942, the Japanese were no longer in a position to attack the Western hemisphere. With that danger removed and with the Allies taking the initiative in Europe, the Rios government could move toward rupture. But it still required the Sumner Welles' speech to prod the Chileans out of their neutral position.

After diplomatic relations were severed, Chile continued to move slowly relative to the Axis nations. War was not declared for another two years and then only on Japan. Chile again hesitated, but once again the United States wanted all Latin American nations to declare war on the Axis. U.S. will eventually prevailed but only after additional lengthy diplomatic maneuvering. Chile's democratic government could not be pushed into action quickly, but when Santiago concluded that an anti-Axis policy was in its own best interest, it acted. In the case of a declaration of war, the argument that convinced the Chileans was that only by declaring war could Santiago gain an opportunity to participate in the peace negotiations once the Axis surrendered. Beyond that, as participants in the war they were guaranteed a seat on the projected United Nations. With these two incentives clearly recognized, Chile declared war on Japan on April 5, 1945.[58]

Ambassador Claude G. Bowers, who consistently advised restraint on the State Department, handled the entire controversy over Chile's breaking of relations with the Axis powers well. Secretary of State Cordell Hull's patient dealing with Chile was also laudatory. Because of the willingness of both nations to work out their differences peacefully over time, the diplomatic repercussions were minimal. The United States and Chile remained close throughout the remainder of the war and into the post-war era.

Notes

1. For a succinct statement on the unanimity concept in dealing with Latin America, see Sumner Welles, The Time for Decision (New York: Harper and Brothers, 1944), pp. 233-235.

2. An especially harsh critic of Hull's handling of Argentina is Randall B. Woods, "Hull and Argentina: Wilsonian Diplomacy in the Age of Roosevelt," Journal of Inter-American Studies and World Affairs 16 (August 1974): 350-371.

3. Claude G. Bowers, Diary, 25 September 1941, Lilly Library, Indiana University, Bloomington, Indiana.

4. Claude G. Bowers, My Life: The Memoirs of Claude Bowers (New York: Simon and Schuster, 1962), p. 306.

5. For an examination of Chile's neutrality in World War I, see Enrique Rocuant, The Neutrality of Chile: The Grounds that Prompted and Justified It (Valparaiso: Sociedad Imprenta y Litografía Universo, 1919) and Gustavo Vargas Molinare, En Defensa de Chile (Santiago de Chile: Imprenta Universitaria, 1942).

6. Augusto Iglesias, Alessandri, Una etapa de democracia en America: Tiempo, Vida, Acción (Santiago de Chile: Editoral Andrés Bello, 1960) p. 363.

7. Senator Joaquín Azocar, Speech of August 19, 1942, Senate Record, Ordinary Session, 1942, III, p. 1475.

8. "La Junta Central Radical por unanimidad proclamo candidato a la presidencia de Chile al senor Pedro Aguirre Cerda," La Hora (Santiago), 22 December 1937. For a discussion of a portion of the nominating convention's deliberations, see Tancredo Pinochet, "Grove y Ibáñez," Asies (Santiago), 4 May 1938.

9. O.S.S./State Department Report #42, "Axis Aliens and Citizens of Axis Descent in the Latin American Republics, September 25, 1942," O.S.S./State Department Intelligence and Research Reports, Part XIV, Latin America, 1941-1961, microfilm reel #1.

10. For a discussion of German immigrants throughout Latin America, see Symphronio de Magalhaes, Contra hitlerismo: Por la integridad de las naciones americanos, translated into Spanish by Alberto Secco Ellauri (Montevideo: Impresora L.I.G.U., 1940), pp. 65-69.

11. "Survey of the Elements of Instability in the Latin American Sector, January 30, 1942," O. S. S./State Department Intelligence and Research Reports, Part XIV: Latin America, 1941-1961, microfilm reel #1, p. 30. See also Michael J. Francis, The Limits of Hegemony: United States Relations with Argentina and Chile During World War II (Notre Dame, Ind.: University of Notre Dame Press, 1977), pp. 93-94 and 108.

12. Bowers wrote three autobiographical books, My Mission to Spain: Watching the Rehearsal for World War II (New York: Simon and Schuster, 1954); Chile Through Embassy Windows: 1939-1954 (New York: Simon and Schuster, 1962); and My Life: The Memoirs of Claude Bowers (New York: Simon and Schuster, 1962).

13. The President's Papers, Roosevelt Library, Hyde Park, New York, reveal that Bowers did correspond with Roosevelt.

14. Only Secretary of State Hull and a few others in the Department continued to believe that Washington followed the correct policy in dealing with the Spanish Civil War. See Arnold A. Offner, American Appeasement: United States Foreign Policy

and Germany, 1933-1938 (Cambridge, Ma.: The Belknap Press of Harvard University Press, 1969).

15. Ibid., pp. 272-279.

16. For an interesting contemporary account of the massacre of the Nazi students, see "Como se desarrollaron los trágicos sucesos del 5 de septiembre de 1938," Hoy (Supplement), 29 November 1938. This special edition of Hoy, which went on sale two days before the regular edition appeared, dealt exclusively with the Nazi youth rebellion in sixty-four pages of text and pictures.

17. Florencio Duran Bernales, El Partido Radical (Santiago: Editorial Nascimento, 1958), p. 233.

18. Ricardo Donoso, Alessandri, agitador y demoledor: Cinquenta años de historia política de Chile (Mexico City: Fondo de Cultura Económica, 1954), II, p. 371.

19. Bowers, Chile Through Embassy Windows, p. 98.

20. Ibid., p. 93.

21. Bowers to Secretary of State [Hull], 11 December 1944, Foreign Relations of the United States, 1944, Vol. XVII: The Americas (Washington: Government Pringing Office, 1967), p. 696, hereafter Foreign Relations volumes will be cited as FRUS.

22. Correspondence dealing with Lend Lease negotiations between Chile and the United States, FRUS, 1941, Vol. VI, pp. 559 and 571-576.

23. Ambassador Bowers to Secretary of State [Hull], 6 August 1941, FRUS, 1941, Vol. VI, p. 573. See also "Special Report--The Spanish Falange in Latin America," O.S.S./State Department Intelligence and Research Reports, Part XIV, Latin

America, 1941-1961, microfilm reel #1.

24. Bowers Diary, 8 September 1939.

25. Ibid., 10 and 30 May and 6 June 1940.

26. Ibid., 1 and 3 June 1940.

27. "Chile Continues Inquiry," New York Times, 14 June 1940, p. 8.

28. Bowers Diary, 6 July 1940.

29. Russell B. Porter, "Nazis are Ready for Coup in Chile," New York Times, 13 July 1940, p. 3 and Bowers Diary, 16 July 1940.

30. Porter, New York Times, 13 July 1940, p. 3.

31. Ibid.

32. Jorge Rios Igualt, Hacia una coordinación de la Economía Sudamericana (Valparaiso: Imprent Litografía Universo, 1941), p. 13.

33. Bowers Diary, 25 September 1940 and 24 May 1941.

34. Ibid. and 10 August and 12 September 1941.

35. J. Alvarez del Vayo, "Mas sobre el caracter de la Guerra," La Nación (Santiago), 21 November 1941.

36. Bowers Diary, 19 April 1942.

37. Ibid., 15 May 1942 and "Nazi Wire Tapping Alleged in Chile," New York Times, 15 May 1942, p. 9.

38. "Chile Seizes Bombs in Raids Upon Nazis," New York Times, 23 May 1942, p. 7.

39. Ibid.

40. "Nazi Sabotage Linked to Bombs in Chile," New York Times, 24 May 1942, p. 21.

41. Bowers Diary, 26 May 1942.

42. "Chile Opens Inquiry into Nazi Activities," New York Times, 11 June 1942, p. 11.

43. Bowers Diary, 3 October 1942 and "Chile Clears Writer of Security Charge," New York Times, 6 December 1942, p. 59.

44. Duran, El Partido Radical, p. 358.

45. Cordell Hull, The Memoirs of Cordell Hull (New York: Macmillan, 1948), II, p. 1384.

46. Bowers Diary, 8 October 1942.

47. Ibid., 9 October 1942.

48. Donoso, Alessandri, pp. 370-371.

49. Bowers Diary, 11 October 1942.

50. Ibid., 20 October 1942.

51. Duran, El Partido Radical, p. 345.

52. Ibid., p. 346.

53. "Reich Resigned to Break with Chile, Vichy Reports," New York Times, 1 November 1942, p. 8.

54. Persio Celeste Franco, "Chile and the Axis," letter to the editor, New York Times, 3 February 1943.

55. Duran, El Partido Radical, pp. 347-348.

56. "Chile Breaks Ties with Axis Powers," New York Times, 21 January 1943, p. 8.

57. "100,000 Celebrate Chile's Break with the Axis," New York Times, 28 January 1943, p. 7.

58. Bowers Diary, 6 April 1945.

Aid to Families with Dependent Children in Texas, 1941-1981
by James H. Conrad

Over the past decade and a half, social work historians have given considerable attention to the administration of the Aid to Families with Dependent Children (AFDC) program at the national level, particularly to the explosive increase in the rolls in the late 1960s, offering various theories to explain the forces responsible for the dramatic increase in the number of families entering the AFDC system.[1] Recently historians have begun to investigate the techniques employed by AFDC families to cope with and manipulate the overall system.[2] But the study of the administration of AFDC at the state level--though while not completely neglected--has yet to be explored in detail. The state level approach to AFDC provides insight into the complex interplay of pressures and forces between state regulations and state bureaucracy administering the AFDC program. The administration of AFDC in Texas since 1941 affords a fascinating case study. In many respects typical of other Southern states in culture, economics, and tradition, the Texas case illustrates the various legislative strategies used to regulate AFDC and the efforts of the Department of Human Resources, the state agency responsible for AFDC, to adjust to the financial constraints on the program.

Texas, relatively late in taking advantage of Aid to Dependent Children (ADC, predecessor of AFDC) federal matching funds available through the Social Security Act, instituted a number of legal and financial restrictions on AFDC families. This placed enormous pressure on the Texas Department of Public Welfare to adjust its operation to conform to restrictive legislative mandates. The statistics tell much of the story. ADC families during the first decade fluctuated from a high of 22,000 in early 1942 to a low of about 10,000, leveling out to about 17,000 in the late 1940s. Despite the displacement of thousands of black and white farm families and a growing population, Texas rolls hardly went up at all in the ten years from 1950 to 1960, though the number of blacks on the rolls increased from 37 percent to 49 percent between 1950 and 1960. The number of families on ADC showed a general increase through the 1960s, but literally skyrocketed in 1968-1972, reaching a crisis in 1968-1970 that required the state legislature to pass several emergency appropriation bills and forced the governor to shift funds from higher education to AFDC. In the mid and late 1970s, however, the Texas Department of Human Resources (the new name of the Department of Public Welfare) actually succeeded in bringing the number of families on AFDC down from the pre-1972 level. The early 1980s witnessed a gradual, but not spectacular, increase in AFDC clients on Texas rolls.

The pre-1940s attitude in Texas toward child welfare was characterized by the belief that poor relief was best handled by the family, the church, the fraternal order, or when all else failed, the local community. Indeed, most of the governmental responsibility for the care of dependent and neglected children rested in the local community through the elected county commissioners courts. Specifically, the 1876 constitution--still the basic primary written instrument of Texas today though amended many times--placed responsibility for care of the dependent on county government. Article XVI, section 8 specifically mentioned local responsibility: "Each county must provide in such manner as may be prescribed by law, a manual labor poorhouse and farm, for taking care of, managing and employing and supplying the wants of its indigent and poor inhabitants."[3] State law also authorized local institutions to establish detention on parental homes for neglected or to pay board for neglected and dependent children.[4] For cases of dependent and neglected children which the county could not handle, or did not wish to handle, the state maintained eight institutions for orphaned children and four primarily adult institutions which provided specialized institutionalized care for children in special cases.

Following a nationwide trend, in 1917 the Texas legislature authorized the county commissioners courts to grant to widows with children as much as fifteen dollars per month for one child and six dollars per month for each additional child in the family, but counties usually appropriated only enough revenue to operate the regular welfare functions and granted little aid to widows with children.[5] In 1934, for example, only eight counties offered mother's pensions out of 254 counties in Texas.[6]

The Great Depression forced Texas and other states to become more directly involved in assistance payments to indigent and destitute children through the Social Security Act (SSA). Representing a new alignment of responsibility in the field of public welfare away from local control to federal/state partnership, the

1935 Social Security legislation provided grants to states on a matching basis in three categories of needy persons: Old Age Assistance, Aid to the Blind, and Aid to Dependent Children (ADC).[7] Initially, ADC provided federal aid to states on a matching basis for care of dependent women with children to assist, broaden, and supersede existing mother's aid programs. Under SSA, money payments went to dependent mothers in their own homes to help families stay together.

Although the Social Security Act set the general framework for the administration of ADC and the two other assistance programs, states had considerable latitude over how the program was organized, who was eligible for benefits and even the level of assistance payments provided. Texas and other states took full advantage of those provisions to shape a welfare system to meet the ideological bent of the state.[8]

Another factor accounting for the restrictive nature of ADC in Texas was the nature of the Texas Constitution, enacted during the aftermath of the Reconstruction with its severe restrictions on state appropriations, which made it easy--perhaps even natural--for the legislature to restrict public spending. Any changes in spending for public welfare and any grants to individuals had to be done by constitutional amendment. Throughout the history of AFDC in Texas, this one mechanism--the constitutional amendment on welfare spending--more than any other single factor kept assistance at a starvation level. In turn, the Department of Public Welfare, State Department of Human Resources, the state agency responsible for administering the program, had to devise strategies and mechanisms to cope with this chronic shortage of funds.

The payment of pensions to the aged, the first of the SSA assistance programs, faced fewer ideological difficulties from the Texas legislature and people than did ADC. The general feeling was that the elderly had contributed to society in their lifetime and therefore "deserved" a pension in old age. Anticipating passage of the Social Security Act, the Texas legislature passed a resolution calling for a constitutional amendment to provide for assistance to the needy aged under the terms of the SSA. The amendment was approved by the voters on August 24, 1935, just ten days after the federal Social Security Act became effective, permitting payment of fifteen dollars monthly, the maximum the national government would match, for each indigent aged citizen over sixty-four years of age.[9] The first payments began in July 1936.

Aid to the blind and children was later in coming to Texas. In 1937, the forty-fifth Texas legislature sent to the voters a constitutional amendment authorizing assistance to the needy blind and needy children under ADC.[10] The amendments were restrictive in nature. Under the proposed amendment, the state's total share of ADC assistance could not exceed $1,500,000 yearly and only children under fourteen years of age could receive benefits.[11] The federal act set the age limit at sixteen, or eighteen if the dependent child were attending school. The constitutional amendment further limited state appropriations to not more than eight dollars for one child or twelve dollars for two or more children in any one family. On the other hand, the

Social Security Act permitted federal contributions of one-third of the total grant either the maximum limit on the grant set at eighteen dollars for the first child and twelve dollars for each additional child.[12] Strong precedent existed for restricting through a constitutional amendment the amount of money paid for welfare in the case of Confederate pensions. The 1894 amendment to Confederate pensions placed a ceiling of $100,000 a year for the establishment and maintenance of a home for indigent and disabled Confederate soldiers and sailors who were residents of Texas. An 1898 amendment mandated that direct grants were not to exceed eight dollars per month per veteran.

Although the voters approved the amendment to authorize aid to dependent neglected children, the next legislative session failed to pass the enabling legislation for ADC, though money was appropriated for aid to the blind. Finally in 1941 the forty-seventh legislature enacted the Public Welfare Act which set the general statutory guidelines for the administration of ADC in the state of Texas for the next forty years.[13] Under the act, ADC recipients had to be citizens of the U.S. and "have resided in the state for one year if the child was under one year of age and does not have sufficient income or other resources to provide a reasonable subsistence compatible with decency."[14] As though anticipating shortage of funds for ADC, section 28 of the 1941 law provided for the prorating of money. Under this provision, if the funds available for the legislature failed to meet the needs of ADC, the department was required under the law to ration the funds among the ADC families.[15] The first ADC payments were made in late 1941.

Though the law required the Texas Department of Public Welfare (DPW) to prorate the funds, the department at first experimented with a variety of methods of coping with the shortage of funds. In the first years of operation, nearly 22,000 cases were on the rolls which quickly exhausted the appropriations. Obviously, a total of 22,000 was too high a level to substantiate with the funds available. Some method was needed to control the number on the rolls yet still fairly distribute the money, so the DPW began prorating funds. In September 1942, the DPW discontinued prorating in favor of concentrating all funds on the neediest families, a plan that came to be known as the "30 percent policy." The department decided to pay maximum grants to the 12,000 families most in need rather than completely inadequate grants to some 22,000 families. The 30 percent plan worked in the following manner: if the monthly income of a child from the household was sufficient to meet 30 percent of the budgetary requirements, the applicant was ineligible for ADC.[16] With the adoption of this drastic measure, the roles were reduced by over one-third. Because of increasing funds from the federal government, in April 1944 the DPW discounted the 30 percent policy and began payments in full to meet budgeted needs.

In 1945 the voters approved a new amendment expanding assistance to the needy aged, needy blind and needy children. This amendment deleted the annual limitation of $1,500,000 for the ADC program, the eight and twelve dollar limitations on grants, and the fourteen-year old age limit. But it added to the constitution a residence requirement of one year, a citizenship requirement, an age limit of sixteen (these had been incorporated in the Public Welfare Law of 1941, but not in the 1937 amendment for ADC) and an annual ceiling of $35 million on the total state appropriations for assistance to the needy blind, the needy aged and the needy children of the state. The $35 million increased the maximum amount payable for ADC to twenty-four dollars for the first child eligible for assistance, but DPW policy limited the maximum amount of money per family to seventy-five dollars.

While the 1945 amendment seemed to liberalize the ADC expenditures, little had actually changed. The DPW had pressed for lumping Old Age Assistance, Aid to the Blind, and ADC together in the ceiling because separating them would make voters more likely to support the amendment. The same strategy was used for the biennial appropriations. Though the constitutional amendment deleted the $1,500,000 ceiling on ADC, the annual ADC appropriations were not raised until 1947, at which time it was increased to $2,500,000 and later increased in 1948 to $3,000,000.

In December 1945, Texas reinstituted measures to cut back on ADC, but this time the family income plus the ADC grant could not exceed 60 percent of the estimated needs of the family.[17] Between November 1945 and February 1946, more than two thousand grant denials and nearly three hundred denials of applicants resulted from the 60 percent rule, resulting in a decrease of three thousand families from the caseload of DPW. This policy lasted until 1946, when the department again instituted appropriations with cuts determined each month on the basis of the ratio of available funds to ADC obligations. The first prorating of payments amounted to 18 percent in April 1946 and reached 38 percent in February 1947 when the Texas legislature made more funds available. Grants were paid in full for the next six months, but in September 1947, the DPW had to invoke the prorating again. Similar reductions have been made throughout the entire history of ADC and AFDC. Almost every year for the past forty years, the budgeted needs of ADC families overran the funds available from the Texas legislature.[18] After the 1945 amendment, the legislature almost every three to four years put before the voters amendments to increase the ceiling on Old Age Assistance, Aid to the Blind, and ADC. In 1953 per capita expenditure for public assistance of state and local funds, Texas ranked forty-eighth in payment on ADC. ADC payments were limited to a maximum of ninety-six dollars per family. On September 1, 1953, the average grant was $22.60 per child.

On November 5, 1957, a constitutional amendment passed raising the limit to $47 million per year for assistance to the needy aged, blind and children. The amendment again stipulated the maximum payment for state funds for each category of assistance. A 1963 amendment removed all residency requirements, authorizing the legislature to set them, and increased the spending ceiling to $60 million.

Yet another indirect result of the restrictions on money for welfare was the shortage of welfare workers, resulting in a higher number of ADC cases per workers than almost any other state in the union. For several years Texas had the highest caseload per worker in the nation. In 1949-1950 the average caseload for public assistance in Texas was a whopping 386; the average for the nation was 192.[19] These high caseloads continued throughout most of the early history of the ADC program, until the federal government imposed a reduction in 1963. Even then, Texas maintained a higher than average number of cases per worker compared to other states.[20]

Not surprisingly, the turnover rate for Texas DPW workers was also exceptionally high. In 1946-1947, the Department reported 423 separations out of a total personnel force of 1,245.[21] This trend continued through the 1960s and 1970s. The vast majority of caseworkers and supervisors had no professional social work education other than what they received at DPW--usually a week of training at a regional education center plus on-the-job instruction from fellow workers and occasional refresher courses. What impact this high caseload, high turnover rate and lack of training had on the administration of ADC is unclear. However, the heavy caseloads and lack of professional training prevented DPW workers from rendering additional social services to ADC clients.

Probably the most crucial result of the rapid turnover of workers was the lack of acculturation of the DPW employees to social work professionalism. Employees brought with them the biases and prejudices found in some white Southerners in the pre-civil rights era and after. One net result was a not too subtle discrimination against blacks and hispanics. Though there is not exact data on the social composition of clients on ADC rolls until 1948, there were substantially fewer blacks than whites on the rolls in Texas. In 1949 the U.S. government exerted some pressure for a relaxation of discriminatory practices, requiring states to adopt a federal application process, thus making it difficult for state welfare officials to brush off applicants by treating them as casual inquiries. After increases in the late 1940s and early 1950s, the number of blacks on the rolls through the 1950s and 1960s remained more or less constant. The number of blacks on ADC increased, but even when they did get on the rolls they were kept under pressure to work at least part time. Many mothers and children--black and white--left ADC and became self-supporting through seasonal employment, particularly cotton chopping in the spring and cotton picking in the fall.[22]

Some of the prejudices of the caseworkers also discouraged blacks--and not a few whites and Texan-Mexicans--from applying for aid. A 1980 study by W. Norton Grubb and Julian Green Barody found that there were great differences among Texas counties in the certification of needy women and children to draw AFDC benefits. Federal officials who monitored AFDC stated that "it is harder for eligible individuals to receive welfare in west Texas and south Texas because of greater hostility toward welfare recipients and a lack of bilingual caseworkers."[23] Another study reported that hostility toward outreach programs that increased participation rates in AFDC accounted for the low rates. Grubbs and Barody concluded that Texas Department of Human Resources officials were reluctant or unable to impose uniformity of administration upon DHR's regional and local administration.

If some of the DPW workers had deep-rooted misconceptions of ADC clients, treating them in an intimidating manner, many DPW workers, such as James McDowell who worked in Waco, treated ADC families with kindness and dignity. McDowell remembers rescuing one divorced mother with an illegitimate child from the efforts of her small rural community to put the child in an orphanage.[24]

Support services increased as one way of attempting to keep rolls manageable. In 1960 the Department of Public Welfare placed more mature and experienced workers on the ADC cases and reduced the number of ADC cases per worker. The Annual Report for 1961 justified the new reduced loads: "specialized caseworkers were able to meet and overcome some of the problems facing ADC families and thereby produced a marked reduction in the number of families and children on the rolls of that program at the end of the year."[25] A public hearing on the welfare budget in 1960 provided a glimpse of the condition of ADC twenty years after its introduction in Texas. John Winters, director of the DPW, told the House Appropriation Committee that in 1942, "14 percent of every Texas dollar went for welfare and that the figure for 1961 was 6 percent."[26]

Rolls increased gradually in the 1960s. From 1960 to the spring of 1968, the number of families on ADC increased from 21,000 to 28,000. In 1968 the voters unexpectedly defeated a constitutional amendment to raise the limitations on state welfare spending from $60 million to $75 million which precipitated a severe crisis for the state and DPW. The DPW, which instituted procedures for sorting out the funds available to meet this new development, cut allotments to 50 percent of a family's recognizable budget needs for housing, food, clothing, and other responsibilities. This cut, setting aid at $12.50 per month per child, caused the federal court to issue an injunction against the state, asserting that if improvements were not made within sixty days all federal AFDC funds would be cut off.[27]

Sit-ins of welfare mothers added to the urgency of getting money for families on AFDC. Starting on November 25, 1968, there was a three-day sit-in in the regional office of the DPW in Dallas, sponsored by the National Welfare Rights Organization and supported by the Student Nonviolent Coordinating Committee. On May 1, 1969, welfare mothers demonstrated in the Houston Regional Office of the DPW. A third demonstration in June occurred in San Antonio for two nights and two days.[28] Responding to these extreme pressures, the Texas legislature made a special transfer of funds to AFDC and again submitted to the voters a proposed constitutional amendment to increase the ceiling on welfare spending to $80 million. A special committee headed by Houston lawyer Leon Jaworski was created to lobby for the amendment. Leading newspapers in the state supported the amendment.[29] Voters approved the amendment on August 5, 1969. Under the amendment, the new level of funding permitted the DPW to increase payment from 54 percent to 75 percent of the budgeted needs of AFDC families.[30]

The director of the DPW, Burton G. Hackney, offered his reasons for the drastic increase:

> Among them were the normal growth rate as expected because of population growth; the advent of medicare in Texas the previous year, providing government purchased medical care for needy citizens and thus a new incentive to apply for public assistance under one of the department's four categorical programs; and to some extent the U.S. Supreme Court ruling that AFDC benefits could not be denied to families nor "substitute fathers." Also some of the increase can be attributed

to efforts of federally funded "anti-poverty" agencies and other groups to locate potential recipients in the communities and inform them of the benefits available.[31]

To complicate matters, the federal court ordered the state to eliminate residency requirements for welfare applicants, to disregard income in families earned by children fourteen years or under, and to pay benefits to mothers of dependent children even if there were an able-bodied man living in the house.[32] All of these contributed to the expansion of AFDC in Texas. The dramatic rise in the rolls in Texas was matched by an increase in rolls nation-wide. In February 1969, there were 1,545,000 families on the combined AFDC rolls. By October 1970 some twenty months later, the case load had risen to 2,400,000 families, an increase of 55 percent in the United States.

The additional money proved only a temporary cure as the rolls continued to outstrip the funds available. From September to October 1969, 14,000 more persons were added to the AFDC rolls than the same time the year before. Herbert C. Wilson, deputy welfare commissioner, stated, "Instead of an increase of 5,000 the rolls have gone up an increase of almost 10,000 between September 1969 and February 1970. Since the state constitution prohibits overspending, we had nothing to do but cut."[33] The spectacular growth continued in the fall of 1970. In August 1970, 68,000 families received aid; in August 1971, the DPW had 100,300 families on the rolls, representing 292,000 children under age eighteen (or twenty-one if in school.)[34] The number of cases continued to increase into 1972 as did the number of applicants.

To meet this new crisis, Governor Preston Smith took the unprecedented step of transferring $7.5 million from the appropriation for a new medical school in Lubbock and another $6 million from the new University of Texas at Houston medical school to AFDC. The legislature also put before the voters yet another amendment to the constitution to remove the ceiling on assistance to the elderly, blind and disabled, but still placing a $55 million ceiling on AFDC.[35] But voters defeated the amendment on May 18, 1971.

Starting in 1971, the DPW instituted efforts to tighten controls on eligibility for AFDC programs to stop the spiraling number of families on the rolls. In addition to expanding vocational training and day care to help AFDC mothers find jobs, DPW administrators strengthened the program to ferret out those suspected of welfare fraud.[36] On June 9, 1972, the State Welfare Commissioner, Raymond Vowell, stated that he was going to

> cleanse Texas welfare rolls of ineligible recipients... I am now ready to place this unwanted child, the ineligible welfare recipient, where it belongs--on the doorstep of the U.S. Department of HEW in Washington, D.C. Since January 1971 our legal division has referred to county and district prosecutors a total of 254 cases of suspected welfare fraud. So far 97 felony indictments or misdemeanors have been handed down. Information has been returned by grand juries in 17 counties. Twenty-nine convictions have been obtained. There will be more.[37]

Another DPW program, supported by federal legislation and recent changes in Texas law, stepped up efforts to locate fathers responsible for child support payments. This resulted in reduction in the number of cases and substantial savings in the 1970s according to the DPW.

In September 1973, urged on by federal regulations, the

department adopted a mass recertification effort on each case to spot those ineligible families on AFDC.[38] Also a special validation section was added to the department's financial service division to spot-check the accuracy of cases with a primary focus on the AFDC program. The DPW found that the AFDC error rate in Texas was 10.4 percent and overpayment 16.35 percent, but by fiscal year 1975 eligibility error rate had dropped 2.6 percent and overpayment to 6.5 percent.[39]

After 1969-1971, the rejection rate of applicants for AFDC sharply increased. Many of the denials were justified, though a substantial number were dismissed for apparently frivolous reasons. In the DHR 1973 Annual Report, 14,000 were denied for "refusal of applicant to furnish information or follow agreed plan... more than 9,000 because of earnings of parent or person acting in parent's place... more than 5,000 for failing to keep an appointment... more than 3,200 location of applicant unknown", and 529 because the applicant was "unable to establish continued absence of father."[40]

Many of these regulatory activities were often punitive, very expensive, and cost inefficient, while diverting the limited staff from the main purpose of AFDC. In 1981 the effort to track down fathers cost the DHW $11.1 million for collection of $10.9 million in child support payments. Some of these efforts succeeded, nevertheless, as rolls began to decline in 1972-1973 and continued to decline throughout the remainder of the 1970s.[41]

In 1981 the number on the rolls showed a modest increase for the first time in seventeen years. The reasons given in the annual report were rising population and inflation.[42] Because of growth in the rolls and its share of payments for the AFDC payment, again Texas almost ran out of money. A ceiling on welfare only through fiscal year 1983 was still only $80 million. After an organization called "Citizens Concerned about Children" rallied behind the amendment in November 1982, the voters approved an amendment raising the ceiling to 1 percent of the state budget, though the legislature established the exact funding level within 1 percent of the constitutional restriction through biennial appropriation. After passage of the amendment, the legislature approved increased AFDC grants of forty-eight dollars per person from the previous thirty-eight dollars per person. This was the first special payment made possible by the legislature in fourteen years to recognize the need for increases in the living standard for poor families.[43]

The rise in the number of applicants in 1982-1983 prompted the DHR to develop a brochure to discourage anyone from coming to Texas unless he or she already had a job lined up by indicating the readiness of the state's public assistance programs.[44] The bottom line was that the maximum monthly payment was $140 for a parent and three children if the parent was absent or disabled.

The roots of the restrictive AFDC policy in Texas can be traced back to the 1876 Texas Constitution with its prohibition on direct grants to individuals. The only exception was grants to veterans of the Confederacy. This meant that welfare spending had to follow the arduous route of constitutional amendment. In framing constitutional amendments for pensions to veterans, the legislature devised the concept of ceilings on the total amount appropriated for pensions and a ceiling on individual grants as further safeguards against raids on the state treasury. Later in the 1910s and 1930s, amendments permitting mother's pensions, Old Age Assistance, and Aid to the Blind had similar provisions. Not surprisingly, the legislature imposed similar--though harsher-- limitations on ADC and AFDC.

Since ADC supposedly involved moral issues such as non-working mothers and illegitimate children, the Texas legislature set very severe eligibility requirements in amendments and statutory laws dealing with ADC. The legislature seldom, if ever, took advantage of optional federal ADC programs and services. Created to administer these Social Security Act grants, the Texas Department of Public Welfare had to learn to work within these legal mandates. Devising strategies to cope with lack of money and still deliver services in the early years, the Department used prorating and an informal system of intimidation. In the 1960s and after, in part because of changes in federal regulations and development of a professional staff, the DPW turned to more formal and legal methods of control--fraud investigation, recertification and work programs--while compensating for inadequate grants by expanding ancillary services. Still the Department had few options to induce change in the system. The strategies--legal and administrative--worked. The number of families on AFDC remained stable throughout the 1940s and 1950s and increased slightly in the 1960s despite growth in the population of Texas. After the crisis of 1969-1972, the rolls stabilized again and declined during the 1970s. Payments per family and individual child changed very little over the first forty years of AFDC in Texas.

Notes

1. Frances Fox Piven and Richard A. Cloward, Regulating the Poor: The Functions of Public Welfare (New York: Vintage Books, 1971); Social Welfare or Social Control? Some Historical Reflections on Regulating the Poor, ed. Walter I. Trattner (Knoxville: University of Tennessee Press, 1983); Eugene Durman, "Have the Poor Been Regulated: Toward a Multivariate Understanding of Welfare Growth," Social Service Review 47 (September 1973): 339-359; Jan Mason, John S. Wodarski, and Jim Parham, "Work and Welfare: A Revolution of AFDC," Social Work 30 (May-June 1985): 197-203.

2. Clarke A. Chambers, "Toward a Redefinition of Welfare History," Journal of American History 72 (September 1986): 407-433.

3. Texas Constitution (1876), art. XCI, sec. 8.

4. To receive aid, a child had to be under sixteen, a citizen and a resident of the county in which he or she received aid. The maximum grant was set at fifteen dollars per month for the first child and six dollars per month for each additional child. General and Special Laws of the State of Texas, 42nd Legislature Regular Session, 1931, p. 759.

5. University of Texas, Bureau of Research in the Social Sciences, Texas' Children (Austin: University of Texas Press, 1938), p. 578.

6. In 1934 the per capita expenditures for Mothers' Pensions in Texas was the lowest of all states having such programs; Texas ranked 39th among all states in the average grant per family, 33rd in the number of families per 10,000 aided, 41st in

the per cent of counties in which mothers' pensions were in effect, and 42nd in the maximum grant allowable for a family with three children.

7. Title IV, Sec. 402, The Federal Social Security Act, August 1935. On January 1, 1974, Old Age Assistance, Aid to the Blind, and Aid to Dependent Children became federalized with administration passing to the federal government.

8. The general federal requirements that placed restrictions on the states included the following: public assistance to be distributed on the basis of need, programs to be state-wide in coverage, no requirement pertaining to citizenship that would disqualify a United States citizen, rights to a fair hearing before the state agency if claimant is dissatisfied with action taken, names and other information about applicants for aid to be safeguarded, and mandated a state agency to administer public assistance with its personnel selected under a merit system.

9. Texas Constitution, art. 3, sec. 516.

10. The amendment was interpreted by a variety of state attorney general opinions to cover only cash allocations to recipients and to exclude costs of program administration and many medical costs where recipients received service rather than dollars.

11. Texas, Legislature, S.B. No. 36, 46th Legis., 1937.

12. Texas, Senate, Journal, Part I, 1937, p. 1166.

13. Public Welfare Act of 1941, Vermons Statutes, Article 695 c.

14. Texas, Legislature, H.B. 611, Section 17-c, 47th

Legis., 1941.

15. Ibid.

16. Texas, Department of Public Welfare, Manual of Policies and Procedures, November 1, 1942, Section III, p. 4.

17. Texas, Department of Public Welfare, Annual Report (1970), pp. 2-3, hereafter cited as TDPW, Annual Report.

18. Ibid., (1949), Table 10.

19. In 1954 and 1955 the DPW had the highest caseload in the nation. Ibid., (1954), p. 3 and (1955), p. 3.

20. The U.S. Department of Health, Education and Welfare stipulated that a case load of sixty cases was the maximum to be carried by any ADC worker; the Department of Public Welfare adjusted the work loads on May 1, 1963 to meet this new requirement. In 1962 the average case load was 111 for AFDC workers; in 1963 the number had been reduced to 62. Ibid., (1963), p. 3.

21. Ibid., (1946) and (1947).

22. Ibid., (1954).

23. W. Norton Grubb and Julia Green Brody, "Spending Inequalities for Children's Programs in Texas," The Annals of the American Academy of Political and Social Sciences 461 (May 1982): 60.

24. Interview with James McDowell, 11 July 1986, Commerce, Texas. In the case of Anglos or Texas-Mexicans, the state had the power to declare a child dependent and neglected and place the child in an adoptive or foster home or in an institution. Such programs and institutions for blacks were limited in Texas in the 1940s and the 1950s, and so the department of welfare had to keep the families on the rolls.

25. TDPW, Annual Report (1961), pp. 1-2.

26. "Child Welfare Plea," Texas Observer, 25 February 1961, p. 1.

27. "Texas Welfare System Teetering on the Brink," Texas Observer, 1 August 1969, p. 19.

28. TDPW, Annual Report (1969), p. 3.

29. Ibid.

30. Ibid., (1970), p. 2.

31. Ibid., (1969), p. 1.

32. "The Welfare Crisis," Texas Observer, 6 March 1970, pp. 2-3.

33. TDPW, Annual Report (1970), pp. 2-3.

34. Ibid., (1971), p. 2.

35. "The Welfare Crisis," Texas Observer, 6 March 1970, p. 2.

36. Texas, Department of Human Resources, Annual Report (1975), p. 4.

37. "Door Step Babies," Texas Observer, 7 July 1972, p. 19.

38. Texas, Department of Human Resources, Annual Report, (1975), pp. 25-27. Until 1971, the U.S. Department of Health, Education, and Welfare encouraged states to use an oversimplified system of establishing eligibility for AFDC. This meant accepting an applicant's statement for assistance at almost face value.

39. Recertification HEW encourages state to use a simplified system; Ibid., p. 26.

40. Adequate or excess earnings under the DHR's formula of

need accounted for only one-third of all reasons for denial of AFDC payments.

41. Texas, Department of Human Resources, Annual Report (1978), p. 15.

42. Ibid., (1980), p. 2.

43. The legislature approved increases in AFDC grants to $44.80 per person from thirty-four dollars. This was the first special payment made possible by the legislature in fourteen years. Ibid., (1983).

44. "Broke? Don't Come to Texas, Official Pamphlet Warns," Denton Record Chronicle, 27 May 1982, p. 1-A.

C. Wright Mills' "Letter to the New Left":
A Radical's Critique of American Liberalism
by Frank Annunziata

To reconsider recent historical events is to be reminded that writing contemporary history is especially treacherous. Where the history of the distant past, say of the Renaissance or the Reformation, stands as starkly ribbed as a cathedral, that of the recent past seems blurred and amorphous. Precisely because it has not settled into a permanent part of our historical memories, contemporary history seems elusive even when we try to organize specific details. Perhaps one of the best examples of this problem for historical analysis, in 1980s America, is the way in which we are formulating scholarly assessments of the New Left era. By emphasizing its role in the Vietnam war protests and other developments marking the 1960s, we have overlooked the crucial relationship that the origins of the New Left movement had with the dominant intellectual ethos of post-World War II American culture. Now, however, as we mark the twenty-fifth anniversary of C. Wright Mills' "Letter to the New Left," we can begin to glimpse the shifting patterns of post-1945 American social thought. We are also coming to see Mills as neither the patron saint of the New Left nor "the quintessential fifties maverick," but, rather, as one who anticipated much of the debate of the last two decades and especially the role that neo-conservatism would come to play.[1]

In the aftermath of World War II, an understandable and perhaps predictable satisfaction with American ideas and institutions could be discerned among intellectuals. The politically conservative and economically content Truman-Eisenhower years were characterized by containment and consensus; the shared convictions about the malign intentions of the Soviet Union and an appreciation, if not a celebration, of American ideas and institutions. An ensemble of themes marked the postwar intellectual mood: "the god that failed" reminiscences of ex-Communists and Socialists; the revival of religion; the invocation by liberals of the legend of FDR and his New Deal; the apparent vitality of capitalism; the alliance between labor and the Democrats and the acceptance (maybe grudging acquiescence by certain conservative Republicans) of the welfare state and an "internationalist" foreign policy.

When the leading intellectual figures of the era are recalled--Max Eastman, Sidney Hook, Reinhold Niebuhr, Dwight Macdonald, Edmund Wilson, Lionel Trilling, Philip Rahv, William Phillips, Arthur Schlesinger, Jr., David Potter, Richard Hofstadter, Oscar Handlin, Daniel Boorstin, Clinton Rossiter, Louis Hartz, John Kenneth Galbraith, Talcott Parsons, Daniel Bell, Seymour Martin Lipset--it becomes evident how multi-faceted and prevalent the consensus paradigm was. That it embodied an unmistakable politics of caution could be seen in several of the leading book titles of the period--The Vital Center (Schlesinger); The Genius of American Politics (Boorstin); and People of Plenty (Potter)--and in the characteristic warning provided by Lionel Trilling. In The Liberal Imagination Trilling invoked the label of "moral realism" for his stance and defined the intellectuals' task as the willingness to work for change combined with the recognition of "the dangers" that "lie in our most generous wishes." Beware especially, said Trilling, of the lamentable tendency to reduce others to "objects of our pity, then of our wisdom, ultimately of our coercion."[2] As Daniel Bell was later to note, the key terms which dominate discourse today are "irony, paradox, ambiguity, and complexity."[3]

Such a posture had, of course, necessary correlatives and the 1950s saw pluralism supplanting Progressivism's class-conflict model. The benefits of liberalism, the politics of bargaining and compromise, the praise for the mixed economy, the notion that technical and administrative problems rather than ideological debates ought to predominate on the intellectual agenda--these were the leitmotifs of the era. But for C. Wright Mills, these were the incontrovertible indications that American liberalism had grown into administrative and managerial routinization.

Post-World War II American social thought was dominated by Reinhold Niebuhr's theological proposition that the decisive seat of evil in this world resided neither in social nor political institutions but in the weaknesses and imperfections of the human soul. Linked with this revived Christian sense of original sin was the conclusion by many leading American Jewish intellectuals (like Richard Hofstadter and Daniel Bell) that the Holocaust had aroused the Judaic chayim--fear of the animal. Although some scholars, like the philosopher Morton White in Social Thought in

America (1957), lamented how it was a sad commentary on the social thought of today that two of the most popular social thinkers on the American scene (Walter Lippmann and Reinhold Niebuhr) can produce nothing more original or natural than the doctrines of original sin and natural laws as answers to the pressing problems of the age, most did not find the contours of the contemporary intellectual debate objectionable.

Into this celebratory, complacent and self-congratulatory culture came the provocative challenge of C. Wright Mills. Who among America's post-World War II intellectuals was more estranged and more adversarial toward the reigning set of intellectual convictions? When Mills' "Letter to the New Left" is placed in its appropriate historical context--as a critique of the consensus intellectuals who dominated the debates of the Truman-Eisenhower years--we can detect what Morris Dickstein has called "the rise of a new sensibility of how the Fifties broke up"; we can see that the decline of the Cold War consensus owed much to Mills.

Professor Morris Dickstein, author of one of the best histories of the 1960s, recalls what Mills meant to undergraduates in the 1950s:

> I can well remember the impact that C. Wright Mills' work had on us as undergraduates in the late fifties. He seemed like the one bold spirit in the gray, gray crew of American social science. As it happens I wasn't much interested in social science but Mills' polemical tract of 1958, The Causes of World War Three, captured the irrational atmosphere of that era perfectly: the cold war, the Dulles policy of armed deterrence and "massive retaliation," the cheerful preparations for nuclear Armageddon. When Mills (like Sartre) also took up the cause of Castro's Cuba--against an increasingly hostile American policy there--

we cheered. (Castro in his pre-Leninist phase was another of our idols: the compleat hippie revolutionary.) I knew that my elders at Columbia considered Mills shallow and unsound, a dangerous simplifier--and the part of me that was innoculated against ideology, that considered the world too ambiguous and complex for any sweeping theories, shared their misgivings. Later, after his death, when his collected essays were published in 1963, one reviewer could assert complacently that poor Mills had disintegrated well-meaningly from a crack professional to a crude polemicist in his last years.[4]

When Mills' "Letter" was published, he had spent almost twenty years as a sociologist and possessed an international reputation. He grew up in Texas, had studied philosophy as an undergraduate at the University of Texas and then did his doctoral study in sociology at the University of Wisconsin. After four years (1941-1945) at the University of Maryland, he received an appointment at Columbia which he held until his death in 1962 at age forty-five. Mills' diverse interests and research subjects could never obscure his primary and enduring fascination with American pragmatism and the role of liberalism in contemporary American and world politics.[5] Although Mills is often linked with American Populism or with Thorstein Veblen, he was haunted by many of the same problems which engaged John Dewey. Mills, like Dewey, believed that industrialization had dislocated the individual from the delicate and fragile web of customary relationships. Now the democratic polity was dissevered from community and a new network of regional, national and international relationships were preventing the vast majority of the democratic public from understanding what bound them to their fellow citizens. A mass community, Mills felt, fostered mass subservience. Later Mills would fuse his concerns about what

Dewey called the "public and its problems" with the critiques of the mass media rendered by two of his Columbia colleagues--Robert Merton and Paul Lazarsfeld. They had contended that the media exposed the individual to a flood of mostly superficial information, making him think that "knowing about [the] problems of the day" was the same as "doing something about them," and therefore accentuating his passivity. Popular culture was a "respectable and efficient" narcotic, fostering social apathy and perhaps seducing the masses into receptivity for authoritarian leadership.[6]

It is, of course, well known that Mills' notions of class, status and party derived from his theory of power. From his dissertation on pragmatism through his later work, Mills was preoccupied with the connections between culture and politics. When Mills' subjects--the moral and psychological costs of affluence, the anxieties of the middle class, the impact of mass communications, conformity, alienation and ennui are separated from their underlying analytical framework viz., the structure of the economy, his central point can be obscured. Mills' "Letter" makes clear above all that he wanted to have intellectuals perform the crucial task of challenging the complacent orthodoxies of the university/ business/ government/ military elites. Immanuel Wallerstein observed in his essay on Mills for the International Encyclopedia of the Social Sciences, "Mills was a utopian reformer. He thought that knowledge properly used could bring about the good society and that if the good society was not yet here, it was primarily the fault of men of knowledge."[7]

Whatever other themes emerge in Mills' "Letter," the fundamental controversy is about the relationship of intellectuals to social change. To re-examine the "Letter" and the sharp responses it drew is to be reminded of how the rise of the academician in late nineteenth-century America was linked with a secularizing of moral concern and of the moral career. This displacement of personnel from the clergy to the academy--from pulpit to lectern--is especially evident in the work of twentieth-century academic intellectuals who have provided radical critiques of their own societies. Mills preferred a conception of the intellectual as a moral catalyst rather than a technical functionary serving the power structure.

Throughout the corpus of Mills' sociological scholarship, there are links to what he regarded as the enduring problems identified by earlier scholars. If his caveats about bureaucratization, rationalization, capitalism and socialism reflected an indebtedness to Weber, there was always Mills' fascination with the dichotomies of a self-balancing, decentralized, liberal society with the corporate, labyrinthine, bureaucratic mass society of the twentieth century. Political consciousness had been supplanted by mass indifference as liberalism had become routinized. This is the problem Mills wanted a New Left to overcome.

Earlier in <u>The New Men of Power</u> (1948), he had warned about politically active and alert elites manipulating a mass of politically passive people. In other books, <u>White Collar</u> (1951), <u>The Power Elite</u> (1956), <u>The Sociological Imagination</u> (1959), he further developed his objections against "The Ones Who Decide" with their folklore of pluralism, their betrayal of the true function of intellectuals and their anti-communist negativity.

With the enlargement and centralization of administrative authority, said Mills, the power holders owned not merely the means of production, they dominated decision making as well. They deliberately held themselves, as Richard Pells has summarized Mills, as "remote, impersonal, inaccessible, anonymous":

> They conducted their affairs in private; they rarely engaged in "public or even Congressional debate"; they relied neither on force nor "reasonable discussion" but on the techniques of psychological manipulation (and when all else failed, the allusion to the "official secret") to pacify the electorate. Thus their policies could not be effectively opposed; there were now no explicit "targets for revolt." Here Mills was not merely weighing the difficulties of defying the organization or the peer group. Where William Whyte and David Riesman had treated the problem of resistance primarily as a personal and moral question, Mills wanted to point out its political ramifications. When power was "hidden" and actions were taken "behind men's backs," when people's lives were transformed without their knowledge or consent, the choice between other-direction and autonomy hardly mattered. Democracy itself had become a hoax.[8]

To isolate but one instance of Mills' work, his "Letter to the New Left," is not to suggest that it can be understood apart from the entire corpus of his scholarship. It obviously reflects his settled beliefs, developed over two decades of scholarship. Yet, if it recapitulated the enduring themes in his sociological thought, the essay also contained provocative clues as to how Mills was aiming to invest intellectuals with the responsibility to forge a renascent radicalism.

Lewis Feuer attributes the "Mosaic myth" to Mills[9]--calling on intellectuals to make the revolution. Mills himself, however, had no such grandiose formulations in mind. He was so honestly committed to understanding the connections between culture and politics that he saw intellectuals performing an indispensable function--becoming the "real live agencies of historic change."

Mills' "Letter" implored the Left to abandon the "labor metaphysic," to forget thinking that a liberal/ labor social welfare democratic alliance would bring fundamental change; to transcend pragmatism and Marxism; to recognize that the end of ideology proponents were exhausted ex-socialists now bankrupt of political philosophy in a posture of "false consciousness"; to reject their "fetishism of empiricism" and to force the differentiations between Left and Right:

> The Right, among other things, means--what you are doing, celebrating society as it is, a going concern. Left means, or ought to mean, just the opposite. It means: structural criticism and reportage and theories of society, which at some point or another are focused politically as demands and programs. These criticisms, demands, theories, programs are guided morally by the humanist and secular ideals of Western civilization-- above all, reason and freedom and justice. To be "Left" means to connect up cultural with political criticism, and both with demands and programs. And it means all this inside <u>every</u> country of the world.[10]

Mills' "Letter" provoked a storm of criticism and an extensive reconsideration of the end of ideology posture. Daniel Bell's "Vulgar Sociology" rejoinder essay became perhaps the most famous response to Mills' "Letter." Bell and Seymour Martin Lipset, although unmentioned in Mills' essay, were clearly on Mills' mind when he wrote his essay. Whatever misunderstanding Mills made of their use of ideology, he accurately caught the spirit of their counsel with its inevitable political implications. Mills managed to push them to the Right as defenders of the status quo and exposed the beginnings of what would be a confrontation of Old Left (1930s radicals) with the New Left radicals. Quite apart from how effective Bell's rebuttal was, he did not take up Mills' central challenge--that intellectuals had to create a political philosophy or ideology. When Bell designated Mills' prophecy, passion and polemics as "vulgar sociology," as a romantic protest against contempoary society, with points not argued or developed, but only asserted and reasserted so that they become only a strategy of rhetoric, he was, in fact, pleading for a more "professional" sociology. Mills, said Bell, was "basically an American anarcho-syndicalist, a Wobbly."[11] How could such a stance square with the demands of a professional sociology? Yet this was precisely the role that Mills had repudiated in his life as a sociologist. Mills and Bell essentially differed in their definitions of what the sacred and profane taskes were for sociologists and intellectuals. Notice how Mills welcomed the "utopian" designation:

> We are frequently accused of being "utopian"--in our criticisms and in our proposals; and along with this, of basing our hopes for a New Left politics "merely on reason," or more concretely, upon the intelligentsia in its broadest sense.
> There is truth in these charges. But must we not ask: what now is really meant by utopian? And: Is not our utopianism a major source of our strength? "Utopian" nowadays I think refers to any criticism or proposal that transcends the up-close milieux of a scatter of individuals: the milieux which men and women can understand directly and which they can reasonably hope directly to change. In this exact sense, our theoretical work is indeed utopian in my own case, at least, deliberately so. What needs to be understood, and what needs to be changed, is not merely first this and then that detail of some institution or policy. If there is to be a politics of a New Left, what needs to be analysed is the structure of institutions, the foundations of policies. In this sense, both in its criticisms and in its proposals, our work is necessarily structural--and so, for us, just now--utopian.[12]

Let the emerging new young intellectuals throughout the world lead the way "out of apathy" away from the "Age of Complacency" into an era when the ideologies, the "new theories of structural changes" will forge a renascent radicalism.

That the New Left would use Mills' insights and language in the 1960s to mount a substantive and effective critique of the welfare state and the foreign policy orientation of American liberalism is a provocative reminder of how the "celebration of America" in the 1950s and the Cold War consensus had taken a reform vision away from American liberalism. In becoming technical, administrative and managerial, liberalism had been victimized by its own successes. Whether Mills would have accepted the legacy wrought by the American New Left over the decade after his death is uncertain. What is certain, however, is that he would have been heartened by the challenge of New to Old Left. Indeed, in the two decades since Mills' death, a revised estimate of his role has been forming. Irving Louis Horowitz's biography helps to make Mills' case and Lewis Coser has rendered what may represent an emerging and enduring consensus. "His formulations," concluded Lewis Coser, "often tended to lack precision, and many of his generalizations have hardly stood up under the test of subsequent research. But his distinctive version of 'conflict theory,' with its central emphasis on macrosociological forces and the contentions of power between classes of corporate actors, helped revise an almost buried radical perspective within the sociological tradition."[13]

Notes

1. For a range of historical judgments on Mills as "the intellectual who most influenced the early new left," see Allen J. Matusow, The Unraveling of America: A History of Liberalism in the 1960s (New York: Harper and Row, 1984), p. 311; Stanley Aronowitz, "When the New Left Was New," The 60s Without Apology, ed. Sohnya Sayres, Anders Stephanson, Stanley Aronowitz, Fredric Jameson (Minneapolis: University of Minnesota Press, 1984), pp. 11-43; The New Left: A Collection of Essays, ed. Priscilla Long (Boston: Porter Sargent Publisher, 1969), pp. 14-25. For good introductions on the subject of "influences" on the New Left, see Staughton Lynd, "Towards a History of the New Left," The New Left, ed. Long, pp. 1-13; William L. O'Neill, Coming Apart: An Informal History of America in the 1960's (New York: Quadrangle/ New York Times Book Company, 1971), pp. 275-276; Ralph Miliband, "C. Wright Mills," C. Wright Mills and the Power Elite, ed. G. William Domhoff and Hoyt B. Ballard (Boston: Beacon Press, 1968), pp. 3-11.

2. Lionel Trilling, The Liberal Imagination (New York: Doubleday, 1953), pp. 212-215.

3. Daniel Bell, The End of Ideology (New York: Free Press, 1960), p. 300.

4. Morris Dickstein, Gates of Eden: American Culture in the Sixties (New York: Basic Books, 1977), p. 58.

5. Mills, "Liberal Values in the Modern World," Power, Politics and People: The Collected Essays of C. Wright Mills, ed. Irving Louis Horowitz (New York: Oxford University Press, 1963),

pp. 187-195.

6. Paul F. Lazarsfeld and Robert K. Merton, "Mass Communication, Popular Taste, and Organized Social Action," Mass Culture: The Popular Arts in America, ed. Bernard Rosenberg and David Manning White (New York: Free Press, 1957), p. 464.

7. Quoted in Irving Louis Horowitz, C. Wright Mills: An American Utopian (New York: Free Press, 1983), p. 7.

8. Richard Pells, The Liberal Mind in a Conservative Age: American Intellectuals in the 1940s and 1950s (New York: Harper Row, 1985), pp. 253-254.

9. Lewis A. Feuer, Ideology and the Ideologists (New York: Harper Torchbooks, 1975), p. 7. See p. 121 on the New Left and p. 160 for Mills' critique of labor. See also T. B. Bottomore, Critics of Society: Radical Thought in North America (New York: Pantheon Books, 1968), pp. 53-65.

10. Mills, "Letter to the New Left," The End of Ideology Debate, ed. Chaim I. Waxman (New York: Funk & Wagnalls, 1968), p. 133. Mills' letter was addressed to the English New Left and appeared first in New Left Review. Subsequently it was published in the American journal, Studies on the Left. It is reprinted in The End of Ideology Debate, pp. 126-140 and many other New Left collections.

11. Daniel Bell's rejoinder to Mills can be found reprinted in his The Winding Passage: Essays and Sociological Journeys, 1960-1980 (Cambridge, Ma.: ABT Books, 1980), pp. 138-143; and John Eldridge, C. Wright Mills (New York: Tavistock Publications, 1983), pp. 110.

12. Mills, "Letter to the New Left," The End of Ideology Debate, p. 134.

13. Horowitz, C. Wright Mills, pp. 314-316 and Lewis A. Coser, Masters of Sociological Thought (New York: Harcourt Brace Jovanovich, 1977), pp. 579-580.

Robert H. Bremner's Publications

Books

"The Civic Revival in Ohio: The Fight Against Privilege in Cleveland and Toledo, 1899-1912," Ph.D. dissertation, Ohio State University, 1943.

With M. M. Adams and L. Greenberg, American Red Cross Services in the War Against the European Axis. Washington, D.C.: American Red Cross, 1950.

From the Depths: The Discovery of Poverty in the United States. New York: New York University Press, 1956.

American Philanthropy. Chicago: University of Chicago Press, 1960. The Chicago History of American Civilization edited by Daniel J. Boorstin. Revised edition, 1988.

Editor with John Braeman and Everett Walters, Change and Continuity in Twentieth-Century America. Columbus: Ohio State University Press, 1964. Modern America Series, No. 1. Reprint, New York: Harper & Row, 1966.

Editor, Essays on History and Literature. Columbus: Ohio State University Press, 1966.

Editor and introduction, Anthony Comstock, Traps for the Young. 1883; Cambridge, Ma.: Belknap Press of Harvard University Press, 1967.

Editor with John Braeman and David Brody, Change and Continuity in Twentieth-Century America: The 1920's. Columbus: Ohio State University Press, 1968. Modern America Series, No. 2.

Editor with John Braeman and David Brody, Twentieth-Century American Foreign Policy. Columbus: Ohio State University Press,

1971. Modern America Series, No. 3.

Compiler with the assistance of Richard M. Friedman and Donald B. Schewe, American Social History Since 1860. New York: Appleton-Century-Crofts, 1971. Goldentree Bibliographies in American History.

Editor with Associate Editors John Barnard, Tamara K. Hareven, Robert M. Mennel, Children and Youth in America: A Documentary History, 3 vols. Cambridge, Ma.: Harvard University Press, 1970-1974.

Editor with John Braeman and David Brody, The New Deal: The National Level and The New Deal: The State and Local Levels, 2 vols. Columbus: Ohio State University Press, 1975. Modern America Series, No. 4.

The Public Good: Philanthropy and Welfare in the Civil War Era. New York: Alfred A. Knopf, 1980. The Impact of the Civil War, the Civil War Centennial Series planned by Allan Nevins and edited by Harold M. Hyman.

Editor with Gary W. Reichard, Reshaping America: Society and Institutions, 1945-1960. Columbus: Ohio State University Press, 1982. U.S.A. 20/21: Studies in Recent American History, Number One.

Editor with Gary W. Reichard and Richard J. Hopkins, American Choices: Social Dilemmas and Public Policy Since 1960. Columbus: Ohio State University Press, 1986. U.S.A. 20/21: Studies in Recent American History, Number Three.

Articles

"Background of the Norris-La-Guardia Act," The Historian 9

(1947): 171-180.

"The Civic Revival in Ohio," American Journal of Economics and Sociology 8 (1949): 61-68.

"The Civic Revival in Ohio: Samuel M. Jones: The Man without a Party," American Journal of Economics and Sociology 8 (1948): 151-161.

"The Civic Revival in Ohio: Reformed Businessman, Tom L. Johnson," American Journal of Economics and Sociology 8 (1948): 299-310.

"Honest Man's Story: Frederic C. Howe," American Journal of Economics and Sociology 8 (1949): 413-422.

"The Civic Revival in Ohio: The Artist in Politics, Brand Whitlock," American Journal of Economics and Sociology 9 (1950): 239-254.

"Tom Loftin Johnson," Ohio State Archaeological and Historical Quarterly 59 (1950): 1-13.

"The Civic Revival in Ohio: The Single Tax Philosophy in Cleveland and Toledo," American Journal of Economics and Sociology 9 (1950): 369-376.

"The Civic Revival in Ohio: Self Government," American Journal of Economics and Sociology 10 (1950): 87-91.

"The Civic Revival in Ohio: The Street Railway Controversy in Cleveland," American Journal of Economics and Sociology 10 (1951): 185-206.

"Tax Equalization in Cleveland," American Journal of Economics and Sociology 10 (1951): 301-312.

"The Civic Revival in Ohio: Gas and Ice Monopolies in Toledo," American Journal of Economics and Sociology 10 (1951):

417-428.

"The Civic Revival in Ohio: The Fight for Home Rule," American Journal of Economics and Sociology 11 (1951): 99-110.

"The Civic Revival in Ohio: The Political Techniques of Progressives," American Journal of Economics and Sociology 12 (1953): 189-200.

"The City: Hope of Democracy," American Journal of Economics and Sociology 12 (1953): 305-310.

"Harris P. Cooley and Cooley Farms," American Journal of Economics and Sociology 14 (1954): 71-74.

"Penal and Parole Policy in Cleveland and Toledo," American Journal of Economics and Sociology 14 (1954):387-398.

"Civic Revival," American Journal of Economics and Sociology 15 (1955): 195-202.

"'Scientific Philanthropy,' 1873-93," Social Service Review 30 (1956): 168-173.

"The Big Flat: History of a New York Tenement House," American Historical Review 64 (1958): 54-62.

"The Business Spirit in Philanthropy," in Business History Conference, Michigan State University, 1962, America as a Business Civilization. East Lansing, Mi.: Michigan State University, Bureau of Business and Economic Research, 1962.

"'An Iron Scepter Twined with Roses': The Octavia Hill System of Housing Management," Social Service Review 39 (1965): 222-231.

"The Impact of the Civil War on Philanthropy and Social Welfare," Civil War History 12 (1966): 293-303.

"The Prelude: Philanthropic Rivalries in the Civil War,"

Social Casework 49 (1968): 77-81.

"The State of Social Welfare History," in Herbert J. Bass, editor, The State of American History. Chicago: Quadrangle Books, 1970.

"Other People's Children," Journal of Social History 16 (1983): 83-103.

"The Foundation and Its Operation," in Thomas Langevin, editor, Batelle Memorial Institute Foundation, 1975-1982. Columbus: Battelle Memorial Institute Foundation, 1983.

"Children's Bureau," in Donald R. Whitnah, editor, Government Agencies. Westport, Ct.: Greenwood Press, 1983.

"The New Deal and Social Welfare," in Harvard Sitkoff, editor, Fifty Years Later: The New Deal Evaluated. Philadelphia: Temple University Press, 1985 and New York: Alfred A. Knopf, 1985.

"Benjamin Franklin," in Walter I. Trattner, editor, Biographical Dictionary of Social Welfare in America. Westport, Ct.: Greenwood Press, 1986.

"Advocacy and Empowerment Movements in Philanthropy Since 1960," in 1985 Spring Research Forum Working Papers. Washington, D.C.: 1985.

"Charities for Children," in Richad Magat, editor, Philanthropic Giving. New York: Oxford University Press, 1987.

Robert H. Bremner's Ph.D. Students at The Ohio State University

David J. Maurer, "Public Relief Programs and Policies in Ohio, 1929-1939" (1962).

Jack R. Thomas, "Marmaduke Grove: A Political Biography" (1962).

William C. Berman, "The Politics of Civil Rights in the Truman Administration" (1963).

Roger Eugene Bilstein, "Prelude to the Air Age: Civil Aviation in the United States, 1919-1929" (1965).

Max Welborn, Jr. "Victor Schoelcher's Views on Race and Slavery" (1965).

Tamara K. Hareven, "The Social Thought of Eleanor Roosevelt" (1965).

Philip C. Ensley, "The Political and Social Thought of Elmer Davis" (1965).

Ronald G. Lora, "Conservatism in American Thought, 1930-1950" (1967).

Thomas C. Coulter, "A History of Woman Suffrage in Nebraska, 1856-1920" (1967).

Frank Annunziata, "The Attack on the Welfare State: Patterns of Anti-Statism from the New Deal to the New Left" (1968).

Joseph L. Arnold, "The New Deal in the Suburbs: The Greenbelt Town Program, 1935-1952" (1968).

James N. Giglio, "The Political Career of Harry M. Daugherty" (1968).

Robert Earl Moran, "The History of Child Welfare in Louisiana, 1850-1960" (1968).

John P. Resch, "Anglo-American Efforts in Prison Reform, 1850-1900: The Work of Thomas Garwick Lloyd Baker" (1969).

Phillip R. Warken, "A History of the National Resources Planning Board, 1933-1943" (1969).

Robert R. Mennel, "Attitudes and Policies Toward Juvenile Delinquency in the United States, 1825-1935" (1969).

James S. Saeger, "The Role of Jose de Antequera in the Rebellion of Paraguay, 1717-1735" (1969).

Donald L. Zelman, "American Intellectual Attitudes Toward Mexico, 1908-1940" (1969).

Bruce C. Flack, "The Work of the American Youth Commission, 1935-1942" (1969).

John W. Hevener, "A New Deal for Harlan: The Roosevelt Labor Policies in a Kentucky Coal Field, 1931-1939" (1971).

Albert N. Keim, "John Foster Dulles and the Federal Council of Churches, 1937-1949" (1971).

Donald B. Schewe, "A History of the Postal Savings System in America, 1910-1970" (1971).

Roy T. Wortman, "The IWW in Ohio, 1905-1950" (1971).

Clarence J. Geiger, "Peace in War: American Social Thought and the First World War" (1972).

Felix James, "The American Addition: The History of a Black Community" (1972).

Wayne D. Lammie, "Unemployment in the Truman Aministration: Political, Economic, and Social Aspects" (1973).

Embrey B. Howson, "Jacob Sechler Coxey: A Biography of a Monetary Reformer, 1854-1951" (1973).

Jane Harriet Schwar, "Interventionist Propaganda and

Pressure Groups in the United States, 1937 to 1941" (1973).

William Gibson, "John Rogers: Religion and Politics in the Life of a Puritan Saint" (1973).

James H. Conrad, "Health Services of the United States Children's Bureau, 1935-1953" (1974).

Patricia Terpack Rose, "Design and Expediency: The Ohio State Federation of Labor as a Legislative Lobby, 1883-1935" (1975).

Thomas E. Williams, "The Dependent Child in Mississippi: A Social History, 1900-1972" (1976).

Stephen P. Geitschier, "Limited War and the Home Front: Ohio During the Korean War" (1977).

Angela Howard Zophy, "For the Improvement of Our Sex: Sarah Josepha Hale's Editorship of Godey's Lady's Book, 1837-1877" (1978).

Calvin F. Ruskaup, "The Other Side of Broadcasting: A History of the Challengers to the Use of the Airwaves" (1979).

Joseph Mark Stewart, "A Comparative History of Juvenile Correctional Institutions in Ohio" (1980).

Patricia Grace Zelman, "Development of Equal Employment Opportunity for Women as a National Policy, 1960-1967" (1980).

Frank R. Levstik, "History of the Education and Treatment of the Mentally Retarded in Ohio, 1787-1920" (1981).

Patrick D. Reagan, "The Architects of Modern American National Planning" (1982).

William Lewis Young, "The John F. Kennedy Library Oral History Project: The West Virginia Democratic Presidential Primary, 1960" (1982).

Contributors

Frank Annunziata is chairman of the Department of History at the Rochester Institute of Technology, Rochester, New York. He held a National Endowment for the Humanities post-doctoral fellowship at the University of Michigan, 1975-1976, received the Thomas Jefferson award for work with honors sections in history, and holds membership in the National Humanities Faculty. He has been a visiting professor at Hobart and William Smith Colleges. His continuing research interests include American intellectual history, the history of social reform, the New Deal legacy, and conservative critiques of the New Deal and the welfare state. He has contributed articles to a number of historical publications.

James H. Conrad coordinates oral history and archives at East Texas State University, Commerce, Texas. He is compiler of Reference Sources in Social Work: An Annotated Bibliography (Metuchen, N.J.: Scarecrow Press, 1982) and co-editor with Thad Sitton of Every Sun that Rises: Wyatt More of Caddo Lake (Austin: University of Texas Press, 1985). He has published articles in The East Texas Historical Journal and Texas Libraries and writes a weekly column on local history for two area newspapers.

Albert N. Keim teaches recent American history and ethics at Eastern Mennonite College, Harrisonburg, Virginia. He is the author of Compulsory Education and the Amish: The Right Not to Be Modern (Boston: Beacon Press, 1975), Conscientious Objection and the Historic Peace Churches (Scottdale, Pa.: Herald Press, forthcoming), and essays in Journal of Church and State and the Mennonite Quarterly Review.

Ronald G. Lora teaches American intellectual history and recent U.S. political and cultural history at the University of Toledo, Toledo, Ohio. He is the author of Conservative Minds in America (Chicago: Rand McNally & Company, 1971 and reprinted Westport, Ct.: Greenwood Press, 1980). Among his articles in intellectual history is "Conservative Intellectuals, the Cold War, and McCarthy," in The Specter: Original Essays on the Cold War and the Origins of McCarthyism, eds. Robert Griffith and Athan Theoharis (New York: New Viewpoints/ Franklin Watts, 1974). More recently, he has completed studies in the history of American education including "Education, Public Policy, and the State," in American Choices: Social Dilemmas and Public Policy Since 1960, eds. Robert H. Bremner, Gary W. Reichard and Richard J. Hopkins (Columbus: Ohio State University Press, 1986). He is the editor of America in the 60s: Cultural Authorities in Transition (New York: John Wiley & Sons, 1974) and The American West: Essays in Honor of W. Eugene Hollon (Toledo: University of Toledo, 1980). In 1976 the University of Toledo honored him with an Outstanding Teaching award. In 1987 the Ohio Academy of History named him the recipient of its Outstanding Teacher award.

Richard Magat is president of the Edward W. Hazen Foundation. He is the editor of Philanthropic Giving (New York: Oxford University Press, 1987) and serves as book review editor of Foundation News.

David J. Maurer teaches twentieth century U.S. history and museum administration and curatorial management in the graduate program in Historical Administration at Eastern Illinois University, Charleston, Illinois. He has published an annotated bibliography, U.S. Politics and Elections (Detroit: Gale Co., 1978), and essays in The Emerging University: A History of Eastern Illinois University, ed. Donald F. Tingley (Charleston, Ill.: Eastern Illinois University, 1974), Essays in Illinois History in Honor of Glenn Huron Seymour, ed. Donald F. Tingley (Carbondale: Southern Illinois University Press, 1968); The New Deal: The State and Local Levels, eds. John Braeman, Robert H. Bremner, and David Brody (Columbus: Ohio State University Press, 1975), Biographical Dictionary of American Mayors, eds. Melvin G. Holli and Peter d'A Jones (Westport, Ct.: Greenwood Press, 1981), and Historical Dictionary of the Progressive Era, ed. John D. Buenker (Westport, Ct.: Greenwood Press, 1987). Currently, he is working on research projects associated wih the American Association for State and Local History.

Robert M. Mennel teaches American history at the University of New Hampshire, Durham, New Hampshire. He served as associate editor of Children and Youth in America, 3 vols., ed. Robert H. Bremner (Cambridge, Ma.: Harvard University Press, 1970-1974). His writings include Thorns and Thistles: Juvenile Delinquents and Their Care in the United States, 1825-1940 (Hanover, N.H.: University Press of New England, 1973) and articles in Crime and Justice: An Annual Review of Research, vol. 4 (Chicago: University of Chicago Press, 1982); Social Welfare in America: An Annotated Bibliography, eds. Walter Trattner and Andrew Achenbaum (Westport, Ct.: Greenwood Press, 1983); History of Education Quarterly, and Ohio History. Currently, he is editing the correspondence between Felix Frankfurter and Oliver Wendell

Holmes, Jr.

Patrick D. Reagan teaches American economic and labor history and twentieth century U.S. history at Tennessee Technological University, Cookeville, Tennessee. He has published essays in *Historical Dictionary of the New Deal*, ed. James S. Olson (Westport, Ct.: Greenwood Press, 1985); *Voluntarism, Planning, and the State: The American Experience, 1914-1946*, eds. Jerold E. Brown and Patrick D. Reagan (Westport, Ct.: Greenwood Press, forthcoming); *Mid-America* and *Ohio History*. Currently, he is working on a book-length study of American national planning in the New Deal.

John P. Resch teaches history and humanities at the University of New Hampshire at Manchester. He is also the acting Associate Dean for Academic Affairs. He has published articles in *Social Service Review*, *Ohio History*, and *Prologue*. He is a recent recipient of a National Endowment for the Humanities Fellowship to complete his book on *Politics and the Formation of Public Culture in the Early Republic: The 1818 Revolutionary War Pension Act*.

J. Mark Stewart is a consulting teacher in the Columbus Public Schools' Peer Assistance and Review Program, Columbus, Ohio. He has written a variety of social studies curriculum materials for several major textbook companies as well as for the Columbus Public Schools. In 1985, he was a National Fellow for Independent Studies in the Humanities, a program jointly sponsored by the National Endowment for the Humanities and the Council for Basic Education. He is currently working on a book that explores the implications of each American president's health to the affairs of the time.

Jack Ray Thomas teaches Latin American history at Bowling Green State University, Bowling Green, Ohio. He has published Latin America (New York: Oxford University Press, 1972), Varieties and Problems of Twentieth Century Socialism with Louis Patsouras (Chicago: Nelson-Hall, 1981) and Biographical Dictionary of Latin American Historiography and Historians (Westport, Ct.: Greenwood Press, 1984). He has written articles for Americas: A Quarterly Review of Inter-American Cultural History, The Historian, Revista/ Review Interamericana, Americas (Pan American Union, The Journal of Library History, Social Science, The Hispanic American Historical Review and the Journal of Inter-American Studies. In addition he has published six articles as chapters in historical anthologies. Currently, he is completing Abroad in Yankeeland: Latin American Travel Accounts of Nineteenth Century Life in the United States (Westport, Ct.: Greenwood Press, forthcoming).

Roy T. Wortman teaches American history at Kenyon College, Gambier, Ohio. His course offerings include seminars in labor and rural history and classes in American civilization. He has published articles on labor and ethnic history and From Syndicalism to Trade Unionism: The IWW in Ohio, 1905-1950 (New York: Garland Publishing, 1985). Currently, he is researching the history of the National Farmers Union.

Angela Howard Zophy teaches U.S. and Women's history at the University of Houston-Clear Lake, Clear Lake City, Texas. She has published "UAW Local 72: Assertive Union" in Kenosha

Retrospective: A Biographical Approach, eds. Nicholas C. Burckel and John A. Neuenschwander (Kenosha, Wi.: Kenosha County Bicentennial Commission, 1981); and entries in The Holy Roman Empire: A Dictionary Handbook, ed. Jonathan W. Zophy (Westport, Ct.: Greenwood Press, 1980); Biographical Diciontary of Modern Peace Leaders, ed. Harold Josephson (Westport, Ct.: Greenwood Press, 1985); and Dictionary of Afro-American History, ed. R. M. Miller (Westport, Ct.: Greenwood Press, forthcoming). Currently, she is editing An Encyclopedic Handbook of American Women's History (New York: Garland Publishing, forthcoming).